GENERAL INTELLECTS

GENERAL INTELLECTS

Twenty-One Thinkers for the Twenty-First Century

McKenzie Wark

VERSO
London • New York

A Public Seminar book

First published by Verso 2017

1 3 5 7 9 10 8 6 4 2

Verso
UK: 6 Meard Street, London W1F 0EG
US: 20 Jay Street, Suite 1010, Brooklyn, NY 11201
versobooks.com

Verso is the imprint of New Left Books

ISBN-13: 978-1-78663-190-9 (PB)
ISBN-13: 978-1-78663-283-8 (HB)
eISBN-13: 978-1-78663-192-3 (US)
eISBN-13: 978-1-78663-191-6 (UK)

British Library Cataloguing in Publication Data
A catalogue record for this book is available from the British Library

Library of Congress Cataloging-in-Publication Data

Names: Wark, McKenzie, 1961– author.
Title: General intellects : twenty-one thinkers for the
twenty-first century
/ McKenzie Wark.
Description: New York : Verso Books, 2017. | Includes
bibliographical
references.
Identifiers: LCCN 2016048999 | ISBN
9781786631909 (alk. paper)
Subjects: LCSH: Intellectuals—History—21st century. |
Philosophy—History—21st century.
Classification: LCC HM728 .W365 2017 | DDC
109.2/2 [B] —dc23
LC record available at
https://lccn.loc.gov/2016048999

Typeset in Minion Pro by MJ & N Gavan, Truro, Cornwall
Printed and bound by CPI Group (UK) Ltd, Croydon, CR0 4YY

For my students at the New School—
the general intellects to come

Contents

Introduction

Where are the *public intellectuals* like we used to have back in the good old days? Whenever one talks about the figure of the public intellectual, one is supposed to talk about their decline.[1] There is no more Sartre nor de Beauvoir, no more Pasolini, no more James Baldwin. One might ask why the figure of the public intellectual always seems linked to this sense of decline. Or, one might ask about who is writing right now who ought to be part of some sort of general discussion.

To sidestep the whole mélange of habitual feelings and assumptions about the public intellectual, let's call it something else. Let's talk about *general intellects*. There's a famous text by Marx, now usually called the "Fragment on Machines," in which he talks about *the general intellect*. I'll come back to that later. To shorthand it for now, the general intellect might be Marx groping for a way to think the role of something like intellectual labor in the production process.

For now, let's just pose the problem of the public intellectual in relation to the general intellect. Perhaps the story of the decline of the public intellectual has to do with intellectual labor being finally absorbed into the production process. It isn't a question of the personal failings of the intellectuals of today to live up to the fabled standards of yore. Today's intellectual workers have to work in a different system. A system which in a much more refined way slots them into processes of extracting value from their work. One just doesn't get to be a Sartre or a de Beauvoir even if one wanted to be.

1 Russell Jacoby, *The Last Intellectuals: American Culture in the Age of Academe*, New York: Basic Books, 2000.

To follow that example just for a bit: they were able to make a living by their pen and typewriter. There was a culture industry based on mass printing. There was a rapidly expanding field of higher education producing readers for their books.[2] And, let's not forget: they were products of an elite education system, in countries where that still bestowed an aura of prestige and entitlement. Of course, this is a crude sketch, but the basic point is that doing intellectual work today confronts very different circumstances. It would be pretty much impossible to write intellectually challenging books and make a living from it. Today one needs a day job, and usually in the university.

The university is not what it used to be, either. Rather than being a distinct kind of institution that produces people who could run a capitalist society, it's becoming itself a business.[3] Academic labor has to work within systems of management that are derivative of other kinds of management of intellectual labor. It is becoming quantified and stratified. Much of the labor is becoming casualized. In some cases, the university seems to imagine it can get along quite nicely without the traditional disciplines that tried to think about historical, social or political events.

So there could be reasons for the decline of the public intellectual, and not all of them self-inflicted. Those who think the problem is that today's academics write too much "jargon" should look at the business press. Was ever there a language more filled with spurious, made-up words of indeterminate meaning? But rather than engage with the standard stories of the public intellectual, let's think instead about *general intellects*. By general intellects, I mean something a bit different to Marx's formula of *the* general intellect, although they might be connected. By general intellects, I mean people who are mostly employed as academics, and mostly pretty successful at that, but who try through their work to address more general problems about the state of the world today.

They are, on the one hand, part of *the general intellect*, in that they

2 Regis Debray, *Teachers, Writers, Celebrities: The Intellectuals of Modern France*, London: Verso, 1981.

3 Bill Readings, *The University in Ruins*, Cambridge, MA: Harvard University Press, 1997.

are workers who think and speak and write, whose work is commodified and sold. But they are, on the other hand, *general intellects*, in that they try to find ways to write and think and even act in and against this very system of commodification that has now found ways to incorporate even them. They try to address a general *situation*, one that many people find themselves in today. And they try to do so intelligently, by applying their training and competence and originality.

I have chosen to write about twenty-one such general intellects. Most are academics, but they come from different disciplines. They are not the only people one might usefully read at the moment as talking about some part of the puzzle of confronting the contemporary situation. That situation, most people might agree, is rather bleak. Unless you are part of that tiny handful—the so-called 1 percent—whose fortunes have soared, then things are likely to appear as a spectacle of disintegration.[4] The forward momentum of commodification seems to result mostly in the destruction of both nature and social life.

And so what follows are readings of general intellects who I think have made some progress on thinking about such things. But it seems likely that if general *intellects* have to work under conditions in which they are just component parts of *the* general intellect, whose sole function is to keep commodification going and profits flowing, then this will in some way disfigure the work and limit its ability to grasp the general situation.

This is why the readings I offer are appreciations, but critical ones. Two things seem to me to need more attention than they usually get. One is the development of new *forces of production*. Information technology seems to me something qualitatively different to previous regimes of mechanical and thermodynamic means of production. Moreover, information technology seems to me to be transforming the whole social formation, permeating everyday life and shaping strange forms of surveillance and control.

The second thing is an unexpected effect of how information technology has also found its way into the sciences.[5] We now know the

4 McKenzie Wark, *The Spectacle of Disintegration*, London: Verso, 2013.

5 Paul Edwards, *A Vast Machine: Computer Models, Climate Data and the Politics of Global Warming*, Cambridge, MA: MIT Press, 2013.

global consequence of endlessly commodifying all the resources of the planet: it will crash. Climate change is just the most pressing aspect of what are now often grouped together as the signs of the *Anthropocene.*

A consequence of the first of these two situations is that I don't think one can bracket off the question of *techne* from questions about the social, the historical, the political and the cultural and so on. A consequence of the second situation is that one can no longer treat social phenomena as if there was a stable background of natural phenomena that can be bracketed off and ignored. In the essays that follow, I try to bring both these aspects of the situation into the writing of leading general intellects.

For while I have begun here by defending today's intellectual work from the narrative of their decline, it has to be said that the heavy dependence on the university as a context for support has left its scars on the work general intellects get to do. It may be a good thing that in the training of these general intellects there was a discipline they had to master. But the boundaries of disciplines are arbitrary, and much of the current situation calls for thinking that exceeds them.

It may be a good thing to know and cite leading authorities, but the paradox is that the reason someone like Marx becomes an authority is because of their ability to break with the authorities of their own time and formulate a new problematic within which to think and act.[6] It has to be said that much of this work has tenuous and distant relations to social movements and sites of struggle. There is a trade-off between intellectual rigor, power and coherence and capacity to engage directly in the issues of the hour. In a more subtle way, there's a hardening of the division of labor, wherein general intellects lose touch with other kinds of labor, even intellectual labor, or even other kinds of work in the same universities, such as in the sciences, engineering and design.

I want to address this first by putting a bit of pressure on the received idea of the general intellect, as it has been picked up from Marx. After that comes a series of critical appreciations of particular

6 Louis Althusser, *For Marx*, London: Verso, 2006. However, I prefer how Wendling thinks about changing problematics in Marx, as we shall see.

general intellects, which can be read in any order. The book starts with two imaginative readings of Marx: Wendling on the mode of production; Karatani on modes of exchange. Then some Italian and French workerist and autonomist thinkers, Virno, Boutang, Lazzarato and Berardi. Then Anglophone cultural studies, with McRobbie and Gilroy, followed by psychoanalysis with Žižek and Dean, then political theory with Mouffe, Brown and Butler. Then there're two unique takes on the body politic with Azuma and Préciado, media theory with Chun and Galloway, speculative realism with Morton and Meillassoux, and finally science studies with Stengers and Haraway.

There are some significant omissions. These are general intellects of what Gilroy calls the overdeveloped world, although they do span several European countries, the United States and Japan.[7] Questions of race, gender and sexuality come up, but in the context of thinking about politics, media and so forth, rather than as organizing principles. Here is probably a good place to stress that general does not mean universal.

Nearly all of these general intellects do theory of the middle range: not pure philosophy, but not case studies either. Something in between. While they succeed in a large measure at bringing concepts to bear on the current situation, they might be a bit too tied to traditional interpretive practices. So I want to read these texts against themselves, bringing some of the same critical tactics to bear to find their limitations.

While I would defend them against the rather unthinking complaint about the decline of the public intellectual, I would level a slightly different charge. I think it has to do with importing into the space of academic life texts that don't really belong there—of which Marx is a signal example. It should not be controversial to point out that Marx was not a philosopher.[8] His work might not be an appropriate object for the techniques of exegesis and commentary of continental theory.

7 Gilroy wrote to me that he borrowed the term overdeveloped world from André Gorz and Murray Bookchin. It can also be found in the writings of the Situationist International.

8 A point not lost on Étienne Balibar, *The Philosophy of Marx*, London: Verso, 2014, 2–6, but still.

It might call for a slightly different kind of critical reading practice. Rather than import him into the homogeneous time and space of a discipline, be it philosophy or political theory or whatever, perhaps it might be more useful to connect it up to quite other ways of working and thinking in the world.

For instance, I have lately been trying to connect the reading of Marx back up to the practices of rather different kinds of general intellects, be they from media practices outside the university, or from scientific disciplines within it.[9] Both might be ways of introducing a more practical knowledge of the role technical change played in the history of the nineteenth and twentieth centuries and beyond.

I want to illustrate this issue with a reading of a famous Marx text, the so-called "Fragment on Machines" of 1858, from the *Grundrisse*, from which the expression *general intellect* derives. Marx's interest here is in the passage from the use of simple tools to machine systems. In other words, he is trying to grasp the advanced forces of production of *his* day, which is to say the backward industry of our own times. He starts with a phenomenon in the world—machine systems—and brings concepts to it. This is of course the opposite of how Marx is now usually read: starting with his thought, in the form of texts like this "Fragment," and interpreting the phenomena through the text.

If one understands the difference between these two approaches, it is not hard to see how the now more common one results in the discourse of *eternal capital*, which is where many readers of Marx seem to want to reside today. Marx is taken as revealing a deep philosophical core of capital through the study of its historical and phenomenal forms. In this approach, it is admitted that capital is historical only to the extent that it may take on new historical *appearances*, but its *essence* remains eternal and unchanging.[10] In this traditionalist, old-testament Marxism, the eternal form of capital then awaits its *negation* by that which is in-and-against it, labor.

9 McKenzie Wark, *The Beach Beneath the Street*, London: Verso, 2015; McKenzie Wark, *Molecular Red*, London: Verso, 2015.

10 I develop this argument in McKenzie Wark, "The Sublime Language of My Century," *Public Seminar*, May 14, 2016, at publicseminar.org.

There is a tension in this philosophical reading of Marx. It wants to hang on to some way of using the category of eternal capital. It does not quite want to admit that if capital is indeed continually mutating and self-modifying, then it has no essence, and "appearances" need to be taken seriously as not mere phenomenal forms but as actual forms in the world. In short: there can be no "Marxism" as a philosophy produced by means of philosophy, which takes the essence of capital as its subject. The modifications in so-called phenomenal forms need to be understood as more than mere phenomena, and that requires a more modest approach to the forms of knowledge it might possess of those modifications.

In short, intellectual work after Marx could only be a *collaborative* practice of knowledge among different but equal ways of knowing, where philosophy is not the *ruling party.* Or to put it in a quite different language: the statement "the essence of technology is nothing technological" is fundamentally untrue and a barrier to thought.[11] Technology really does need to be understood through the collaboration of specialized forms of knowledge about what it actually is and does. The attempt to make philosophy a ruling "technology of essence" is retrograde: *the technology of essence is nothing essential.*

Read as *low theory*, rather than philosophy, Marx's 1858 "Fragment on Machines" turns out to be interesting but of its time.[12] He is bamboozled by this new machine system form of tech. He describes it, in mystified form as "a moving power that moves itself" (53).[13] Actually it isn't. A whole dimension is missing here: the forces of production are also *energy systems*. Entirely absent from this text is the simple fact that industrialization had run through all the forests of Northern Europe and then switched to coal, which was in turn more or less exhausted by our time. This is connected, as we shall see, to

11 Contra Kostas Axelos, *Introduction to a Future Way of Thought: On Marx and Heidegger*, Meson Press, 2015.

12 On low theory, see Judith (aka Jack) Halberstam, *The Queer Art of Failure*, Durham, NC: Duke University Press, 2011.

13 Karl Marx, "Fragment on Machines," in Robin MacKay and Armen Avanessian (eds.), *#Accerate: The Accelerationist Reader*, Falmouth: Urbanomic, 2014.

Marx's failure here to think through the metaphor of *metabolism* in this text.

Most of the text is about the transfer of the worker's skills into the machine in a form apparently designed by capital. It is "the appropriation of living labor by objectified labor." Living labor in "subsumed under the total process"—one which here remains only partially thought (54). The actual value-producing power of living labor becomes a vanishing quantity over and against that of fixed capital in the form of machinery.

Marx here grasps, in a mystified form, something important: the knowledge of the "social brain" appears as an aspect of capital rather than of labor (55). Or in a formula that is not much better: "general social knowledge" has become a "direct force of production" (64). But rather than inquire as to how what appears as this fetish of "social brain" or "general intellect" (64) is actually produced, Marx himself falls under the spell of it as a fetish. The social brain becomes part of capital, but who or what actually *makes* the social brain?

For Marx, science will appear to the laborer as something alien to him. Science appears in the form capital dictates. Science is a *productive force*: "all the sciences have been pressed into the service of capital." But who makes science? "Invention has become a business," says Marx, but who does the inventing (61)?

It is worth bearing in mind the rather rudimentary state of the merger of science and industry in Marx's time. Actually it wasn't science that led to that stage of the industrial system. The energy system part—steam power—was the product of craftsmen and self-taught engineers rather than science. Indeed, thermodynamics as science will largely arise out of the steam power industry rather than vice versa.

A somewhat different story is the rise of the German chemical industry, where a rather more organic co-development of the experience-based engineering side and the lab-based scientific side took place. A different story again in an industry Marx doesn't mention at all, and which is important rather later—electricity. Here Faraday and Maxwell's scientific discoveries and theories really did lead more directly from science to industry, although with a considerable lag.

The problem is that as actual organized social activities, science and technology do not fit so neatly into the schema of labor and capital. Hence in Marx they simply come from without as a reified thing called "science" which then becomes part of the machine system as fixed capital. Here is where one or other of two kinds of knowledge of actual science can help us. One is science studies, but the other is the rather more Marx-inflected Social Relations of Science movement, which preceded science studies, and about which science studies is curiously rather silent.[14]

Thus, we can turn to JD Bernal's *Science in History*, a landmark work in the Social Relations of Science, which usefully shows how modern science arises out of the coming together of advanced forms of technical labor, on the one hand, and forms of gentlemanly culture which used its leisure time to crack the secrets of God's universe. Or in short, its class origins are hybrid, and not quite locatable in any preexisting class—indeed, it points towards a new kind of class.

For what Marx could have no inkling of, given his times, is the way science itself would become not just a force of production, but in its own right a kind of industrial system, and one which works quite differently to the factory system. The factory system is based on quantified labor time, making standardized products. But what of those (non-)labor processes that make *nonstandard* things? New things? Or as Asger Jorn understood it: What about those who make not content but forms?[15] To what class do they belong?

I was not the first to propose that we think of these people as belonging to another class, although I did attempt to come up with a contemporary-sounding name for them: the *hacker class*.[16] JD Bernal, for example, had already come close in his theory of the *scientific*

14 See Mario Biagioli, *The Science Studies Reader*, New York: Routledge, 1999; on the social relations of science, see Gary Wersky, *The Visible College: The Collective Biography of British Scientific Socialists of the 1930s*, New York: Holt, Rinehart & Winston, 1979.

15 Asger Jorn, *The Natural Order and Other Texts*, New York: Routledge, 2016, 123ff.

16 McKenzie Wark, *A Hacker Manifesto*, Cambridge, MA: Harvard University Press, 2004.

worker.[17] But I did at least offer a thought about how the relations of production mutated to absorb them into the commodity system: the rise of intellectual property as a mutation in the private property form, that encloses the commons of information and spawns whole new categories of *potential* commodities.

And so: to rethink Marx's fragment outside of its historical time and into our own, we need to pay much more attention to at least two things: firstly, the contribution of science (and knowledge-work more generally) to the *design* of the form of industrial systems. And secondly: energy systems, about which Marx is here mostly silent.

Putting energy back into the picture helps refine a metaphor Marx uses twice in this fragment but in an unsatisfactory way—*metabolism*. Marx identifies only circulating capital with "metabolism" and understands it in too restricted a way, not as an energy system but as a matter of distribution (58). This is particularly problematic when he links metabolism to agriculture, which "becomes merely the application of the science of material metabolism, its regulation for the greatest advantage of the entire body of society" (62).

One can connect this in turn to the inkling Marx has of labor no longer as that which contributes energy to production, but that which *controls* it through *information*. He uses the term "regulator" for this, possibly thinking of the regulator of the steam engine—sometimes also known as the accelerator—an early instance of the negative feedback of information, the function of which is to maintain equilibrium (62).

Here we can connect Marx's writings on the general intellect to his later attempt to develop the category of metabolism, and in particular, *metabolic rift*. His real breakthrough (as John Bellamy Foster has shown) is to understand that in commodified agriculture and perhaps elsewhere, labor is *not* functioning as the regulator of a metabolism, but quite the reverse.[18] It may be that collective social labors, as incorporated in the machine systems of capital, are "deregulators,"

17 JD Bernal, *The Social Function of Science*, Cambridge, MA: MIT Press, 1967.

18 John Bellamy Foster, *Marx's Ecology: Materialism and Nature*, New York: Monthly Review Press, 2000.

exacerbating metabolic rifts—of which, as we now know, climate change is just one.

So the Marx of 1858 does not know yet the full contours of what he is groping for. He is like the blind man with the elephant. And as in that parable, it is only through the combined efforts of all kinds of blind researchers feeling out different parts of the beast that is social labor that the contours of the thing can be known, and the elephant in the room described and conceived: *metabolic rift*. The commodity regime treats matter, energy and information as the materials for accumulating wealth as exchange value on an ever increasing scale and velocity, despite the havoc this wreaks on the natural systems and even social ones.

One task for general intellects might be to imagine a kind of common hacker class interest among those whose efforts end up being commodified as some sort of intellectual property: artists, scientists, engineers, even humanist and social science academics. We could imagine all of these as belonging to the same class from the point of view of the commodification of information. We all process information that is part of a complex natural-technical-social-cultural metabolism. But nearly all of us get to see a ruling class of a rather unprecedented kind extract most of the value from the combined efforts of hackers and workers worldwide. As general intellects, maybe we could stick our heads above our little cubicles, look around, and figure out how to cooperate with others who understand different parts of the labor process.

Marx did not have the intellectual tools to think about information as a regulator, and he was only just beginning to grasp how metabolic rifts were opening up due to commodified production's disregard of its natural conditions of existence. Without input from those with more practical knowledge of those emerging developments, Marx allows his conceptual apparatus to overshoot the available data, and in the end to become a hostage to philosophizing. He constructs a false relation between a partially grasped totality and a future conceived via a merely abstract, formal, dialectical negation. He tries to do alone what only the *cooperation* of many kinds of general intellects could really do.

There is however something of use in the "Fragment on Machines" in the way Marx thinks the relation between the machine, labor and time. For Marx, machinery is mostly a way of capturing more time from the worker (and here he neglects the science part he has elsewhere so presciently intuited). Marx: "capital here—quite unintentionally—reduces human labor, expenditure of energy, to a minimum. This will redound to the benefit of emancipated labor" (59). Notice how *energy* finally appears here, but only the energy of human labor. He has not grasped the extent to which the replacement of human energy with fossil-fuel energy is very central to how capitalism unfolded.[19]

The machine system means a reduction of necessary labor time to a minimum, and the replacement of labor by capital. Wealth can be created independently of labor time. This ought to increase the amount of real wealth, which for Marx is freely disposable time, but it doesn't. The result is rather "not-labor time" for the few, for a ruling class. The machine system "is thus, despite itself, instrumental in creating the means of social disposable time" (64). Moreover: "The saving of labor time is equal to an increase of free time, i.e. time for the full development of the individual, which in turn reacts back upon the productive power of labor as itself the greatest productive power" (66).

It is a neat dialectic, and at least the beginnings of a way of thinking capitalism that is not romantic, which does not simply want to run away from the whole question of the means of production into some idle idyll. (The *eros* of Marcuse, and so forth.[20]) Marx:

> While machinery is the most appropriate form of the use value of fixed capital, it does not follow that therefore subsumption under the social relation of capital is the most appropriate and ultimate social relation of production for the application of machinery. (57)

Machinery could be something else. Capital calls machinery into existence in the form of fixed capital, but it could take *another form*.

19 Andreas Malm, *Fossil Capitalism: The Rise of Steam Power and the Roots of Global Warming*, London: Verso, 2016.

20 Herbert Marcuse, *Eros and Civilization: A Philosophical Inquiry into Freud*, Boston: Beacon Press, 1974.

This is a point that needs insisting on in the tech-phobic world that is so much of the humanities and social sciences. There *politics* is the magic answer to all our problems. But not this *actual* politics whose dismal rituals we see all around us. Some other politics, a *virtual* politics that is a possibility latent in mere actual politics. For these general intellects, politics has this dual character, virtual and actual, but technology never does. Only the first part of Marx's thinking on this is acknowledged—that science and tech, or today's techno-science, is absorbed into capital and takes its form. That tech too is both virtual and actual, and could have other forms, is not up for discussion. General intellects might have to figure out together how all of the particular domains in which we work or which we study, from politics to culture to science to technology, are all at one and the same time part of the problem and part of any possible solution.

But to make progress in this direction means dispensing with a bit of Marx's *obiter dicta* that became holy writ: the notion of "the general intellect" (64). This is an idealist residue, a fetishistic half-thought, not a concept. *There is no general intellect.* There are only the concrete and specific practices of the production of knowledge. These become "general" only in fetishistic form: as intellectual property. This stage of capitalism—if that is what it still is—developed a whole apparatus for commodifying the results of all our hacker activity, codified in relatively new property forms, which are used not only in producing industrial systems over and against labor, but *against the hacker class as well.* Hence one has to think about both cooperation among different kinds of hacker class knowledge production, but then also about an alliance between the hacker as class (creators of new form) and the worker as class (creators of standardized content).

No kind of knowledge production, whether of science or culture or even philosophy, is exogenous to the commodity form any more. But neither is it as simple as saying that "invention becomes a business" (61). Rather, it became *a new kind of business, which changed all the others.* There is no eternal capital. It has no transhistorical essence. It mutates in both its particulars and its abstract forms. It can neither be negated from without, nor does merely accelerating it do anything other than open metabolic rifts. There can be no Promethean leap.

The task before us, rather, is to work out how different kinds of knowledge of different parts of the metabolism might cooperate, other than via the commodification of knowledge as intellectual property. Then we might *extrapolate* from what we know of how metabolic systems of all kinds operate, and design a better one—a survivable metabolism. This is a task not entirely made easier by atavistic philosophy, trying to steal fires it does not even know how to light. Nor is it helped by scriptural reverence for the old texts, even of Marx. For he too was a product of his times.

And so in *General Intellects*, I treat a range of intellectual work, in philosophy, political theory, cultural studies and so forth, as *partial totalizations*. Each sees the world from the point of view of a certain way of working, and generalizes that way of working into a whole worldview. Unfortunately, these have a habit of spending a certain amount of intellectual energy trying to maintain the *sovereignty* of their own point of view over all others. To the political theorists, politics is ontological; for the theorists of culture, everything is always cultural—and so on. Even our general intellects remain rather bourgeois thinkers to the extent that they keep making ambit claims to the totality as being their particular private property.

I prefer to set these claims aside and look for ways in which these partial totalizations might be connected to each other in a more comradely fashion. While as individual hackers of information we are caught within the process of reproducing the commodity form, with all its tendencies to separation and fetishism, how might one nonetheless begin to produce, not a totally totalizing view of history, but rather a language of connection between partial views? To make progress on that question might be to begin the politics of knowledge in our time.

1.

Amy Wendling: Marx's Metaphysics and Meatphysics

The mark of a major body of work is that it will support more than one interpretation, all of which are coherent and persuasive, and each of which is open-ended enough for still further elaboration. So it is with Marx. Rather than squabble over what is the true and total interpretation, it seems to me more useful to think of the *Marx-field* that he enables. The Marx-field would then be a matrix of variations on themes, each more or less useful in particular situations. On that view, there may be as yet unexplored quadrants of the Marx-field that might be of more help in constructing a critical thought for the times.

Marx's work clearly draws on German idealist philosophy and its sources, such as Spinoza. It also draws on the scientific thought of his time in physics and other sciences.[1] The latter are now technically obsolete, known only to specialists. So the general tendency in elaborating Marx has been to retreat from that engagement with the sciences and their consequences, and to go *back* to German idealism or back even further to Spinoza.

But what if, in contrast, we went *forward*? What if rather than ignore the conceptual elaboration of modern science in Marx, we updated it? Marx got as far as the revolution in physics which added thermodynamics to mechanics and its worldview. What if we thought through what modern biology, earth science and information science

1 I found Frederick Beiser, *After Hegel: German Philosophy 1840–1900*, Princeton, NJ: Princeton University Press, 2014 to be a very useful guide to German scientific materialism.

added to the picture? A first step might be to reconstruct a plausible version of Marx's relation to two neglected sources. The first is the scientific materialism of his time; the second is his investigations into engineering and machinery. For this, we can turn to an excellent book by Amy Wendling, *Karl Marx on Technology and Alienation.*[2]

For Wendling, Marx's relation to the great books of the philosophical canon is a kind of *performance* that draws its energy not from continuing them, or even critiquing them from within another philosophical system. Rather, it is closer to what I would call a *détournement* which works by appropriating elements from different information sources and holding them in tension against each other.[3] In this sense, Marx is not a Hegelian or a political economist but an activist-writer who cuts these (and other) tainted sources against each other tactically in the interests of constructing the labor point of view. Or more precisely, the point of view of the *overcoming* of wage labor.

As I see it, the texts Marx samples for détournement change through time, as different sources come into play in the general conflict of communication. Rather than being an incomplete "epistemological break" with the work of the "young Marx," the later work plays off a different mix of samples to different effect to the earlier work.[4]

Wendling sees it a bit differently. For her, the earlier, "humanist" Marx is still deploying the residual category of a spirit or essence that separates the human from the natural. The later or "older" Marx (must we call him mature or scientific?) uses sources for whom the human is part of the natural world, interchangeable with animals or machines. The humanist bits don't go away altogether, however. They are occasionally deployed against the scientific material to dislodge it from its own implication in a more advanced stage of capital.

Perhaps the transition from younger to older Marx is one of the changing resources available to him. Wendling: "Capitalism, not

---

2 Amy Wendling, *Karl Marx on Technology and Alienation*, New York: Palgrave, 2009.

3 On détournement, see Guy Debord, *The Society of the Spectacle*, New York: Zone Books, 1994, chapter 8.

4 Louis Althusser, *For Marx*, London: Verso, 2006.

Marx, invalidates the earlier humanist conceptual frameworks" (5). Their ideological function had changed. As Berardi shows, for readers of the "young Marx" in the '60s, Marx could be read as longing for the restoration of a precapitalist world, but for Wendling this was not Marx's position even then. Rather, capitalism *itself* produces both a romantic desire for restoration and also the scientific worldview that makes it obsolete.

Wendling calls this romantic longing, provocatively, a "capitalist humanism." Wendling: "Marx's use of this humanism, like his use of scientific materialism, would then be a performance: a performance designed to show that capitalism cannot account for its own activity without recourse to the humanistic notions that it supposedly banishes" (7). This is not to say that a certain humanism is entirely banished, even in the older Marx. He deploys readings and rewritings of both capitalist humanism and capitalist scientism in *Capital* to tease out capitalism's own contradictory nature.

But he is not always in control of this performance, and his major texts such as *Grundrisse* and *Capital* have different and somewhat open-ended versions of this method—surely a strength rather than a weakness.[5] The difficulty is that Marx is struggling for something other than old philosophical categories of the human—which capital has abolished—and also for something other than the reduction of the human to exchange value, which capitalism has all but achieved even in his time. Hence his tactics of performing one against the other.

Marx deploys the category of the human against that of capital through a theory of *technology*. Marx is one of the first thinkers to try to conceptualize it rather than just describe it. Could science and technology point towards a new kind of species-being? One of Marx's achievements was to think technology as having *affordances*, as being a space of possibility. Intellectuals will make all sorts of claims for the possibilities of reason or culture or politics, but technology is usually just stubbornly stuck in its current form. For Marx, at least at certain

5 One could connect this to Alexander Bogdanov's insight that Marx's texts are in a certain sense collectively authored.

moments, it could be other than what it is, even if not quite an infinite object of Promethean acceleration.[6]

There's a slight decentering here, from labor to the labor-tech encounter. Marx tried to create a kind of meta-science, which would try to understand how the "science" of political economy, for example, used concepts grounded in material and social and technical realities it did not perceive. Wendling: "The illusions produced by capitalist making come to determine the possible range of human thinking" (13). This is a very useful line of thought for our times, when *both* so-called techno-utopianism and its supposed critics seem to share exactly the same horizon formed by the ideological materials of the humanism-scientism complex of capitalist thought itself.[7]

Wendling winds the story back to some key samplings from Hegel, particularly the distinction between *objectification* and *alienation*. Objectification is a social process of shaping the world for human needs. Alienation refers not to objectification by labor, but to the separation of the object of labor from the laborer. Alienation is a break in the pattern of subjective transformation of the world into its object and the object's reciprocal production of the subject. Alienation is what happens to wage labor when it is divorced from its own agency as producer, and produces mere things separated from it, and itself as separated and thing-like. This is why in Marx there can be no question of just redistributing unequal wealth. It is not enough to redistribute what is alienated from labor (although some might argue that it's a start); one has to change the way it is produced in the first place. Writing about that, even as a possibility, takes some textual tactics.

Marx builds this position through a series of détournements from various sources, all cut and collaged to perform their effects. From Aristotle comes the bit about justice as equal exchange, where exchange that is not for use is unnatural and monstrous. From Rousseau comes the bit about an imbalance not of goods but of political right and the

6 Although perhaps the Prometheus figure could be read in more interesting ways. See Jared Hickman, *Black Prometheus: Race and Radicalism in the Age of Atlantic Slavery*, New York: Oxford University Press, 2016.

7 This is the problem with Evgeny Morozov, *Click Here to Save Everything*, New York: PublicAffairs, 2014.

problem of class for liberal society. From Locke comes the bit about the laboring act as the foundation of wealth, or at least of property, against which feudal life can be made to appear artificial. From Smith comes the bit about labor being more social than in Locke, dependent on tools and land.

The naturalism of labor in Locke and Smith is a tactic that enabled a critical denaturalizing of feudalism. Marx wants to denaturalize capitalism in turn. Hence labor becomes a social and historical category, not (or not just—it's slippery) a natural one. Labor is a product of alienated society. But throughout Marx there are lingering bits of the idea of equal exchange for labor and the idea of labor as a kind of self-creation.

Marx wants a critique of the apparent naturalness of labor. He deploys a distinction from Aristotle, then expands it. To use value / exchange value, he adds labor / labor power. The former in each pairing produces wealth (use value) and has qualities; the latter produces exchange value and does not. For Wendling, Marx is not uncritically repeating the labor theory of value but trying to get some leverage on it to analyze the alienation of labor from itself. The crucial thing is not labor as source of both wealth and exchange but the *split* between wealth and exchange.

Alienation is built into production and produces social activity in the form of labor under capitalism. Labor cannot be redeemed through redistribution, as what alienation produces is a crippled and stunted life for the majority. Moreover, labor is dominated not just by the commodities it produces but also by the tools used, the instruments of production. The worker is made peripheral. Commodity fetishism in exchange is doubled by *machine fetishism* in production. Occult qualities are ascribed to both commodities *and* machines, omitting the labor that mediates them.

Wendling: "The machine is the final 'metaphysical object' of the Marxist account of alienation, occupying the same structural position as God in Feuerbach or the absolutist state in Rousseau" (57). Wendling here very usefully recenters our thinking not on the commodity but on the machine. Marx's research on machines starts to change his concepts of labor and nature. The older Marx will then try to layer a scientific-materialist and thermodynamic model of labor onto his earlier ontological one drawn from Hegel and Feuerbach on alienation.

In the thermodynamic worldview, human labor is just one type of energy among others. Instead of humans working on a passive world, the world is actively working on itself, and human action is a subset of that action. It is already, if you like, a modern multi-agent worldview that includes nonhuman agents, or at least forces.[8] Wendling: "Labor changes from a creative endeavor wrought by human spirit on inanimate nature, as conceived in Aristotle, Hegel, Smith and Locke, into a mere conversion of energy in which nature goes to work on itself" (61).

Here Marx was working with the materials of his time, recoded in his own way. Labor is no longer self-realization in the alienating conditions of capitalist production. It is rather an expenditure of energy, to the point of fatigue. "The individual develops not in doing labor, as with Locke, but in liberation from it" (59). Hence Marx's distinctive view of freedom as freedom *from* labor—for everybody, at least part of the time.[9]

Labor is not spirit realizing itself in the world, but maybe an individual artistic or scientific thought might still remain free. But eventually, commodification subsumes that as well and makes it function for capital accumulation. But like labor, creative or scientific endeavor—what I call the hacker class—puts up a fight in and against its distinct forms of commodified exploitation—as, for example, intellectual property.[10] But Marx was not able to think these phenomena which had not fully taken form in his time.

---

8 In other words, Bruno Latour is not quite correct in thinking that critique always involves a split between nature and culture. Nor is Jane Bennett in imagining that her own multi-agent perspective offers something not thinkable in the Marx-field. See Jane Bennett, *Vibrant Matter*, Durham, NC: Duke University Press, 2010.

9 See Kathi Weeks, *The Problem With Work*, Durham, NC: Duke University Press, 2011.

10 McKenzie Wark, *A Hacker Manifesto*, Cambridge, MA: Harvard University Press, 2004.

Sometimes, Marx deploys the Lockean notion of labor to critique what labor becomes under capitalism. He pipes up for *living labor.* But he also undermines this perspective via a later view of labor as energy expenditure, within a worldview that sees the body and its energetic exchanges with an environment, probably drawn from Ludwig Büchner.[11]

In the production paradigm, the laboring body is a productive machine like any other. But Marx did not quite accept the leveling of the human/animal/machine in a general theory of *energetics*. He is not quite a "post-human" thinker. "Marx never leaves behind the Hegelian thesis of the progressive spiritualization and rationalization of the natural" (65–66). Yet he tactically triangulates the paradigm of work, the paradigm of production, and the thermodynamic worldview in which "Capitalism is a steam engine with a design flaw… which will precipitate an explosion, no matter what anyone does or thinks" (66).

The tactical development of the difference is Marx's distinctive *materialism*, although it is not one that rests on a metaphysical claim about the world. "Instead Marx turns to investigating the historical accidents by which the world and nature are built up and transformed through labor" (67). To achieve that, Marx drew on the scientific materialism that was current in Germany after the failure of the 1848 revolutions.[12] Scientific materialism was a progressive force in the absence of a liberal public sphere. But Marx rejected its vulgar materialism and was not attracted to its naïve realism, or its determinism—on that score he hewed to the Epicurian swerve, the subject of his doctoral thesis.[13]

Scientific materialism had roughly two generations. The first included Feuerbach and von Liebig. The second included Ludwig Büchner, Karl Vogt, Jacob Moleschott and Hermann von Helmholtz, one of the discoverers of the law of the conservation of energy. This

11 See Beiser, *After Hegel.*

12 Here Wendling confirms the intuitions of Anson Rabinbach, *The Human Motor*, Berkeley: University of California Press, 1992.

13 Karl Marx, *Collected Works*, vol. 1, London: Lawrence & Wishart, 1975, 25ff.

writing had its political side. For Büchner, the universe itself is not a monarchy but a republic, governed by its own laws and not ruled by will from above. Energy seemed to imply a kind of natural equality in a monist universe governed only by its transformations. "The political realm is reconceived not as an anti-physics, in opposition to nature, as it was by the contract theorists. Instead, the political realm is woven from nature construed as an energetic system" (74).

In this worldview, all energy is derived from the sun. All is matter as motion and—same thing—heat. Rather than forces that begin and end in time, energy is constantly transformed from one state to another. Vitalist forces are increasingly excluded from this picture—which as Haraway notes, was an objective Joseph Needham was still working on seventy years later.[14] The steam engine supplants the clock as a governing metaphor, including its design problems of efficiency, durability and safety.

Energetics transforms discourse about labor: workers don't resist it out of lack of spirit, but lack of energy. There are objective limits to labor, and hence there can be a science of work—ergonomics. Moleschott, who worked on nutrition, even wrote a cookbook for workers. There was an alliance of scientific materialists and labor-reform politics, of which Marx was highly suspicious of course.

Instead, he used energeticist notions to start thinking about *surplus value*—or what the capitalist gets from the worker without giving in return. But Marx still draws on an older scientific materialism in the form of Liebig's vitalism, which was a non-divine but still nonmaterial notion. He still sometimes thinks of human agency as special, as a kind of "living, form-giving fire," as he wrote in *Grundrisse*. Seen from the labor point of view, labor is not just one energy node among others. Latent in this notion of form-giving is the possibility of a concept of information, but one still assumed to be a human prerogative.

Marx insists on a moral critique of the reduction of a part of the human species to the mere reproduction of its labor power. For him, poverty and wealth are connected, and mere redistribution does

---

14 Donna Haraway, *Crystals, Fabrics and Fields*, Berkeley: North Atlantic Books, 2004.

nothing to change exploitation and alienation at work. But there's a limit to how far he gets with this. "Among Marx's most under-theorized ideas is his notion that human activity is not reducible to labor" (87).

Energetics complicates Marx's view of the good life. He opposed his son-in-law Paul Lafargue's *Right to Be Lazy*. He resisted Charles Fourier's utopian replacement of work by play.[15] Energetics seemed to point to the necessity of the social production of the means of existence, even if not necessarily in capitalist form. But perhaps the time that social production requires can be shared equally, and minimized.

Wendling:

> Marx's critique of political economy becomes possible because the concept of labor on which Locke, Smith and Hegel founded, respectively, autonomy, property and subjectivity is irreparably changed. Instead of dignifying the human being and setting him or her at the apex of the universe, instead of spiritualizing nature via a human force different in kind, labor situates the human in continuity with nature and natural force. (84)

Borrowing from the energetic worldview, capital becomes an entropic system:

> Capitalism is like a poorly designed steam engine that must be run at top speed, despite the fact that this speed contributes to a greater overall loss of heat. This increased overall heat can be neither transformed into productive work nor released in adequate quantities. Instead it threatens to blow up the engine itself. (91)

In the older Marx there is less on the theory of political agency "against nature" and more on the theory of crisis. Wendling: "the capitalist way of life is unsustainable...it squanders the very energy it should struggle to preserve" (92).

---

15 Paul Lafargue, *The Right to Be Lazy*, Chicago: Charles H. Kerr, 2011; Charles Fourier, *Theory of the Four Movements*, Cambridge: Cambridge University Press, 1996.

Useful but problematic here is Marx's critique of the "natural" constraints on human flourishing. Overpopulation is a threat to peace in Hobbes, and in Malthus, scarcity is the will of God. Marx rightly saw these supposedly natural constraints as also social ones. Liebig's agricultural science had shown how to raise agricultural productivity through artificial fertilizers. Wendling does not connect this to Marx's other borrowing from von Liebig: *metabolic rift*. He was at least partly aware of the limits to the overcoming of limits. It would have to wait for Sartre to show how *scarcity* could be a concept freed from either an essentialist anthropology or assumptions in advance about nature.[16]

From Liebig and elsewhere Marx tries to sustain a difference between human and animal relations, in and against nature. The human is a distinctive power, in that it can make a technical relation to nature on a rational and scientific basis. Humans can apply "intellect" to the design of a technology. Hence technology sometimes has a double aspect in Marx, trapped in a capitalist mode of production, and yet having a wider potential, if intellect could be applied to its design.

If for Locke feudalism was unnatural, for Marx it is capitalism that is unnatural. It is a jerry-built steam engine that will sooner or later blow a gasket. It is an alienated form of objectification that can't last, because of the rifts that traverse it. Wendling: "Marx's prediction of crisis is also nature's revenge" (97). But this is a logic of postponement, of waiting for the engine to blow, rather than of trying to make improvements to the engine while it runs. "Scarcity" will inevitably operate, but as a social rather than natural constraint in Marx.

In *Grundrisse*, Marx sees in the affordances of technology the possibility of producing wealth for the whole of our species-being. Freed from capitalist relations of production, a redesigned tech might objectify without alienating. But as I argued in the introduction, in the famous "Fragment on Machines" Marx's thinking is still too tied to a *vitalist* idea of the human essence augmented by machines. Humans are a tool-using species that is being used by its tools. Workers are

---

16 Karl Marx, *Capital*, vol. 3, London: Penguin, 878ff; Jean-Paul Sartre, *Critique of Dialectical Reason*, vol. 1, London: Verso, 2004.

alienated from their essence, and need their tool-using nature restored to them.

In communism, machines can then be for the production of wealth, defined as the expansion of free time and human needs, or alternately as net productivity not dependent on human labor for its measure. Wealth is also science, which Marx sometimes understood as a social force in the world. "Marx…links science to political change, offering one of the first syntheses of the technical and the political" (103). Where capitalism forks value into use value and exchange value, via the separation of labor from labor power, or the qualitative from the quantitative, communism realizes the wealth created, but suppresses the regime of exchange value.

The "Fragment" distinguishes fixed and circulating capital, where fixed capital is embodied in a particular use value (machines) and circulating capital realizes its value in exchange (money). Like natural resources such as water and air, the general level of technology is something capital gets "free of charge" from the commons. But capital has interests in fettering tech and science, which can undermine as well as augment a given regime of accumulation.

Fixed capital replaces labor, raising productivity and profits, but capital is chasing its own tail, and as fixed capital grows, the rate of profit (supposedly) falls. Workers become obsolete. Pushing up profits is a matter of intensifying work or lengthening the working day. Capital's problem—as Georges Bataille well knew—is not scarcity but abundance, or rather the attempt to maintain scarcity within abundance.[17] Against this, Marx sketches only the faintest outline of communism as noninstrumentalist use value, a theme picked up in different ways by Bataille, Marcuse and Haraway, where use value becomes the gift or pleasure or situations.[18]

Marx offers an unusual picture of human-machine symbiosis under communism, different to the usual antagonistic or alienating narratives. Wendling:

---

17 Georges Bataille, *The Accursed Share*, vol. 1, New York: Zone Books, 1991.

18 Perhaps the most radical version of this vision is Constant's. See Mark Wigley, *Constant's New Babylon*, Rotterdam: 010, 1999.

> Marx will want to portray the human as a material thing, not a spiritual one, and to make a case for the worth of its materiality. This means that human beings will have to remain envisioned as the complicated material-like structures of nineteenth-century science, a science which portrays human being as machine-like, and also as worthy. The human being will have to be materially honorable without recourse to God or the divine within. Moreover, human activity can retain none of the occult qualities that inhere in the vitalist explanations of the creative acts of labor. (118)

It is a matter of thinking that the human-machine material mesh—Haraway's cyborg—could be quite other than as it appears under capitalism.

The mark of a good society would be both the elaborated forms of humans and tech it would make, and perhaps not being able to tell them apart anymore. Hence for Marx maybe humans *should* be treated as fixed capital—and accorded the respect of machines. Wendling: "As a regulative ideal, humans do not seek to become more like their gods, but more like their machines" (119). Or as I would put it: the objective is more a *meat*-physics than a *meta*-physics.

Grundrisse includes an expansive notion of what technology could become; *Capital* does not. In *Capital* Marx limits himself to the negative effects of tech within capitalism. But in *Capital* there's still a certain slippage between competing narratives of continuity and discontinuity, or between energeticist and vitalist worldviews. The vitalist strand alone supports the theology of communism as a leap out of nature.[19] Wendling: "revolutions are indebted to the vitalist metaphysics of the pre-thermodynamic era: they reassert human priority over the natural world" (126).

It might be more useful these days to start from Marx's energeticist tactics, and turn back and take a more critical stance towards the vitalist one, at least as it came to float various forms of what Wendling calls capitalist humanism as reactionary responses to thermodynamic

---

19 Of which Andrey Platonov was a particularly brilliant critic. See *The Foundation Pit*, New York: NYRB Classics, 2009.

leveling. In an interesting move, Wendling argues that misogyny, anti-Semitism and racism are ways of making claims to the human at the expense of a category of other humans in the face of an all-enclosing and alienating system in which no particular kind of labor has any special claim on the human.[20]

Wendling makes good use of Marx's 1850s notebooks on engineering and the sciences, which he later redacted into *Grundrisse*. These notebooks were largely unknown until published in German in the 1950s. David Riazanov, founder of the Marx-Engels Institute, did not think them worth including in the original collected works. Particularly interesting are Marx's notes on Charles Babbage's *On the Economy of Machinery and Manufactures*. Babbage—also inventor of the proto-computer the Difference Engine—had done extensive "fieldwork" in factories and had a quite unique knowledge of them for the time.[21] He understood technology conceptually as having three parts: the motor, the means of transmission and the working tool. This simple scheme helped Marx think the morphology of tech.

The first component, the motor, had changed a lot. "In nineteenth-century science and technology, no changes are as frequent as changes in available energy sources" (138). Steam engines must have mystified a generation used to wind and water power, even if they seem quite explicable a generation later. Just as Jameson thought the computer could not be figured, whereas my eleven-year-old son understands not only their operative parts but how to program them.[22]

Steam power changed people's worldview. It did not depend on the gods to make the wind blow or the river flow. The human labor accumulated in the machine could replace natural sources of energy and distribute it smoothly. This was no Promethean triumph, however. Human capacity over nature improved, but at the expense of working humans. For Marx, under capital, machines are vampires. Labor is

20 Wendling draws from Moishe Postone, *Time, Labor and Social Domination*, Cambridge: Cambridge University Press, 1996.

21 Nick Dyer-Witheford, *Cyber-Marx*, Champaign, IL: University of Illinois Press, 1999.

22 Fredric Jameson, *Postmodernism, Or, The Cultural Logic of Late Capitalism*, London: Verso, 1991.

deskilled and reduced to "watchman and regulator" (i.e., interestingly cybernetic) functions. Boring work is an affront to the worker's "animal spirits."

Wendling picks up on the disturbing side to these technophobic notes in *Capital*, which pits monstrous machines against natural humans. It's a romantic version of capitalist humanism passed on to many subsequent Marxisms (although not to Bogdanov and Platonov, or to Bernal and Needham—forgotten as those strands often are). There's an anti-Semitic side to the vampire, for example, tied to those "outsider" figures who threaten a pastoral norm. However, "we must ask whether a non-anti-Semitic critique of economic life was possible in the nineteenth century" (152). Marx performs the pastoralism and technophobia of the age, perhaps unwittingly, but can be read, after Haraway, as using monsters more as *demonstrations*.[23]

Wendling is particularly good on Marx's anxieties about working women. Steam power had reduced the need for strength in labor, and the modern tool system was superseding male-control crafts, hence the "troubling" entry of women into paid work.[24] Wendling:

> If, unlike these reformers, we interpret the laboring, actively sexual female body as a positive rather than a negative monstrosity, we might even conclude that industrialization has conditioned certain aspects of women's liberation…A girl at work is not, necessarily, a rough, foul-mouthed boy. She might simply be a rough, foul-mouthed girl, or, better still, a rough and foul-mouthed hybrid creature whose very existence challenges the rigid norms of Victorian gender. (166–67)

A line of thought rather lusciously extended by Préciado. On the other hand, Marx did have some clues as to how gender and race emerge as new means of social differentiation under capitalism where a chunk of labor has been leveled and homogenized. A woman or a person of color is no longer distinguished by a lack of guild skills, but as Gilroy stresses, by physiology alone.

---

23 Donna Haraway, *Modest_Witness*, New York: Routledge, 1997, 213ff.

24 One could connect this to Lyotard's brilliant reading on Marx and the "little girl" in *Libidinal Economy*. Marx shared the Victorian anxieties of his time.

In his tech notebooks, Marx perceives science and tech as "thick, historically sedimented practices" (180). He got this from a selective reading of Babbage. Both shared an interest in class and the social role of science. Babbage thought tech would educate the workers; Marx, that tech would alienate the workers, but form them into a class as abstract labor. Unlike Marx, Babbage did not neglect the question of the reskilling as well as deskilling of workers. Babbage wanted cooperative enterprises; Marx of course thought there was no solution but to let the whole engine blow.

Interestingly, Babbage stressed working-class *agency* in technical change, which Marx excludes. In writers such different as Virno, Dean and Chun, this perspective drops out, and labor becomes either a pure antagonist to tech or a mere effect of it. One could perhaps use Babbage to write a new chapter of E. P. Thompson's *The Making of the English Working Class* on its role in the making of tech itself—which is to say to do *science studies from below.*[25]

Oddly, Marx follows the line of thought of Malthus et al. in the notion of the need to sacrifice and to not interfere in the workings of "nature," where "nature" here is the nature of capitalism itself. Another fork in the matrix of the Marx-field might follow Liebig or Babbage, for whom nature is to be interfered with in the interests of the common good. As I read her, Wendling offers an understanding of Marx where he performs a series of tactical appropriations from two broad traditions: one philosophical; the other a scientific materialism. Both are ideological. Marx's tactics use these ideologies against each other to suggestively mark out a path beyond.

Wendling does not highlight the *metabolic rift* theme, which is another of Marx's borrowings from Liebig. That might be a place to push back from the energetics side against some residual forms of capitalist humanism in the Anthropocene, where all will be well if we ride organic bamboo bicycles and buy locavore cheese. From the brilliant start Wendling has made, a path opens up to think Marx through the major scientific discoveries after his time, in biology,

25 E. P. Thompson, *The Making of the English Working Class*, New York: Vintage, 1966.

earth science and information science—which would be to repeat and revise his tactics for a critical theory of the present situation. Capital's reliance on labor to exploit is anachronistic. But this opens up onto a strange worldview. "Human agency does not do the groundwork for a better society; instead, society lays the groundwork for future human agency behind the backs of its human agents" (135). The monstrosity of capital is the condition of possibility of its overcoming.

2.

Kojin Karatani: Structure of the World

There're a lot of different ways to weave new strands out of the Marx-field. Wendling did it by reconnecting Marx to a neglected strand of scientific materialism. Kojin Karatani does it with the well-worn fibers of Marx's debt to German idealism, but he does it in a strikingly original way. His *The Structure of World History* is an astonishing work of synthetic historical theory.[1] Karatani views world history as a history of *modes of exchange*. He rejects the classical Marxist view of history as successive modes of production forming an infrastructure, to which political, religious and cultural levels are superstructures.[2]

The Marxist base and superstructure model always conjures up for me an image of the social formation as a three-story building, with an economic ground floor and politics and ideology (or culture) as the second and third. Karatani's alternative model is more like three elevator shafts running through the social formation from top to bottom. The inadequacies of the base-and-super three-story image led Marxists such as Althusser to stress the *relative autonomy* and material specificity of the political and cultural "levels," an idea taken even further in Mouffe and Butler towards an absolute autonomy and even priority of the political. Karatani sees two problems with this. One is a loss of a totalizing and systematic approach to history. The

1 Kojin Karatani, *The Structure of World History: From Modes of Production to Modes of Exchange*, Durham, NC: Duke University Press, 2014.

2 Marx, "Preface" to the *Contribution to the Critique of Political Economy*.

other is that it is really only in the West that politics could even be imagined as autonomous from economics at all.

So rather than the three horizontal levels, Karatani thinks three (or perhaps four) elevator shafts, running vertically through the social formation, and conceived as modes of exchange. Mode A is *association*, or rather the reciprocity of the gift. Mode B is *brute force*, or rule and protection. Mode C is *commodity exchange*. There's also a Mode D, which transcends the others, but more on that later. Rather than criticize Marx, Karatani thinks it is time to complete his historical materialist project, by doing for Modes A and B what Marx did for C.

Since Marcel Mauss, mode of exchange A is assumed to be dominant in archaic societies, but did not really exist among nomadic peoples.[3] They could not stockpile goods. They pooled them as pure gift. It was a society of mobility and equality. Clan society only really developed the reciprocity of the gift once there was settlement. Clan society members were made equal by the reciprocity of the gift but were no longer free.

This is relevant to Marx's notion of primitive communism, which is hard to support with anthropological studies. Marx and Engels looked to Lewis Morgan, who studied clan societies, when they should have been looking not at sedentary clans but nomads.[4] Karatani's project is to envision a return to a kind of nomadism, equal and free.

Most of the study concerns not mode D but the interactions of modes A, B and C, or association, brute force and commodity production. Karatani thinks these first as something like elevator shafts running through the social formation from top to bottom, but then loops them into each other in something like a Borromean knot. It was Hegel in the *Philosophy of Right* who first articulated this three-part model. Marx began his historical materialism with a critique of Hegel on this.[5]

---

3 Marcel Mauss, *The Gift*, Chicago: HAU Books, 2016.

4 Lewis Morgan, *League of the Iroquois*, New York: Citadel, 1984.

5 Karl Marx, *Early Writings*, Harmondsworth: Penguin and New Left Review, 1975, 243ff.

> But in doing so Marx regarded the capitalist economy as constituting the base structure, while he took nation and state to be part of the ideological superstructure. He was never able to grasp the complex social formation that is Capital-Nation-State. This led him to the view that state and nation would naturally wither away once the capitalist system was abolished.

But these are not just superstructures and cannot be dissolved "simply through acts of enlightenment" (xvi).

And so Karatani revisits Marx's critique of Hegel and Hegel's idealist view of state and nation, "to turn them on their head the way Marx did via a materialist approach" (xvii). He claims to extend the methods of Marx's *Capital* to state and nation, or rather to modes of exchange A and B of which they are the current forms. Materialism here means mode of exchange, not of production. "If we posit that economic base equals mode of production, we are unable to explain pre-capitalist societies" (4). I am not convinced by this argument, but let's rather see what Karatani's modes of exchange can explain.

A constant of Karatani's thought is that it is always a *world-system* approach, rather than one that takes social formations as having internal developmental processes that take priority over their external relations.[6] (Although as we shall see, there is one strange exception to this). The Borromean knot of Capital-Nation-State is the product of a world system, not of any one nation-state, as were the previous arrangements of the three modes.

So while Karatani follows Mauss in thinking that Mode A dominates premodern societies, he thinks Mode A's gift exchanges arose not within, but between societies: "reciprocity is not so much a principle of community as it is a principle for forming larger, stratified communities" (5). Mode B, brute plunder and force, also has a critical role between societies. The conquered come to accept protection in exchange for plunder, and peace is kept with gestures of redistribution. Interestingly, he sees Carl Schmitt's friend-enemy relation of

6 Immanuel Wallerstein, *World System Analysis: An Introduction*, Durham, NC: Duke University Press, 2004.

Politics as just a subset of mode of exchange B, and hence in a sense actually "economic."[7] What is particularly delicious about Karatani is that it is a more, not less "economistic" theory than most now current. All three modes are "economic" modes—but of exchange, not of production.

Mode C is commodity exchange, or mutual consent between parties, but with neither the reciprocal obligation of Mode A or the brute force compulsion of Mode B. In Mode C each recognizes the other as a free being owing nothing more to community or ruler once the transaction is done. This freedom from constraint in Mode C is constitutive of the city as social form.

There is no separate sphere of politics or culture or ethics in this theory. All historical social formations include all three modes. Modes A, B and C produce different kinds of power, which are successively community, state and international law. Not all forms of power are based on coercion. The reciprocal gift of Mode A is also a power, and so too is the "natural law" of trade and money characteristic of Mode C. While Karatani implies it rather than directly states it, Modes A, B and C seem to make possible successive *scales* of organization.

Karatani makes external relations at least as constitutive as internal ones for social formations at all historical stages. With one exception. He mentions in passing that Marx drew on the work not only of Hegel but also of Moses Hess, who advanced Feuerbach's critique of religion even further toward a critique of nation and state. Karatani notes that Marx borrowed from Hess the concept of an exchange between the human and nature as *Stoffwechsel*, usually translated as *metabolism*.

In the footnotes at least, Karatani is aware of how this leads towards things like the work of John Bellamy Foster on Marx's ecology, towards thinking human history as part of natural history, with a stress on what Marx in *Capital* vol. 3 called the *metabolic rift* that opens when collective human labor interrupts the cycles of molecular flow within the planetary system. For example, Marx knew from Liebig's classic

7 Compare to Gopal Balakrishnan, *The Enemy: An Intellectual Portrait of Carl Schmitt*, London: Verso, 2002.

studies that modern agriculture disrupted the nitrogen and phosphorus cycles.[8]

Karatani's historical materialism is entirely focused on social relations—except in odd moments when natural changes enter from without. Karatani has the chutzpah to accuse V. Gordon Childe of not being Marxist enough, but Childe at least thought seriously about labor-nature metabolism. Karatani makes relations of exchange prior to relations of production. Here is the thread of an argument I find interesting, but with which I can't agree.

Unfortunately, Karatani shares a certain humanistic disdain for scientific thought, and remains naively positive about what humanistic thought can achieve on its own. Were it not for science and technology, we would not even be able to produce a knowledge of what climate change is, let alone of other metabolic rifts, which together are the symptomatology of the Anthropocene. So while there is progress here in thinking cultural, ethical and political phenomena in a materialist manner, it is not quite materialist *enough* for me, even in Wendling's nuanced sense of the term. And while there is attention to externalities that impinge on social formations, the externalities of the engagement with the natural world are never an integral part of the theory. Whether the social formation is imagined on the three horizontal levels model or the three elevator shaft model, all too often what's lost from view is the foundation pit dug in the earth underneath.[9]

One enduring bugbear of historical materialism is Marx's sketchy idea of an "Asiatic mode of production." Refreshingly, Karatani thinks it is a viable concept, just better thought as something not limited to Asia, just as the feudal mode is not limited to Europe. The "Asiatic" is a despotic state or empire where Mode B dominates Modes A and C. In an interesting shift of perspective, China appears as the "normal" developmental form, and Greece and Rome as failed approximations.

---

8 John Bellamy Foster, *Marx's Ecology: Materialism and Nature*, New York: Monthly Review Press, 2000.

9 Andrey Platonov, *The Foundation Pit*, New York: NYRB Classics, 2009.

Borrowing from Karl Wittfogel, Karatani divides the precapitalist world up spatially into the *despotic empires*, their *margins*, their *submargins* and the "out of sphere."[10] Margins get absorbed into despotic states, but submargins need not, even though they often adopt things like the writing systems of the despotic empires. Greece and Rome were submargins to despotic states. Germany was submargin to Rome, where feudalism took root. Trade and cities were able to emerge there outside feudal control. Capitalism arose at the periphery of world empires, giving rise to the modern world system. Russia and China escaped this fate. Socialists unwittingly gave new form to old despotic states.[11]

Within a social formation, the rise of Mode C, commodity exchange, does not mean the abolition of Mode A and Mode B. It was Mode B that became the modern state. Absolutism created the state with a standing army and no reciprocal exchange among ruling elites. Absolutism established what had long existed under despotic states. Mode A then returns in the form of the nation as "imagined community"—once local communities have been weakened or abolished.[12]

This world-systems theory actually has three successive stages. World mini-systems characterized the archaic world, and were dominated by Mode A. The world empires that subsumed them were dominated by Mode B, or what Marx thought of as the "Asiatic mode of production." The modern world market system is dominated by Mode C. Karatani then suggests we are ready for a "fourth great shift: the shift to a world republic" (28).

In a world mini-system, war exists because there is no transcendent power over the clans. Reciprocity is an in-between, it does not

10 Karl Wittfogel, *Oriental Despotism*, New Haven: Yale University Press, 1957. Here I am inclined rather to follow Joseph Needham, *The Great Titration*, Toronto: University of Toronto Press, 1969, 190ff.

11 But see Wang Hui, *China: From Empire to Nation-State*, Cambridge, MA: Harvard University Press, 2014 for a decontruction of all these categories from the point of view of China.

12 Benedict Anderson, *Imagined Communities*, London: Verso, 2006. But see also Harold Innis, *The Bias of Communication*, Toronto: University of Toronto Press, 2008.

dissolve the parties in a higher unity. It can lead to a federal unity, but not a state. So why did hunter-gatherers settle? Climate change. During the Ice Age, humans spread. Warming led to reforestation and decline in game. The stockpiling of smoked fish led to a "sedentary revolution" (45) that produced an agrarian clan society still based on a reciprocity that maintained the independence of social formations from each other.

This reciprocity of the gift extends beyond the human. Magic is a form of the gift. Magic is the attempt to control another through the gift in the form of the sacrifice.[13] "Sacrifices are gifts that impose a debt on nature, thereby sealing off the anima of nature and transforming it into an It" (53). Magic despiritualizes nature. Settlement means coexisting not only with others but with the dead, and the attempt to placate them with gifts.

Karatani dismisses the significance of invention such as that of the deep-furrow plough. "In the terms of the relationship between technology and nature, the innovations achieved by ancient civilizations had little impact" (61). The shift from bronze to iron was for Karatani more important to the rise of the state (weapons) than agriculture. The most important tech in the premodern world was administrative. "The technologies for ruling people don't rely on naked compulsion: instead, they install forms of discipline that make people voluntarily follow rules and work" (61). Religion is about organizing labor—a view that brings Karatani close to Bogdanov.[14]

In another of his reversals of perspective, he argues that "The state did not arise as a result of the Agricultural Revolution: to the contrary, the Agricultural Revolution was a consequence of the rise of the state" (63). Trading and warfare led to city-states, these states then led to agriculture: "the rise of the city cannot be separated from the rise of the state. In other words, mode of exchange B and mode of exchange C are inseparable from one another" (65).

---

13 Alexander R. Galloway, Eugene Thacker and McKenzie Wark, *Excommunication: Three Inquiries in Media and Mediation*, Chicago: University of Chicago Press, 2013.

14 Alexander Bogdanov, *The Philosophy of Living Experience*, Leiden: Brill, 2015.

Interestingly, he views the state as a development of Mode B, as a form of *nonreciprocal* exchange. Hobbes thought the social contract was extorted by fear; Karatani sees it as the transformation of plunder into a mode of exchange, of plunder for protection. The state put an end to horizontal reciprocity, an end to both gift and vendetta. States do not arise from a single community, but in the space of world empire: "the sovereign is something that comes from outside" (71). The state comes from exchange between ruling and ruled social formations.

Agrarian clan communities come after, and are produced by, the state. "Reciprocity does not acknowledge any higher authority. The agrarian communities that formed under Asiatic despotism preserved reciprocity in such aspects as mutual aid and equalization. But they lost the other aspect of reciprocity: their autonomy" (74). While the Greeks, out on the submargin, were making city states, the Qin and Han empires formed the characteristic form of despotic state. "Once a centralized order was established, the despotic state then tried to actively co-opt traditions dating back to clan society. This is why the agrarian community organized by the despotic state took on the appearance of being a continuation of clan society" (75).

Hence Mode B depends on a modified and extended form of Mode A:

> the agrarian community is an imagined community whose framework is provided by the despotic state—just as the modern nation cannot exist in the absence of the framework of the centralized state. Asiatic despotism existed in the form of an amalgamation of the despotic state with the agrarian community. (76)

Dynasties come and go, but the Mode B despotic state and the Mode A agrarian clan remain. Backward Greece and Rome did not develop these forms.

Marx, Weber, Wittfogel and Joseph Needham all argued that the Chinese despotic state was a hydraulic state, that its administrative elaboration was a result of building the technology to control flooding and irrigation, or in short that metabolism determined human-to-human exchange. Karatani disputes this: "The civilization realized by hydraulic societies was not just a matter of technologies for dominating nature; more than that, it consisted of technologies for governing people—namely, state apparatuses, standing armies, bureaucratic systems, written language, and communication networks" (79). One could wonder, however, whether this is a false distinction, and if one can entirely subordinate metabolism to purely intersubjective exchange.

Where do administered and administering people come from? After all, "people do not voluntarily choose to become bureaucrats" (79). A money economy is a precondition for a bureaucratic system. Thus, just as the despotic Mode B state depends on a modified form of Mode A, it also requires the development of Mode C. But money arises not within but between social formations. "Karl Marx repeatedly stressed that commodity exchange began with exchanges between different communities" (81). The form of power of Mode C is money, which the state cannot do without. Karatani stresses the role of money in sustaining standing armies.[15]

For Karatani, money does not require a labor theory of value for its explication. The power of money is grounded in a social contract. Money is king in the same way that the king is king. The king is king because others are subjects, while they imagine they are subjects because he is king. Likewise, money. Money is sovereign, but sovereign as empty position anyone can occupy. Money is minted by the state, but not its power to circulate globally. And in another reversal of perspective, Karatani argues that "the power of precious-metal money to circulate worldwide is not something owing to the state. To the contrary, the state's ability to mint money depends in this power" (92).

Mode B depends on Mode C but tries to limit and contain it.[16] Mode C gets out of hand. "Exchange is pursued to seek not use values but rather exchange values, and for this reason is without limit" (94).

15 As in David Graeber, *Debt: The First 5,000 Years*, New York: Melville House, 2014.

16 Compare to Gilles Deleuze and Félix Guattari, *Anti-Oedipus*, London: Penguin, 2009, 217ff.

Mode C is one of eternal and limitless expansion. But enforcing the repayment of debt calls for both the habits of reciprocity of Mode A and the sanctions of Mode B. These are its real conditions of existence. "The existence of exchange C, far from being a materialist, rational base structure, is fundamentally a world of credit and speculation, a speculative world" (97).

In despotic states such as China, trade was managed by the state bureaucracy, which Greece and Rome lacked. There the market could play a destructive role. In Greece, "letting the market set prices was politically equivalent to letting the masses decide public questions" (101). But Mode C without limits damaged the polis, resulting in inequality and servitude. Democracy in Athens was an attempt to preserve a community of rulers within the polis, backed by an ever expanding slave system.

The despotic states exist within systems of world empire. They exist in contexts of world religions, languages and law that extend beyond and between them. Only some are irrigation based, and here Karatani much expands the concept beyond an Asiatic mode of production. While some were based on irrigation (in China, Peru, Mexico), some were maritime (Rome), some nomadic (the Mongols) and some combined the nomadic with a merchant base (Islam). Karatani: "we come to see that Marx's distinctions between Asiatic, classical and feudal do not mark successive diachronic stages but rather positional relationships within the space of a world-empire" (124). In sum, the three modes of exchange exist in parallel and are interconnected, but in successive historical epochs, Modes A, then B, then C have been dominant.

What then of Mode D? It is the polar opposite of Mode B. Mode of exchange D marks the attempt to restore the reciprocal community (A) on top of the market economy (C). It is an ideal form that never existed in reality, although it is given expression, at least in their formative moments, by the great world religions. But perhaps this line of thought could be made rather more "materialist." In his book *Debt*, Graeber notes that when precious metals are used to ornament temples, it is the withdrawal from circulation of the material means of making the coinage to sustain an army.

The sacrifice of gold to imaginary gods is thus nevertheless a real sacrifice.[17]

Karatani stresses the difference rather than continuity of religion and magic. Prayer is directed, via the priest-king as guardian of the portal, to a transcendent God. It lacks the horizontal and egalitarian aspect of magic. "The development of magic into religion was nothing other than the development from clan society to the state" (131). But religion did not intend to be this: "universal religions originally appeared in the form of a negation of this sort of world empire and religion. As soon as they achieved stable form, however, they found themselves appropriated into the ruling apparatus of a world empire" (133). Religions are part of a history of modes of sacrifice.[18]

World empires (Mode B) need both world religion (Mode A) and world money (Mode C). "The worship of money is, to borrow Marx's language, a fetishism, and with the rise of world money, this fetishism became monotheistic" (134). Money frees individuals from community and reciprocity. But religions are also expressions of something else: "In the process of empire formation, there is a moment when, under the sway of mode of exchange B, mode of exchange C dismantles mode of exchange A; at this moment, and in resistance to it, that universal religion appears, taking the form of mode of exchange D" (135).

Religions both restore, but also abstract, the reciprocity of Mode A. For example, the Jewish god is of a new kind. When their state failed, the people did not abandon Him. "The defeat of a state no longer meant the defeat of its god...This meant the rejection of reciprocity between God and people" (139). This is a power of God that transcends community, state and money.

Christianity stressed Jesus's rejection of state, money *and* community. He speaks of God's love as an absolute gift that cannot be reciprocated. Universal religions gesture beyond the particular reciprocity of Mode A: "universal religions do not become universal by negating the particular. Rather, they become universal through an

17 Graeber, *Debt.*

18 Raoul Vaneigem, *La Résistance au Christianisme*, Paris: Fayard, 1993.

incessant awareness of the contradiction between universality and particularity" (143). What matters about, for example, Saint Paul is not just a transcendent universalism.[19] "The transcendence and immanence of God forms an inseparable, paradoxical unity" (144).

Universal religions arise when Mode C has become generalized, and (as Graeber shows in detail) borrow their metaphors of universality from the market place. World religions are critical of kings and priests, but they become the religion of the state, or fade away. "What Buddha carried out was the deconstruction of existing religions" (152). Confucius taught benevolence, and his social reformism was stressed even more by Mencius. Laozi opposed not only the state but also clan society, pointing back to a nomadic way of life, and Taoism was "a fountainhead of utopianism and anarchism" (156). Karatani's project is in essence to revive not the religious but *social* force of Mode D, to push once again for forms of exchange that are both free and equal, but at a higher level of organization and more extensive scale.

World economy is different from world empire in not being so based on coercion. Karatani thinks Mode C broke out of the constraints of Mode B in Europe because of its marginality rather than its centrality to world history. He cites Needham on the advanced level of technical and social organization in China up until late-modern times. "A world economy emerged in western Europe not because its civilization was advanced but rather because it was located on the submargin" (160). The Mongolian Empire collapsed, after which rose Qing, Mughal and Ottoman despotic states. Europe colonized the margins and out-of-sphere spaces of the empires. Russia and China resisted marginalization, and both tried to build a different world system.

In short, a world economy could only arise where there wasn't a powerful despotic state controlling a world empire. This world economy would be composed eventually of modern nation-states. What made such states possible were the absolutist monarchies,

19 Compare Karatani on Paul to Alain Badiou, *Saint Paul: The Foundation of Universalism*, Stanford CA: Stanford University Press.

which were a bit different to despotic states in that mode C was stronger. There is a union of capital and state in absolute monarchies, in the form of mercantilism. Absolute monarchs rejected higher-order power above them, whether emperor or church, and did their best to abolish the autonomy of communities within their domain.

Absolutism made a more or less homogeneous people under a sovereign, a necessary step prior to that people itself claiming to be sovereign. Absolutism forged the link in the Borromean knot between state and nation. Western powers could not challenge Ottoman, Mughal or Qing power directly, but spread the doctrine of national self-determination and denounced imperial rule. "The existence of a sovereign state inevitably leads to the creation of other sovereign states" (168). The state's essence comes out in war, as a state exists really in relation to other states.

The absolutist state produces the possibility of the modern state's Borromean knot of Capital-State-Nation. The state has to call into existence the means of making a nation, through compulsory education and conscription. Just as Mode B in the form of the state produces Mode A in the form of the nation, it also creates the conditions of possibility for Mode C: "there has never been a time when the state did not intervene in the economy." It is the world market system that produces the modern state, not the other way around. "The state's distinctive form of power will never be understood if we view it only from the perspective of its interior" (174).

Marxists treat the state as superstructure, and expect it to wither away after the revolution. But after the Russian revolution of 1917 it actually got stronger. "Marx had penetrating insight into the nature of capitalism, but his understanding of the state was inadequate" (175). In *Capital* he bracketed off Ricardo's interest in taxation. Karatani turns to Marx's "Eighteenth Brumaire" text for a more nuanced understanding of the Capital-State-Nation knot.[20]

As Karatani reads it, Marx was grappling with Louis Bonaparte's distinctive structural role: "his power as emperor was established

20 Karl Marx, "The Eighteenth Brumaire of Napoleon Bonaparte," in Karl Marx, *Surveys From Exile*, London: Verso, 2010.

by projecting the external appearance of gift-counter-gift reciprocal exchanges onto what was in reality a plunder-redistribution exchange carried out by the state machinery" (178). Karatani takes the structural, sovereign role of both Louis Bonaparte and Otto von Bismarck as evidence of the autonomous power of the state.

Mode C has always existed, but was kept contained until recently by early forms of Mode A and Mode B. As with his analysis of Modes A and B, Karatani sees Mode C as arising within a world system, or between social formations, rather than within a social formation. Commodity exchange that takes place between different value systems can yield a profit. The totality of capital has to engage in an equal exchange with labor and yet it has to extract surplus value. Capital has to go outside and find new consumers. "In order for the accumulation of capital to continue, it has to ceaselessly engage in the recruitment of new proletarians" (192).

The capitalist class prefers finance and merchant capital to industrial capital. (Keynes's *liquidity preference.*) Holland already led in finance and merchant capital, so Britain had to go for industrial, and used the state to make it possible. "The belief that the capitalist market economy develops autonomously, outside the influence of the state, is simply mistaken" (197).

What is distinctive about industrial capital is its discovery of *labor power*. Industrial capital commodifies labor power, which is in the end in limited supply. Industrial capital has to expand across the world system in search of new populations to make over as workers. Moreover, "the emergence of the industrial proletariat is simultaneously the emergence of the consumer" (188).

Industrial capital requires also ceaseless tech-change to improve relative surplus value through rising labor productivity. Capital is rapidly approaching the limits of resources and the ability to process waste. There's an opening here for Karatani to take up the buried theme of metabolic rift in his text, but he doesn't take it. "But the human-nature relationship is of course primary. We need, however, to remain wary of ideologies that stress this and forget about human-human relations" (206). This is of course itself an ideology, and indeed the dominant one among humanities scholars.

One of the most interesting discussion in Karatani is on the nation as a (failed) attempt to revive Mode A in modern form.

> The nation is something that appears within the social formation as an attempt to recover, through imagination, mode of exchange A and community, which is disintegrating under the rule of capital-state. The nation is formed by capital-state, but it is at the same time a form of protest and resistance to the conditions brought about by capital-state, as well as an attempt to supplement for what is lacking in capital-state. (209)

The nation replaces religion as what gives people a sense of the eternal. Nations formed under the absolute monarchs, who united the people by breaking up community within and by refusing any empire or church beyond it. For them, national law trumps empire law (natural law).

The cultivation of nationalism is connected to the management of populations of labor power (or what the Foucauldians call *biopower*). But nationalism was also a form of resistance. The romanticism from which it sprang wanted to restore a sentiment of community lost to capital-state. "Late eighteenth century Europe saw the rise not only of Anderson's 'imagined communities' but also of imagination itself" (214).

The source was Kant, for whom sensibility and understanding are synthesized through imagination. But the romantics lost sight of the imagined status of the nation. They took it for real. "Even in Hegel's philosophy, it is forgotten that this knot was produced in a fundamental sense by the imagination, in the form of the nation; he forgets that the nation exists only in imagination. This also explains why his philosophy was unable to foresee any possibility of superseding this knot" (224). For a tantalizing moment, Karatani maps the triad of Understanding-Sensibility-Imagination onto State-Capital-Nation—as if Kant's categories were a mapping of the organizational forms of modernity itself.

Most modern thinkers read their Marx through the supplement of another philosopher. There are Spinozist-Marxists (Althusser, Negri,

Virno), Hegelian-Marxists (Lukács, Adorno, Žižek), Nietzschian Marxists (Deleuze, Lyotard). The supplement in Karatani is Kant, and in particular Kant's *kingdom of ends*, his regulative idea of treating others not as means but as ends, a reciprocity of freedom itself. "Kant negated religion absolutely—yet he also extracted its basic morality" (230).

This is not the same as distributive justice, which assumes the inequalities generated by Mode C are left intact and dealt with at the second order by a Mode B that has to make concessions to demands usually framed in the Mode A of the nation as imagined community. Rather, Karatani thinks Kant's kingdom of ends implies the abolition of both state and capital. It would be a world republic of peace not just within but between states. This Mode D is no more than a regulative idea, a kind of transcendental illusion. Like the unified self, the kingdom of ends is an idea that makes it possible to think and act but which is not itself real or realizable. "Ultimately, people cannot help but find an end or purpose to history" (232).

Karatani rejects the Jacobin strand of socialism, which saw itself as inheriting and completing the project of the French Revolution, with its imaginary invocation of an ideal Borromean knot of Capital-State-Nation under the slogan of liberty, equality, fraternity—which was only realized under Napoleon as sovereign, and in the form of revolutionary war.[21] Rather, Karatani turns to Proudhon's pre-Marxist socialism and its rejection of statist schemes. "Because equality is realized through redistribution carried out by the state, equality always leads to a greater or lesser extent to Jacobinism and increased state power" (235). Drawing on his more extended argument in his book *Transcritique*, he picks up Max Stirner as a socialist thinker, for whom a higher form of associationism can only come after people free themselves from community.[22]

Marx is much closer to Proudhon on the state than to Lassalle, who is the real origin of state-socialist politics, even though Engels tacked

21 See McKenzie Wark, *The Spectacle of Disintegration*, London: Verso, 2013, 79ff, on my preference for Fourier.

22 Kojin Karatani, *Transcritique*, Cambridge, MA: MIT Press, 2005.

much closer to such a position after Marx's death. Following Engels, Kautsky and Bernstein argued for a statist socialism in Germany, while Luxemburg and Trotsky thought revolution could happen on the margin, due to the necessarily interstate character of the world system and the super-exploitation of the margin. Lenin would pick up this argument and marry it to Jacobin and statist socialism.

Karatani wants to revive a quite other tradition. He agrees with the Leninists that labor unions tend to get absorbed into capitalism and raise only partial and particular demands within its framework. He turns instead to cooperative movements. "Labor unions are a form of struggle against capital taking place within a capitalist economy, while cooperatives are a movement that moves away from the capitalist system. In other words, the former is centered on production, the latter on circulation" (243).

Marx did indeed see the necessity of seizing state power, but in order to make a cooperative commonwealth possible. This Karatani counterposes to the dangers of the Lassalle-type state socialist line. "This was not a product of Stalinism; to the contrary, belief in state-ownership produced Stalinism" (250). Karatani thinks Marx broke with the Jacobin politics that had its heyday in the 1848 revolutions. "The Paris Commune marked its last burst of glory and was not a harbinger of the future" (253). And Marx knew it, despite his fidelity to the Paris Commune.

Contra Žižek, Karatani is opposed to the politics of the leap. There're no shortcuts. "In trying to master capitalism by means of the state, Marxists fell into a trap laid by the state" (257). It is also impossible to supersede capital-state through the nation. That way lies fascism. The opening is rather to rethink Mode D, which would be a "return of the repressed" (xi), or a way for reciprocity to comes back under the dominance of Modes B and C. But Mode D does not really restore community. It is a regulative idea that restores reciprocity after and without community: "communism depends less on shared ownership of the means of production than on the return of nomadism" (xii).

Mode D escapes from particular social formations, not unlike Virno's figure of the *exodus*. The overcoming at a higher level of the

Capital-Nation-State has to be realized in the form of a new world system. The negation of the Capital-State-Nation world system has to come from cooperative practices and from a new imagining of Mode D. But even within the text there're the materials for another kind of historical thought. It would be one that has to pay more attention to both metabolism and production, which are, after all, aspects of the same thing.

Karatani sees the stages of the world market system in terms of the key world commodity of each. Thus for mercantilism it is textiles, for liberalism it is light industry, for finance capitalism it is heavy industry, for state monopoly capitalism it is durable consumer goods, and for multinational capitalism it is *information*. Brown would call this *neoliberalism*, but that's too benign a term for such an imperialistic world system. The current stage, despite appearances, is one of the weakness of the old hegemon, the United States, within the world system. It is an era of the expanded export of capital and corresponding cuts to redistributive justice by the states at the core of the old world system, as "state-capital was freed from egalitarian demands" (279).

The State does not wither away even as Mode C globalizes. State and Nation are no mere superstructures. If there's an end to capital, it may have to do with the entry of China and India into the world market system, and the final exhaustion of the process of making new worker-consumers. Not to mention the waste products of metabolic rift catching up with us all.

Rather than a regulative idea from without, perhaps actual developments from within are key transformative factors. One could imagine the Capital-State-Nation system accelerated from below into a new mode.[23] But it comes up against the systemic constraints of metabolism. Perhaps then one could attempt to describe a shift in levels of organization forced by the confrontation with scarcity. Sartre usefully constructs a world-historical thought on scarcity (which appears nowhere in Karatani), but links it to violence and the practico-inert,

23 McKenzie Wark, "Spinoza on Speed," *Public Seminar*, November 19, 2014, at publicseminar.org.

a kind of repetition of reified and passive affects. But it seems scarcity can lead to a third alternative, which is the extrapolation out of existing forms of organization of new ones.

Bogdanov thought there was a tendency to substitute from one's own labor practices ideas about organization and impose them on the world.[24] Hence Kant's kingdom of ends appears as philosophical practice itself writ large. Other organizational practices might also substitute from their activities to worldviews. Thus it is not only Mode A that might give rise to a regulative idea, but Mode B and Mode C as well. Substituting from Mode B produces what I call the *drone of Minerva*, a reactive policing, particularly by waning states, based on total surveillance and force projected at a distance.[25] Substituting from mode C, we get *financialization* (as in Boutang) and a concentration of all decision-making power in the form of the quantification and pricing of all possibilities.

These regulative ideas, or rather substitutions, all have something in common: an actual infrastructure that would make them possible. They presuppose an actually existing world of communication and computation vectors. So too might attempts to extend Mode A as Mode D. As I argued in *A Hacker Manifesto*, this abstraction of the world is riven with class tensions. The same vector, the same information infrastructure, makes possible both control and commodification, but also more abstract forms of the gift. The politics of sharing free information then becomes the leading form for thinking new possibilities.

While I find Karatani illuminating in many ways, I think what we need is a more vulgar Marxist perspective, or rather two. One is based on Marx's understanding of the labor-nature interaction as metabolism. The second is to revive an old Anglo-Marxist interest in the forces of production. Karatani, like so many others, argues as if this was still somehow the dominant version of Marxism, when it is clear that since the anti-systemic movements of '68 and the rise of New Left

---

24 Bogdanov, *Philosophy of Living Experience*.

25 McKenzie Wark, "The Drone of Minerva," *Public Seminar*, November 5, 2014, at publicseminar.org.

ideologies, the opposite is the case. All of the philosophical schools of Marx join in refusing such a vulgar account. But a dialectic (if it is still that) which connects metabolism, scarcity, waste products and changes in technical-organizational form might seem like a useful perspective in these times.

3.

Paolo Virno: Grammars and Multitudes

Paolo Virno offers a curious diagnosis of the times. In *A Grammar of the Multitude*, he writes of the *communism of capital*.[1] It's a thought that has some pedigree in Marx, who made a similar observation in his own time about the formation of the joint-stock company, which was capital's way of pooling resources and escaping the confines of a narrow form of private property. The crisis of the 1930s led to an analogous socialism of capital, with its hybrids of state and monopoly control.

One could see the recent struggles over the European Union, global trade agreements or the transnational megacorporation as having a similar paradoxical quality. It takes an awful lot of communism to keep forms of private property, exploitation and accumulation afloat. This time the form of communism is rather different to the '30s, less about hegemony and the state, more about transnational infrastructures.

There is a quite conventional understanding of the current mode of production in Virno. He calls it *post-Fordism*. But in many other respects his work is highly original. Like Antonio Negri, he sees its rise through his own experience in Italy as a left militant of the '60s and '70s, activity for which he was imprisoned. And like Negri, he invented a form of Marxist thought at variance with the Gramsci-worship of its more official Italian form.

Virno sees the radical refusal of work characteristic of Italian *workerist* politics of the '70s as a precursor to the form labor takes today.

1 Paolo Virno, *A Grammar of the Multitude*, Los Angeles: Semiotext(e), 2004.

Just as the commodification of agriculture produced vagabonds and highwaymen before it produced the urban, industrial working class, so too post-Fordism first produced the "metropolitans," indifferent to factory labor, tinkering with new communication technologies and forms of urban existence outside the steady life of shift work.[2] Unlike McRobbie, he offers a somewhat masculinist take on this refusal, but it was nevertheless a real one.

Drawing on Marx's "Fragment on Machines," Virno thinks there is finally a "surpassing of the society of labor" (GM101). Virno: "Marx upholds a thesis that is hardly Marxist: abstract knowledge—scientific knowledge, first and foremost, but not only that—moves towards becoming nothing less than the principal productive force" (GM100). In post-Fordism, there is a contradiction between production that draws on qualitative, creative knowledge yet which is still measuring everything in labor-time units. Labor time no longer works as a measure, not least because of hidden, unpaid labor on which it depends.

For Marx, the *general intellect* was congealed into fixed capital, machinery and so forth, but for Virno it is *living labor*, also known as the mass intellectual (as in Berardi), or the *multitude*. The multitude is then addressed via the themes of the *stranger*, linguistic *commonplaces*, the *publicness* of the intellect, *virtuosity* of performance, *individuation*, *biopolitics* as labor power, *opportunism* and *idle talk*.

A *multitude* is not a people, meaning it is a plurality which doesn't become a unity. The state creates a people as one, whereas the multitude was what Hobbes thought of more as a state of nature. (More on that later.) Before the state is the multitude; after the state there is the people as one. "It is a negative concept this multitude: it is that which did not make itself fit to become a people" (GM23). The coherence of the multitude comes from the communal faculties of language and intellect, of generic shared experience.

Virno takes three approaches to the multitude, the first of which is from the point of view of *fear* and *anguish*. Security from fear is in the

---

2 See Christian Marazzi and Sylvère Lotringer (eds.), *Autonomia: Post-Political Politics*, Los Angeles: Semiotext(e), 2007.

hands of a community; security from anguish can only be the province of a religion. Fear is relative; anguish is absolute. But the divide between them has eroded. The state no longer provides comfort from dread. The unity of a people is bounded by fear and a state can secure them against that fear. The multitude lacks this division between an inside and an outside. The multitude is never at home, is always a *stranger*, even if there remains a "dangerous search for protection" (GM35).

The multitude has its home in the *commonplaces* of language, such as the rhetorical figures of more-and-less, of opposites, or of reciprocity. The special places of discourse are perishing, leaving only the commonplaces. The feeling of homelessness and reliance on commonplaces go together. We are now always exposed to the world in its totality. We are all strangers.

The intellect is most often thought of as a private or individual capacity. Virno: "only one thinker takes exception to this long tradition according to which the 'life of the mind' is resistant to publicness; in several pages of Marx we see the intellect being presented as something exterior and collective, as a public good…Marx speaks of a general intellect" (GM37). Where for others the intellect is a solitary figure, a stranger to the community, the general intellect is a *public* of strangers. "The multitude of those 'without a home' places its trust in the intellect, in the 'common places': in its own way, then, it is a multitude of thinkers (even if these thinkers have only an elementary school education and never read a book, not even under torture.)" (GM39)

The public life of the general intellect is far from utopian. Virno:

> If the publicness of the intellect does not yield to the realm of a public sphere, of a political space in which the many can tend to common affairs, then it produces terrifying effects. A publicness without a public sphere: here is the negative side—the evil, if you wish—of the experience of the multitude. (GM40)

Contra Azuma, the multitude does not converge into a *general will* because it is already a *general intellect*. The generic cognitive and linguistic talents of the multitude are deployed within production and don't become a public sphere or political community. The multitude surfaces both in post-Fordist production and the crisis of the state. "So then, the contemporary working class, the current subordinate labor-power and its cognitive-linguistic collaboration, bear the traits of the multitude, rather than of the people. However, this multitude no longer assumes the 'popular' vocation to state-ness" (GM45). Drawing on Marx's remarks about the workers of the American West in *Capital* chapter 33, the instinctive politics of the multitude is *exodus* from the institutions of the state.

A second way to see the multitude is as a breakdown of the differences between labor (poesis), politics (praxis) and intellect. Labor is an organic exchange with nature that produces something. Politics is between social actors, not natural materials, and its result is not external to it. Post-Fordist labor absorbs attributes of politics, becoming a fusion of politics and labor. There is already too much politics in post-Fordist labor, the multitude doesn't need any more: "political action now seems, in a disastrous way, like some superfluous duplication of the experience of labor...Politics offers a network of communication and a cognitive content of a more wretched variety than what is carried out in the current productive process" (GM51).

Virtuosity is activity that finds its purpose in itself without settling into a finished product. It is also activity that requires the presence of others for a performance. Post-Fordist labor becomes like the virtuoso performance, which is already like politics, in being public and lacking a goal outside of itself: "all virtuosity is intrinsically political" (GM53). The split between politics and labor falls apart. Post-Fordist productive labor becomes something akin to performance art.[3]

The culture industry provided the model for post-Fordism. "Virtuosity becomes labor for the masses with the onset of a culture industry" (GM56). Where the peasant moves slowly; the worker quickly; in the cultural industry they wander. There's no visible production of goods that can be measured. Virno:

3 Hito Steyerl, *The Wretched of the Screen*, New York: e-flux, 2013.

> While the material production of objects is delegated to an automated system of machines, the services rendered by living labor, instead, resemble linguistic-virtuosic services more and more...Within the culture industry, even in its archaic incarnation examined by Benjamin and Adorno, one can grasp early signs of a mode of production which later, in the post-Fordist era, becomes generalized and elevated to the rank of *canon*. (GM58)

What Raymond Williams would have called *residual* forms of culture turned out to have emergent possibilities.[4]

> Capitalism...shows that it can mechanize and parcelize even its spiritual production, exactly as it has done with agriculture and the processing of metals. Serialization, insignificance of individual tasks, the econometrics of feelings, these are the recurrent refrains. Evidently, this critical approach allowed, in the peculiar case of the culture industry, for the continuation of some elements which resist complete assimilation to the Fordist organization of the labor process. (GM59)

Which then become the basis of post-Fordism.

Virno has an interesting take on Guy Debord's *Society of the Spectacle*.[5] "The spectacle, according to Debord, reveals what women and men *can* do. While money mirrors in itself the value of commodities, thus showing what society has *already* produced, the spectacle exposes in a separate form that which the aggregate of society *can* be and do" (GM61). It contains and displays its conditions of possibility as well as its negation.

The spectacle, Virno says,

> is human communication that has become a commodity...Thus, the spectacle has a double nature: a specific product of a particular industry, but also, at the same time, the quintessence of the mode of production in its entirety...What presents the spectacle, so to speak, are the productive forces themselves of society as they overlap, in ever greater

4 Raymond Williams, *Culture and Materialism*, London: Verso, 2006.

5 Guy Debord, *Society of the Spectacle*, New York: Zone Books, 1994.

> measure, with linguistic-communicative competencies and with the *general intellect.* (GM60)

The culture industry is the industry of the means of production. "The culture industry produces (regenerates, experiments with) communicative procedures, which are then destined to function also as means of production in the more traditional sectors of our contemporary economy" (GM61).

In post-Fordism, a worker's knowledge is actively sought rather than repressed. "By general intellect, Marx means science" (GM64). But Virno pays attention to only one of the senses in which Marx thought science was becoming the driver of production. For Virno it is all about social cooperation, leaving out Marx's insight into the increasing role of the natural sciences.

Production now depends on a hybrid of the spheres of labor, praxis and intellect. Intellect becomes a productive force and becomes public; labor becomes virtuoso and political. Virno is more interested in the general intellect incarnated in living labor rather than "cast in iron" (GM65). General intellect is not congealed in fixed capital but is elaborating itself in communicative action. The general intellect as the faculty of speech as such, not particular speech acts. It is a virtuosity without a script, a pure potential.

Trapped within the wage relation, the general intellect nevertheless exhibits certain pathologies.

> The crucial question goes like this: is it possible to split that which today is united, that is, the Intellect (the general intellect) and (wage) Labor, and to unite that which today is divided, that is Intellect and political Action?...Rescuing political action from its current paralysis is no different from developing the publicness of the Intellect outside the realm of wage Labor, in opposition to it. (GM68)

Could there be a non-state, non-laboring, nonrepresentative public sphere as an expression of the multitude? Could there be a transition from a servile to republican virtuosity, via civil disobedience, flight, exit, *exodus*?

In the spirit of Adorno, it is often imagined that unhappiness and insecurity result from the alienation of the individual from a world of mass production and domination. Virno follows Gilbert Simondon in thinking of the collective as the condition of possibility for *individuation*, rather than its negation.[6] Simondon draws attention to the pre-individual qualities of perception and language, to which Virno adds the prevailing relations of production. The interest here is not individuals, as if those always and already existed, but *individuation*. This is a process of subject-formation that is never complete. The relation between the pre-individual and individuation is an affective one. Both dread and panic are manifestations of its incompleteness, being respectively the fear of an I without a world and the anguish of a world without an I.

Oddly enough, it is by participating in the collective that the subject has the possibility of individuating. But for the multitude, the collective is not the site of the *general will*, but rather of the *general intellect*. The question is thus one of creating forms of post-political, nonrepresentative democracy outside of the state. These emerge historically in post-Fordism, but may draw on deeper capacities of our species-being to individuate within, rather than against, the collective. "The 'many' persevere as 'many' without aspiring to the unity of the state because: 1. As individuated singularities they have already left behind the unity/universality intrinsic to the diverse species of the pre-individual; 2. Through their collective action they underscore and further the process of individuation" (GM80).

What Marx called the *social individual* is the multitude, made of language, of social cooperation. "It may seem paradoxical, but I believe that Marx's theory could (or rather should) be understood, today, as a realistic and complex theory of the individual, as a rigorous individualism: thus, a theory of individuation" (GM80–81). The question of *biopolitics* is thus for Virno all about labor power, as a generic potential to produce. "Only in today's world, in a post-Fordist era, is the reality of labor-power fully up to the task of realizing itself" (GM81).

6 Gilbert Simondon, *On the Mode of Existence of Technical Objects*, Minneapolis: Univocal, 2017.

Labor power is an unreal potential which is at the same time bought as a commodity. Labor power is a commonplace, not a proper noun.

> Life lies at the center of politics where the prize to be won is immaterial (and in itself non-present) labor-power. For this reason, and this reason alone, it is legitimate to talk about "bio-politics." The living body which is a concern of the administrative apparatus of the State, is the tangible sign of a yet unrealized potential, the semblance of labor not yet objectified; as Marx says eloquently, of "labor as subjectivity." (GM83)

But under wage labor, nihilism has entered production. It is no longer a question of modernization producing rootlessness, contingency, uncertainty, anomie as side effects of a rational core. Rather, productive activity uses those very effects as resources. "Nihilism, once hidden in the shadow of technical-productive power, becomes a fundamental ingredient of that power, a quality highly prized by the marketplace of labor" (GM86). The result is the affective prevalence of *opportunism* and cynicism. As in McRobbie, the post-Fordist worker moves from one thing to another; negotiating rules of the game, responding to rules not facts. Money makes these things equivalent; the general intellect is always something else. It is a *qualitative* potential that forms the basis of all production.

This points to an intriguing revaluation of what for Heidegger was the *idle talk* of the inauthentic life, where the "one" dominates, which Virno reads as the sphere of Simondon's pre-individual. Where for Heidegger, idle talk deflects from the real task, for Virno, "this same lack of foundation authorizes invention and the experimentation of new discourse at every moment" (GM90). Idle talk is performative and connected to curiosity, that perverse form of the love of knowledge. In curiosity, the senses usurp the place of thought, but for Virno as in Walter Benjamin this is an opportunity to expand human sensory capacities, distraction as means of scanning an artificial experience.

In a stunning expansion on his theme, Virno concludes that

> In the multitude there is a full historical, phenomenological, empirical display of the ontological condition of the human animal: biological artlessness, the indefinite or potential character of its existence, lack of a determined environment, the linguistic intellect as "compensation" for the shortage of specialized instincts. It is as if the root had risen to the surface. (GM98)

This repetition of the natural in the historical is a theme taken up more fully by Virno elsewhere.

In *Multitude: Between Innovation and Negation*, Virno touches on a famous (non-)debate between Michel Foucault and Noam Chomsky on the question of a human nature.[7] Virno does not share Chomsky's optimism about the political consequences of the human animal's innate linguistic capability. Rather, he stresses the *instability* of the human, its *evil*. But interestingly, this very instability does not imply the need for the state. On the contrary, criticism of state sovereignty has to rest on a frank understanding of the human as evil by nature, but where evil means the lack of specific habitat and living in culture as nature.

Our species-being is defined by the openness of the faculty for language. For Virno, language is marked by three properties: *negativity*, *possibility* and *infinity*. As in Mouffe, negation leads to separation—you are *not* one of us—and thence a diminution of empathy. Possibility leads to excess and indeterminacy, things could always be otherwise. Infinity leads to an opening to the world and its incompleteness, thence to boredom. Language does not mitigate aggression. All three of these qualities of language can make it worse.

Humans are dangerous by nature because they can *change* their actions and habits. Both evil and virtue stem from the same deficit of instinct. Virno: "truly radical evil, irrepressible and lacerating, is precisely and solely the evil that shares the same root as the good life" (MB21). To give just one example: negation leads to difference: you are not one of us. But then the public sphere could negate that

7 Paolo Virno, *Multitude: Between Innovation and Negation*, Los Angeles: Semiotext(e), 2008; Noam Chomsky and Michel Foucault, *The Chomsky-Foucault Debate: On Human Nature*, New York: New Press, 2006.

negation: you are not one of us, but difference could be the principle of togetherness. Useful institutions don't repress or deny this indeterminacy of our species-being as language animal.

The institutions of the state are in decline. Contra Mouffe, the task is not to repair them but to exit from them and build others. Virno deploys what will turn out to be a non-dialectical understanding of the negative—figured as *ambivalence*, *oscillation* and *perturbation*—to find a path between the openness of species-being and the contingencies of the post-Fordist moment. "In what way can excessive drive and the opening to the world serve as a *political* antidote to the poisons that they secrete?" (MB24).

Why should anyone obey an institution anyway? Virno finds Hobbes somewhat paradoxical on this point. In Hobbes, the obligation to obey is both cause and effect of the state. Hobbes's state of nature is one of prelinguistic drives; for Virno, nature includes language. Whereas for Hobbes natural law is retrospective, an effect of the state; in Virno, language is natural and has its own tendencies to *regulation*. Hobbes's civil state acts as protection from fear, but becomes a pseudo-environment. The connection between drives and language is hidden in Hobbes's concepts of both nature and state. The articulation of drives with language is for Virno both natural and political.

The multitude is antistate and hence a non-people, in that the people is what a state produces, then claims after the fact as its legitimating point of origin. The fragility of the state reveals itself in the *state of exception*, the crisis moment that breaches its pseudo-environment and restores an opening to the world.[8] For Mouffe and other thinkers of the political as necessarily leading to the state, the state of exception is a moment of fear, where the unruly multitude reappears as natural disorder and drive. For Hobbes, there is no rule before the imposition of the state. Virno draws rather on Wittgenstein, for whom there are habits and regularities in the performance of language and the application of rules already, prior to the state. Rules don't have

8 Giorgio Agamben, *The State of Exception*, Chicago: University of Chicago Press, 2005.

rules for their application, or for the application of that application, and so on to infinity. There is always something other, and prior, to the rule.

Hobbes based obedience on overcoming a state of nature; Wittgenstein posits a preliminary regularity rooted in the characteristics of the language animal: questioning, answering, negating, postulating, thanking, hating, praying. Virno: "the concept of regularity indicates the threshold at which language grafts itself repeatedly onto pre-linguistic drives and reorganizes them profoundly...Far from anchoring the application of the rules to the exit from the state of nature, Wittgenstein places natural life at the very heart of historically determined institutions" (MB34).

The prize here is a theory of the institution without the state and its sovereignty, but one which does not duck the question of aggression by claiming a benign state of human nature. For Virno there are already, in the nature of our species-being as language-animals, forms of regularity about the application of rules to cases. This might matter if the post-Fordist era is indeed one of a permanent state of exception, even if it appears as an era in which states become hyperaggressive and vigilant as a result of their crisis.

The crisis of the state comes from an inability to sustain a separate pseudo-environment of political rules apart from regularities. "Regularity, which the institutions of the exodus metabolize, is ambivalent, even perturbing: the opening to the world, negation, the modality of the possible, present themselves, at one and the same time, both as maximum danger and as an authentic resource for warding off evil" (MB38). Rule, against the background of regularity, as both instrument and object of control, is the political equivalent of the linguistic animal: "Sometimes aggressive, sometimes united, prone to intelligent cooperation, but also to the war between factions, being both the poison and the antidote: such is the multitude" (MB40).

In the post-Fordist era, the coherence of the multitude is not the unity of the state, but rather than of the *transindividual* of Simondon and the *general intellect* of Marx. The multitude needs worldly institutions that metabolize ambivalence and oscillation rather than unilateral decision. It needs institutions that don't make a pseudo-environment but are open to the world. Institutions that might restrain evil rather than exacerbate it, or imagine they can expel it.

Language is a pure institution that renders all other institutions possible. Language is both more natural and more historical than all other institutions. It is insubstantial, has no positive reality and is a field of negations. Could there be, based on language, a "non-representative, insubstantial, Republic based upon differences and differences between differences?" (MB51).

The form such an institution might take is a *ritual* form. Ritual has to restrain two extremes: acts without power and power without acts. Ritual has to deal with deficits or excesses of meaning. Ritual is a way of resisting chaos by adhering to it. This might be something like the binding property of the institutions of religion. It might be something like the *immunity* that Robert Esposito writes about, which restrains evil but does not claim it can defeat it. There's no anti-Christ, but no Messiah either. But this means (a theme found also in Haraway) living without innocence. There's no pure state to achieve or return to. Rather it is a safeguarding of *oscillation* between regularity without rules (nature) and rules without regularity (state).

Such institutions might deploy the powers of negativity, possibility and infinity that are attributes of the language faculty of our species-being. From *negation* comes the *negation of the negation*, civil society, and its embrace of the stranger. From *possibility* comes not only the delirium of what might be, but also the tempering talk of what might *not* be. From the *infinite* comes not only the absolute but *ambivalence* toward repetition without end. The problem with the state is that its claim to sovereignty creates a pseudo-environment that prevents an openness to the world.

This is, I think, already a powerful line of argument, deepened even further in *When the Word Becomes Flesh* and *Déjà Vu and the End of History*.[9] There, Virno unfolds a view of our species-being as a language animal and memory animal, able to see and know the ontological conditions of possibility for the faculties of acting and

9 Paolo Virno, *When the Word Becomes Flesh*, Los Angeles: Semiotext(e), 2015; Paolo Virno, *Déjà Vu and the End of History*, London: Verso, 2015.

speaking in the world alongside particular acts and statements. It becomes a rather unique philosophy of natural history.

Here I would like to just mention some caveats. Firstly, it seems rather old fashioned to speak only of the human and not what Haraway calls the *multispecies muddle* we actually exist in and as. And rather than language I would prefer to open up some other categories that define the human as indefinable, whether it be play (Huizinga), ornament (Jorn), or the passions (Fourier).[10] Moreover, in its lack of definition, the human might not be a unique species, but one of many that plays and is open to the world. That world might be less eternal and unchanging were Virno to think about natural history a bit more broadly than Chomsky's naturalistic materialism of a universal grammar. The Anthropocene makes even nature historical and temporary.

Secondly, one might ask if post-Fordism is much of a way of defining the present moment. The fulcrum moment of the mid-twentieth century might be less Adorno's first-hand discovery of the culture industry and more JD Bernal's first-hand discovery of the application of science to production, including information science.[11] The world of the contemporary media and its idle talk grows more out of the latter than the former. The state may be in crisis more because of a technical infrastructure that assumes some of its functions than because of language-based labor.[12] That language-based labor is more an exceptional experience of the overdeveloped world than a general characteristic.

Thirdly, one might also question the fetish of living labor in workerist thought, and ask whether ritual also calls for an embrace of dead labor. But this would mean thinking a bit more about labor. For Virno, intellectual labor, with no end product, "places Marx in an

10 Johan Huizinga, *Homo Ludens*, Kettering, OH: Angelico Press, 2016; Asger Jorn, *The Natural Order and Other Texts*, New York: Routledge, 2016; Charles Fourier, *Theory of the Four Movements*, Cambridge: Cambridge University Press, 1996.

11 Compare Adorno's *Minima Moralia*, London: Verso, 2006, to JD Bernal, *The Social Function of Science*, Cambridge, MA: MIT Press, 1967.

12 Benjamin Bratton, *The Stack*, Cambridge, MA: MIT Press, 2016.

embarrassing situation" (GM54). But only if one thinks it as still the product of the worker rather than the hacker. The former walks fast, while the latter wanders, remember. That might be a different relation to production and property altogether.

All the same, Virno's project of bringing together a conceptual matrix appropriate to the historical moment and which has a speculative grasp on its natural conditions of existence seems like a very timely one as the veneer of democracy starts to fade. Virno approaches the question of the multitude outside the state with rather less optimism than Negri, but their contrasting approachs have proven enabling for a range of general intellects, from Boutang and Lazzarato to Berardi and Préciado.

4.

Yann Moulier Boutang: Cognitive Capitalism

There are broadly three ways of thinking historically about capitalism. One draws on Marx's value theory and pretty much treats capital as eternal. Its appearances may change but its essence is always the same, until the revolution, which, strange to say, never comes.[1]

The second is able to think more historically. For example: the regulation school came up with a convincing portrait of what it called the Fordist regime of regulation.[2] In this version capitalism has stages, each of which is qualitatively different. But this approach tends to be troubled by the current stage, which can only be described negatively as lacking the attributes of the last. Hence it speaks of *post*-Fordism. In general, when change is described via modifiers, such as post or neo or late, one is not really thinking the specificity of an historical period, but merely saying that it is like or not like another.

The third approach is to try and define the specificity of the twenty-first century social formation. An excellent example might be Yann Moulier Boutang's *Cognitive Capitalism*, a book which presents in English the results of a research program that has been going on in French for some time.[3] As Boutang says, "cognitive capitalism is a paradigm, or a coherent research program, that poses an alternative

---

1 McKenzie Wark, "The Sublime Language of My Century," *Public Seminar*, May 14, 2016, at publicseminar.org.

2 Michel Aglietta, *A Theory of Capitalist Regulation: The US Experience*, London: Verso, 2015.

3 Yann Moulier Boutang, *Cognitive Capitalism*, Cambridge: Polity, 2012. And see the journal *Multitudes*.

to post-Fordism" (113). It no longer takes Fordism as the norm, and it certainly does not get bogged down in theories of eternal capital. Its attention is on "new vectors of the production of wealth" (135). This is a challenge, as not even capitalism's biggest fans seem to have much of a clue how to describe it. But Boutang wants to step back from post-situationist thought, whether that of Baudrillard or others, for whom capital becomes an absolute, and all of politics foreclosed: "is this capitalism so absolute?" (3).

Perhaps it calls rather for a fresh analysis, "a kind of small defrag program for Marxism's mental hard drive" (8). "Are we, in particular, going to remain obstinately stuck to the perspective of the value of working time, of the utility or scarcity of resources, in order to measure a wealth that depends on the time of life and on the super-abundance of knowledge?" (4).

Boutang's method is, like that of Virno, Lazzarato and others, shaped by the Italian workerist tradition, and its strong commitment to the point of view of living labor.[4] Like them, his jumping off point is Marx's *Grundrisse*, especially the "Fragment on Machines," and particularly the concept of the *general intellect*. If Marx were to appear by time machine in today's California, he might find that at least some of the work being done there is no longer explainable via recourse to scarcity and physical labor. After mercantilist and industrial capitalism comes cognitive capitalism.

Industrial capitalism at its peak—what the regulation school calls Fordism—was characterized by cheap energy, foreign labor importation, cheap raw materials, full employment, fixed exchange rates, low or even negative real interest rates, price inflation and wage rises in line with productivity. But rather than concentrate on the breakdown of that system as the regulationists do, Boutang is more interested in the features of what replaced it.

Boutang is rather sparing with the term "neoliberal," which is so often used now as a kind of linguistic operator to describe by contrast what this era is supposed to mean. The rise of finance is clearly

4 See Christian Marazzi and Sylvère Lotringer (eds.), *Autonomia: Post-Political Politics*, Los Angeles, Semiotext(e), 2007.

a key feature of our times, but for Boutang (contra Brown) neither economic ideology nor financial speculation is causative. The rise of finance is what has to be explained.

The explanation is an interesting one. With the conversion of intellectual activities into tradable assets, work dematerialized, and the contours of the company became unclear. Financialization is a way of assessing the value of production when production is no longer just about labor and things. Finance both predicts and actualizes futures in which private companies extract value from the knowledge society, where the boundaries of who "owns" what can never be clear.

Cognitive capitalism has its problems, however. Ours is a time in which we witness the crash of unlimited resource extraction against limits. It is a time of "the revenge of externalities" and the predation of the "bio-fund" (20) when "the city turns into a non-city" (22). The global urban crisis is a witness to the exhaustion of positive externalities upon which capital has depended.[5] Which would be another way of figuring what Marx sees as the resources both natural and human that capital uses free of charge.[6]

Those are the problems cognitive capitalism appears completely unable to solve. What it did solve, after a fashion, is the problem of the network effect. Value creation now relies on public goods, on complex processes, and things that it is very difficult to price. Financialization is a response to that complexity.

Boutang follows Lazzarato in speaking of "immaterial labor" (31), a term I never liked, although not quite for the same reasons as some of Boutang and Lazzarato's other critics. I think it is important to hang on to the materiality of information-based sciences and technologies. Indeed, information changes the way one thinks about what the "matter" in materialism might be. For Boutang and Lazzarato, capitalism has changed in that "the essential point is no longer the expenditure of human labor-power, but that of invention power" (32). Now the potential for future innovation is incorporated into the pricing of future possibilities.

5 Mike Davis, *Planet of Slums*, London: Verso, 2007.

6 Paul Burkett, *Marx and Nature*, Chicago: Haymarket Books, 2014.

Immaterial labor is supposed to be an updating of Marx's category of abstract labor, the aggregate of concrete labors that make up socially necessary labor time, or that labor time whose value is realized in exchange value when commodities are successfully sold. But perhaps a more thorough rethinking of the role of information in production is really called for here.

Boutang thinks that in its advanced centers—what Gilroy calls the overdeveloped world—a new form of capitalism has emerged.

> We call this mutating capitalism—which now has to deal with a new composition of dependent labor (mostly waged)—"cognitive capitalism," because it has to deal with collective cognitive labor power, living labor, and no longer simply with muscle power consumed by machines driven by "fossil fuel" energy. (37)

Like the Italian workerists, the emphasis is on living labor, with the twist that for Boutang cognitive capitalism comes to be more dependent on it.

Cognitive capitalism is not limited to the "tech" sector. As I argued in *Telesthesia*, if one looks at the top Fortune 500 companies, it is striking how much all of them now depend on something like cognitive labor, whether in the form of R+D, or logistics or the intangibles of managing the aura of brands and product lines.[7] Moreover, this is not a simple story of the exogenous development of the forces of production. This is not a revival of the "information society" thesis of Daniel Bell and others, a theory which shied away from the complexities of capitalism. There's a story here about power and hegemony, not just pure linear tech growth.

Boutang points towards a more complex way of understanding "capital" than Virno or Negri, for whom it is always more or less the same thing, and always purely a reaction to labor's struggles to make value for itself. Boutang also wants to separate knowledge from information, and to avoid making a fetish of the latter. Knowledge-work

---

7 McKenzie Wark, *Telesthesia: Communication, Culture and Class*, Cambridge: Polity Press, 2012.

is the way information is made. This is salutary. However, I wonder if it might not be the case that just as the dead labor that congealed into fixed capital overtook living labor, so too the *dead cognition* reified into information systems might not have taken over from the living labor of knowledge-workers. This might be what the era of "big data" is really about. Perhaps after an era of "primitive accumulation," based on the circuit K-I-K′, this has now been subsumed into the mature form of I-K-I′, where information systems shape living knowledge production to their form, and for the purpose of extracting more information, I-prime. Hence I am skeptical of one of Boutang's key themes: "the novelty we are witnessing is the centrality of living labor that is not consumed and not reduced to dead labor in mechanism" (54).

It is certainly helpful, I think, to focus on knowledge as a kind of work, rather than to submit in advance to bourgeois categories, where one would speak of "intellectual property" or "human capital" and so on without wondering where and how it was made. Boutang also takes his distance from the state-led schemes of the regulation school, who hanker for a return to something like an industrial world with Keynsian regulatory tools, and for whom finance can only be rent-seeking.

I would have liked to know more about the science-and-labor-alliance policy that Boutang attributes to the French Communists in the postwar years. In Britain this was called "Bernalism," after JD Bernal, its post-effective advocate.[8] What I find useful in this tradition is that, unlike in Boutang and others, it understands the problem as not one of new kinds of labor, but of labor's potential alliance with a quite different class—what elsewhere I called the hacker class.[9]

Given how different Boutang finds cognitive labor to be to physical labor, I question why it has to be thought as labor at all, rather than as the social activity of a quite different class. Boutang at least canvasses this possibility, in mentioning Berardi's idea of a *cognitariat* and

8 Gary Werskey, *The Visible College*, New York: Holt Rinehart & Winston, 1979.

9 McKenzie Wark, *A Hacker Manifesto*, Cambridge, MA: Harvard University Press, 2004.

Ursula Huws's of a *cybertariat*, but the least settled part of attempts to think the current mode of production seems to me to be questions of the classes it produces and which in turn reproduce it.[10]

The symptom of this for me is the emergence of new kinds of property relation, so-called "intellectual property," which became private property rights, and which were extended to cover an ever wider range of information products. Boutang is aware of this:

> One of the symptoms indicating that both the mode of production and the capitalist relations of production are changing is the importance assumed nowadays by institutional legal issues. Never has there been so much talk of property rights, by way of contesting them as well as by way of redefining them. (47)

Perhaps one could press this even further.

Of course, Boutang is not one of those who thinks the "new economy" is somehow magically "weightless." He points out that it does not eliminate material production so much as rearrange it in space and time.

> Not only are the parameters of space and time being radically altered, but the radical overhaul of representations that is underway affects the conception of acting and of the agent/actor doing things, as well as concepts of producing, of the producer, of the living and of the conditions of life on earth. (48)

While Boutang does not go there, I will: What if it was not just a new stage of capitalism but a new mode of production? What if this was not capitalism, but something worse? I think it is a necessary thought experiment, if the concept of "capitalism" is ever to be a valid historical one. We need to have a sense of the conditions under which it could be said to have transformed into something else entirely.

---

10 Ursula Huws, *Labor in the Digital Economy*, New York: Monthly Review Press, 2014.

Whenever one suggests such a thing, the counterarguments quickly default to one or other ideological tropes.[11] One is that if one thinks this is not capitalism, one might subscribe to some version of the California ideology, and be oneself a dupe of various new age PowerPoint-slingers.[12] But why does thinking one thing has ended automatically mean one must believe it was succeeded by a particular something else? That does not follow at all. It points rather to the poverty of imagination of today's Marxists who can only imagine capital to be eternal. They seem to have a hard enough time with Boutang's thesis that it is in a new stage, so needless to say the thought experiment in which something else succeeds it is literally *unthinkable*. Hence I would press even harder than Boutang on this: "Does this not bring immediately into question the capitalist mode of production as a whole, and not just the dominant system of accumulation?" (115).

But I digress. Boutang takes a lively interest in the evident fact that in certain parts of the overdeveloped world, companies have embraced the California ideology, and yet they have "discovered and invented the new form of value" (49). He attempts to inventory them. Cognitive capitalism affects all sectors. Across the board, new tech increases the power of immaterial. But tech change is no longer an exogenous resource, but the very thing accumulation aims at. Value production comes to depend on social cooperation and tacit knowledge.

The complexity of markets means increasing efficiency can't just be solved by economies of scale. Consumption has become a productive part of R+D. Information now manages production cycles in real time. There's a plurality of inputs into most productions, including new kinds of labor. There are new spatial forms, including the clustering of production systems. There is a crisis of property rights, in parallel with attempts by successful firms to capture positive externalities.

---

11 Wark, "The Sublime Language of My Century."

12 Richard Barbrook with Andy Cameron, *The Internet Revolution*, Amsterdam: Institute of Network Cultures, 2015.

Cognitive capitalism looks for spatial and institutional forms that allow it to capture value from things other than traditional labor, including all of those things that some writers call non-labor or digital labor.[13] Hence the rise of the network, as a third organizational form alongside the market and hierarchy.[14] Networks are quick to identify resources when time, attention and care are what are scarce. "Labor" becomes about connectivity, responsiveness, autonomy and inventiveness, and such labor is hard to measure in time units. (But is it still labor?)

What motivates this new kind of (non-)labor besides wealth or power is *libido sciendi*, or the desire to know:

> In cognitive capitalism we are witnessing the emergence of the systematic exploitation of a third passion—or desire—as a factor of efficiency in human activity deployed in an enterprise...What I am referring to here is the libido sciendi—the passion for learning and the taste for the game of knowledge. (76)

Préciado has a quite interesting critique of what he sees as the anti-corporeal and masculinist bias of such a way of thinking about what drives the contemporary economy. The passions might be a broader question, which is why in *The Spectacle of Disintegration* I went back to Charles Fourier and his theory of the twelve passions. It might be better to say that one of the things today's economy is about is the productive use of all twelve of those passions, of which *libido sciendi* might be just one.[15]

As Pekka Himanen showed already in *The Hacker Ethic*, there's a quite different relation to both time and desire at work in what Boutang calls cognitive labor, and what I called the hacker class. They might at times be motivated by libertarian ideologies, but as Gabriella Coleman has shown, the actual ethnography of hackers reveals a

---

13 Trebor Scholz (ed.), *Digital Labor: The Internet as Playground and Factory*, New York: Routledge, 2014.

14 Manuel Castells, *Communication Power*, Oxford: Oxford University Press, 2009.

15 McKenzie Wark, *The Spectacle of Disintegration*, London: Verso, 2013.

more complex ideological field.[16] Not that traditionally ascribed to labor, but not one entirely consumed with petit bourgeois dreams, libertarian or otherwise.

Boutang sees the development of work after Fordism as being about coopting the rebellion from work's alienated form.[17]

> Work comes to dress itself in the clothes of the artist or of the university. The values of creativity only become capable of being exploited by an intelligent capitalism to the extent that they were promoted as a value, first experimentally and then as a norm of living. (88)

Hence, at least in part, "the 'hacker' individual is closer to the creative artist and the ivory-tower professor than to the risk-taker or the possessive individualist" (90). This might not however take full account of the rise of the "Brogrammer," product of elite American universities who studied programming rather than go to business school, and for whom tech is just a means to get into business. The ethnographic realities of class are always complicated.

Even so, while start-up culture is designed to shape a kind of petit-bourgeois personality, not every hacker is persuaded by this. Many will discover that there is now a kind of second-degree exploitation, not of labor per se but of one's capacity to hack, to invent, to transform information. Who knows? Some might even question the split that this emerging mode of production forces between labor and creation, which was the basis of Asger Jorn's very prescient situationist critique of political economy.[18] For Boutang this new division is like that between the "free" worker and the slave in mercantilist capitalism—which I must point out is a division between two different classes.

---

16 Pekka Himanen, *The Hacker Ethic*, New York: Random House, 2001; Gabriella Coleman, *Coding Freedom: The Ethics and Aesthetics of Hacking*, Princeton, NJ: Princeton University Press, 2012.

17 Luc Boltanski and Eve Chiapello, *The New Spirit of Capitalism*, London: Verso, 2007.

18 Asger Jorn, *The Natural Order and Other Texts*, New York: Routledge, 2016.

Perhaps one could even open up the question of whether the tensions within the ruling class point toward the formation of a different kind of ruling class. One part of the ruling class really insists on the enclosure of information within strict private property forms, while another part does not. One part has lost the ability to produce information goods strapped to physical objects and charge as if they were just physical objects. This is the case not just with things like movies or music, but also with drugs and increasingly with sophisticated manufactured goods. You can now buy a pretty good knockoff iPad for a fraction of the price.

And yet there's a tension here, as there is another kind of value production that is all about the leaky and indeterminate way in which social knowledge gets turned into products. One could frame this as an instability for a ruling class which does not know which of these is more important, or whether both tendencies can really occur at once. Or whether it is even a split between different kinds of ruling class: one still dependent on extracting surplus labor power and selling commodities; one dependent instead on *asymmetries of information* and commanding the processes of social creation themselves by controlling the infrastructure of the information vector.

In Boutang, the markets act as a multiplier and a vector for values produced by other means.

> Like the giant Anteus, who could only recharge his strength by keeping his feet on the ground, cognitive capitalism, whose purpose is to produce value (and not commodities or use values), needs to multiply its points of contact with a society that is in motion, with living activity. (108–09)

Entrepreneurial intelligence is now about converting social networks into value. The entrepreneur is a surfer who does not create the wave. Here, like Marx, Boutang understands value creation as taking place offstage, and made invisible by a kind of market fetishism. These days it is not the commodity that is the fetish so much as the Great Man of business. As if the world just issued fully formed from Steve Jobs's brain. Cognitive capital is based on knowledge society, but is not the same thing.

There's a tactical value in seeing cognitive and industrial capital as distinct. "The real challenge is thus to minimize as far as possible this phase during which cognitive capitalism and industrial capitalism can build anti-natural alliances in order to control, restrain or break the power of liberation of the knowledge society" (112). Perhaps there are fissures between them that can be worked in the interests of dispossessed peoples of all kinds.

In a lovely metaphor, Boutang talks about a ruling class that has figured out how to capture the productive labor of its worker bees when they make honey, but is only just figuring out how to capture the value of their efforts at "pollination" (117). What Boutang calls the knowledge society underlying cognitive capitalism is precisely that pollination, that practice of collaborative effort between humans and nonhumans to make worlds. Hence: "Cognitive capitalism reproduces, on an enlarged scale, the old contradictions described by Marx, between the socialization of production and the rules of appropriation of value" (120).

Boutang understands what Butler or McRobbie would call the *precarity* that arises out of the current, rather disorganized stage of the class struggle, and where "getting the multitude to work for free is the general line of cognitive capitalism" (133). Cognitive capital both depends on the pollinating efforts of a knowledge society built on a social-democratic pact and yet undermines it at every turn. "Knowledge becomes the raw material, but it now creates real 'class' divisions" (131).

So far the only way of governing this mess that even partly works is, paradoxically enough, finance. "Finance can be said to be the only way of 'governing' the inherent instability of cognitive capitalism, even if it introduces new factors of instability" (136). Hence "In the cognitive capitalism school of thought, flexible production and financialization are both seen as being subordinate to the achievement of permanent innovation (the substance of value)" (139).

The value of companies has become intangible, and accounting rules don't quite capture the value of knowledge contained in the firm. Finance is a way of assessing and capturing the value of the externalities on which companies actually rely. Price is formed by forming opinion among traders. Financial markets are themselves part of the long-term capture of publics as a resource. "One could even argue that one of the main activities of cognitive capitalism is the production of different kinds of publics, of which the stock market public is not the least" (145). This is an original and provocative thesis.

In a concluding "Manifesto for Pollen Society," Boutang notes that there is now "Wealth in society, but poverty of social organization" (149). The "human cyborg" comes into being as cognitive capitalism acquires power over life itself (150). For Boutang, the privatization of social cooperation is a regression. Particularly given the "urgency of the environmental question," one has to ask about the priorities of a mode of production that seeks more power over externalities for which it does not pay (173). "The only thing that our magicians, pirates and conquistadors of finance have forgotten is that pollination requires the existence of bees!" (189).

5.

Maurizio Lazzarato: Machinic Enslavement

I have a passing acquaintance with the work of Félix Guattari, but the person who may know his work best is Maurizio Lazzarato. His *Signs and Machines: Capitalism and the Production of Subjectivity* shows the ongoing usefulness of the "anti-sociology" that Guattari elaborated, both alone and in his collaborations with Gilles Deleuze[1] (120). The starting point for Lazzarato is what he takes to be a contemporary crisis of subjectivity.

Capitalism launches new subjectivities like new model iPhones, only these days the subjectivities are all basically just bloatware versions of the same model—just like the iPhones. We are all supposed to be entrepreneurs of the self, an impossible task, leading to depression—as Berardi might concur. This version of capitalism—if that is still what it is—no longer promises to be the "knowledge society." All it offers is just debt servitude and lottery tickets. Contrary to the slogans repeated over and over, there's not much "innovative" or "creative" about it.

Lazzarato dismisses those critical theories that deal only with the relation of language to subjectivity while ignoring what he calls "machinic enslavement." His shit list includes Žižek, Virno and Butler. They are all still too caught up in the linguistic. They treat language, subjectivity and politics as if they all happened in a sphere described by Althusser as "relatively autonomous" from production

1 Maurizio Lazzarato, *Signs and Machines: Capitalism and the Production of Subjectivity*, Los Angeles: Semiotext(e), 2014.

itself.[2] Their stances seem "political" but are more strictly idealist. A contemporary critical theory needs rather to investigate—and intervene—in both the domains of social subjection and also machinic enslavement.

Machines have invaded everyday life. There is no autonomous sphere of language, subjectivity and politics. Capitalist cynicism insists we be individual subjects when actually we're dehumanized nodes in indifferent meshes of humans and nonhumans. We are all inside what Lewis Mumford called the *megamachine*.[3] What this demands are not counter-hegemonic ideologies but means of producing a new kind of mesh of both machines and subjects. It's a matter then of keeping two things together: the formation of subjects, mostly but not only in language; and the machines that produce transindividual effects. Subjectivation is always mixed, and includes more than language. Real "innovation" requires more than language games. The dominant signification has to be suspended for anything new to appear at all.

Interestingly, the making of subjects is not something that happens in the superstructure. Lazzarato: "Guattari and Deleuze bring to fulfillment the discoveries of Marx…: the production of wealth depends on abstract, unqualified, subjective activity irreducible to the domain of either political or linguistic representation" (23). It is a move from political economy to *subjective economy*. Marx dealt mostly with the production of commodities, and dealt with the production of workers only as an effect of the production of commodities. Guattari and Lazzarato want to extend that analysis, "sideways," as it were, to a parallel set of production process that make not objects (commodities) but subjects (consumers).

Social subjection provides roles: you are a man, you are a woman, you are a boss, you are a worker, and so on. It produces individual subjects with identities—and ID cards. But this is only part of the picture. The other aspect is *machinic enslavement*, which does the

---

2 Althusser, *For Marx*, London: Verso, 2006.

3 Lewis Mumford, *The Pentagon of Power*, New York: Harcourt Brace Jovanovich, 1974.

opposite. It makes desubjectivized flows and fragments. It turns those subjects into component parts of machines (slave units in the cybernetic sense). Social subjection makes subjects; machinic enslavement makes *dividuals*. It divides up the self and attaches bits of it here and there to machinic processes as less-than-human agents. These machinic assemblages—rather like Haraway's cyborgs—are hybrids of human and machine, but where the human parts are indeed parts rather than subjects, and to the extent that some sort of semiotic code organizes it, this takes the form of what Guattari called an *asignifying semiotics*. It isn't organized by language that means anything or is meant to be interpreted.

Machinic enslavement works on pre-personal, precognitive and preverbal affects, as well as suprapersonal ones. One could think here about how big data deals on the one side with fragmented flows of data and on the other with huge aggregates, which only secondarily identify the subject on which to pin a hope (that they might be a consumer) or a fear (that they might be a terrorist).

Lazzarato mentions all too briefly the role that property rights plays in tying the desubjectivized world of machines to the subject-producing world of discourse. "By ensuring that creation and production are uniquely the feats of 'man,' it uses the 'world,' emptied of all 'soul,' as its own 'object,' as the instrument of its activities, as the means to its ends" (35). The property form makes the individualized subject the author and hence owner of something that is really much more likely the product of a machinic assemblage of different bits of various people's subjectivity, various machines, assorted technical resources. Hence we end up with the myth that Steve Jobs created the iPhone—and reaped most of the rewards from it.

From Guattari, Lazzarato takes the idea of seeking strategies that deal with both subjection and enslavement, which are also in Deleuzo-Guattarian parlance the *molar* and the *molecular*.[4] One can use the machinic, molecular perspective to critique the molar dualisms, but then also take enslavement as an opening to produce something other

4 Félix Guattari, *The Anti-Oedipus Papers*, Los Angeles: Semiotext(e), 2006, 418.

than paranoid consumerism as a corresponding and compensating mode of subjectivity.

Sure, capital has its linguistic dimension, but it may not be as important as flows of labor, money and asignifying signs as a system of production. Dividuals are governed statistically, not as something that operates through ideology or repression. "What matters to capitalism is controlling the asignifying semiotic apparatuses (economic, scientific, technical, stock-market, etc.) through which it aims to depoliticize and depersonalize power relations" (41).

There might still be ideologies, in a sense, but these are second-order effects. "The signifying semiotics of the media, politicians, and experts are mobilized in order to legitimate, support, and justify in the eyes of individual subjects, their consciousness and representations, the fact that 'there is no alternative'" (41). They are not primary. Capitalism isn't really about individuals or language.

It isn't really about people at all. Here Marx was still too anthropocentric, in thinking that surplus value is tied to human agency. Guattari had the nerve to propose that there is such a thing as *machinic surplus value*, too.[5] Capital exploits not workers but machinic assemblages, and is indifferent to their relative organic or metallic composition. All labor is cyborg labor. Productivity depends more on the enslavement of dividual parts than on the formation of proper individual subjects.

Capital exploits the *difference* between subjection and enslavement. It is machines that do the real work, while value remains partitioned between workers who get mere wages, and bosses who get the rest. Here Lazzarato shares a point with Boutang: that value is no longer really assignable to particular subjects as its "author," whether in a labor theory of value, or the equivalent bourgeois ideology, in which genius entrepreneurial "leaders" are the sole agents of wealth creation.

Lazzarato: "it is never an individual who thinks" (44). And it is never a corporation that produces. The corporation appropriates the unassigned values of a machinic "commons," as it were, "free of charge," and captures it in the form of profit or rent. Just as capital

5 Félix Guattari, *Chaosmosis*, Sydney: Power Publications, 2012, 133ff.

appropriates the natural commons, here it appropriates the social commons, or rather a social-machinic one.[6] Meanwhile, the *dividual* agents have to be patched back together as more-or-less whole subjects meant to think of themselves existentially as free agents who are both investors and debtors, trading in the self as currency in a market for souls.

As in McRobbie and as with theorists of the *social factory*, Lazzarato works with an expanded view of the workplace. Marx followed classical political economy in taking the subjective essence of production to be labor. Lazzarato wants a broader concept of that which produces and is produced as human. Capitalism is not just rational calculation, but also the production of desiring machines that are actually not entirely Calvinist rational-choice actors. As any viewer of the *Mad Men* TV show can see for themselves, capital integrates desire into its own functioning.

It is in the highlighting of this theme of the functionality of desire that Lazzarato breaks with Boutang and the theory that this is *cognitive* capitalism. That approach reduces the wider subjective economy to a narrower idea of a knowledge economy. It concedes too much to economics, where knowledge is now supposed to be the endogenous growth factor. But knowledge is less basic to capital than desire. Capitalism doesn't actually need that much knowledge to function. Indeed, recent attacks on schools and universities seem to indicate that it wants to function with much less.

Capitalism needs desiring subjects. But there's a crisis of desire. All it has to go on at the moment is the despotic superego—be your own boss!—which in Berardi's terms keeps collapsing into depression, or worse. Subjectivity is a key commodity that now has to be produced. The preliminary question might then be: how to construct a theory of subjectivity itself. Lazzarato wants to move beyond structuralist, phenomenological and psychoanalytic theories, which tend to privilege the intersubjective and leave out the machinic. Interestingly, he also brackets off base and superstructure theories, which make a prior (molar) cut between what is material and what is ideological, or what

6 Paul Burkett, *Marx and Nature*, Chicago: Haymarket Books, 2014.

is instinctual and what is subjective, or what is a deep structure and what is a particular linguistic sign.

The subject is no mere effect of language, even if language is thought, after Butler, as performative. Capital is now machine-centric, not logocentric. The act of enunciation, where a partition between an enunciator and the enunciation appears, may no longer be unique to humans. "Subjectivity, creation, and enunciation are the results of an assemblage of human, infra-human, and extra-human factors in which signifying, cognitive semiotics constitutes but one of the constituent parts" (63).

In a move parallel to Berardi's rethinking of alienation, Lazzarato writes:

> That objects might start "speaking," start "expressing themselves" (or start dancing, as they do in the celebrated passage from the first book of *Capital*), is not capitalist fetishism, the proof of man's alienation, but rather marks a new regime of expression which requires a new semiotics. (64)

Things really do speak in this world of neo-capitalism, or whatever it is. It is not just the alienation of the worker from her product that one has to look at, but the insistence with which the things she makes talk back to her and demand to be not only bought but loved.

One of the knottiest parts of Deleuze and Guattari's joint work was their disquisition on the linguistics of Louis Hjelmslev, and the categories of *expression* and *content*, which in some ways rework the classic categories of signifier and signified.[7] They refused to make a hierarchy between them. Expression does not depend on content (as some Marxists hold) or content on expression (contra certain structuralists). Rather, the idea is to grasp the content-expression binary by the middle, which is *enunciation*. It is the act of enunciation which produces the relation between expression and content, or between object and subject.

7 Gilles Deleuze and Félix Guattari, *A Thousand Plateaus*, Minneapolis: University of Minnesota Press, 1987; Louis Hjelmslev, *Prolegomena to a Theory of Language*, Madison: University of Wisconsin Press, 1961.

The ground of enunciation is not itself discursive. This opens the door to a general semiotics that extends way beyond language and the language-like. It includes natural asemiotic codings, such as crystals and proteins.[8] It includes human languages too, of course, but where thinking starts from the ground of enunciation. For example, in the political and military forces that shape a "national" language.[9]

Lazzarato calls language a *general equivalent.* Lazzarato: "the semiotics of signification function as both a general equivalent of expression and a vector of subjectivation centered on the individual" (68). Actually I would call it a *general nonequivalent.*[10] I don't think it works the way money—Marx's general equivalent—works. A focus on language tends to leave out the transindividual experiences that in neo-capitalism are only given their due as symptoms of madness, infancy or art. But for Guattari and Lazzarato, those are not keys to a surrealist world of infinite possibility, but rather one with its own asignifying semiotics.

Deleuze and Guattari had a sometimes alarming tendency to generalize from anthropological literature, and Lazzarato picks up on certain distinctions between precapitalist and capitalist social-machinic systems. Eduardo Viveiros de Castro, in his marvelous *Cannibal Metaphysics*, lends some ethnographic dignity to such more speculative accounts of the non-modern subjective machine.[11] In Lazzarato it takes the form of a rather more abrupt juxtaposition. But perhaps it is better to risk saying something too reductive about other cultures, other natures—than to play it safe by saying nothing at all.

---

8 One could read the Marxist science of Bernal and Needham as being about natural asemiotic codings.

9 One might connect this up with Friedrich Kittler's famous work on the quite literal apparatus of the mother tongue and the "machinic" supports for it in things like textbooks for mothers, with diagrams of how the infant should make various sounds of the national language.

10 On the general nonequivalent, see McKenzie Wark, 'Capture All', *Avery Review*, 2015, at averyreview.com.

11 Eduardo Viveiros de Castro, *Cannibal Metaphysics*, Minnesota: Univocal, 2014.

For Lazzarato, in the precapitalist world, social forms precluded the formation of a single homogenous signifying strata. It is only in the modern world that there is a homogenizing of the human, at least within the bounds of the nation, via the imposition of a national language. Such language is the means via which all semiotics appears to become compatible with capital. Lazzarato thinks this means a reduction of polyvalence. Actually I think it is rather the reduction of the *significance* of aberrant meanings. The witch trials and inquisitions recede.

Here too I think he quite misunderstands the role of the mathematical theory of information, which has nothing to do with meaning at all, only with information as statistical probability and the problems of its transmission. Claude Shannon's work is actually at the extreme end of polyvalence, in that meaning is not relevant at all.[12] One can agree with Lazzarato that "There is no language in itself" (76). What mid-century information theory did is call into being statistical operations on asignifying flows via an apparatus where transmission would be relatively (but not absolutely) seamless and where polyvalence could occur in an extreme form—where interpretation no longer matters at all. Except of course for certain patterns of association and usage that will be flagged as potentially "terrorist" in this here surveillance state.

The concept of an *asignifying* semiotics really is intriguing. For Lazzarato it includes computer languages, corporate accounting, but also music, art. For him these are all semiotic flows that don't depend on interpreting subjects, and where the human can be just a component part. For Guattari, unlike Heidegger, the machine does not turn away from being but produces it. The machine runs on kinds of power-signs that do not represent but anticipate and shape the world. They are like diagrams that can accelerate, slow or direct deterritorialized flows of labor, matter, energy or even desire. They are artificial routes to action on the world.

12 Here I think Tiziana Terranova, *Network Culture: Politics for the Information Age*, London: Pluto Press, 2004, better understands the significance of this for the formation of the machinic.

These asignifying semiotic flows mobilize non-reflective subjective fragments, or modular subjective components. They now grid the whole world. Lazzarato:

> In Marx's time, there was only the inside of the factory (with a concentration and intensity incomparably lower to that of today's corporations) and the outside, the latter among a handful of apparatuses such as railroads. Today, they are everywhere except in critical theory. They are everywhere and especially in our daily lives. (91)

There is a broad challenge here to the old theories of a separate political or cultural superstructure, of a quite different kind to Karatani.

Guattari was interested in machines that could take us towards new kinds of subjectivation, even if, in his as in Lazzarato's work, *machine* usually ends up being much too metaphoric a term. We never quite get to any detailed understanding of *actual* machines. Still, it's a compelling conceptual gambit. Mere signifying semiotics has the function of containing deterritorialized and desubjectivized flows that results from asignifying diagrams and symbols and the assemblages of dividuals and machines they organize. The latter idea contains a measure of Spinoza on the transitive nature of affect as a pre-personal category, but not necessarily as a good that one can bank on.[13] The asignifying works via contagion rather than cognition (as it does in Terranova as well).

Part of Lazzarato and Guattari's thinking on pre-individual subjectivity comes from Daniel Stern's work on early childhood.[14] Humans' early experience is transsubjective, and evolves not in stages à la Freud but through a series of levels. Actually there are hints of a base-superstructure model here, except in Guattari that is generally a reversible relationship. Pre-individual subjectivity might start out as a base (except for artists and the insane), but then an individuated one is acquired, at first as a superstructure, but which then

13 Melissa Gregg and Gregory Seigworth, *Affect Theory Reader*, Durham, NC: Duke University Press, 2010.

14 Daniel Stern, *The Interpersonal World of the Infant*, New York: Basic Books, 2000.

becomes the infrastructural layer. The trouble is that this tends to foreclose any genuine learning or creation, which is always destabilizing of constituted subjectivity. Here Guattari and Lazzarato also come close to Gilbert Simondon on the process of *individuation* and its failures.[15]

In Guattari in particular there is an insistence on forms and consistencies of this pre-individual and asignifying ground. It is not a raw world of drives, instinct, animality and spontaneity against which language has to bring the law, structure a lack and make prohibitions. Lazzarato insists that what psychoanalysis presents as a necessary order imposed on raw *id* is actually a political model. This is where his way of thinking forks from so much of contemporary thinking, including: Butler and the necessity of castration; Stiegler and symbolic sublimation; Virno, where speech replaces drive; and Badiou, where spontaneity yields to organization. For Guattari nonverbal semiotics are already organized. Just differently organized.

The strategy is to work not on the layer of language and the subject, but to start from the heterogeneous middle, from *enunciation* as what happens between the pre-individuated, object world and the subjective world where language rules. Although it is unfortunate that Lazzarato's polemics only address biases towards the subject. He has nothing to say on how the deep machinic level is organized. Kittler and Chun, for example, are not addressed.[16]

Unlike Azuma, this method does seem a bit stuck in the past to the extent that its operating example is still cinema. Here cinema appears as a form in which a signifying machine neutralizes, orders and naturalizes an asignifying semiotics. All the same, cinema can show a presignifying semiotics in a postsignifying world. Lazzarato's example is Pier Paolo Pasolini, who perhaps shares with Guattari a kind of "fanatical Marxism" (79).[17] Pasolini worked in Italy, a country

15 Gilbert Simondon, *On the Mode of Existence of Technical Objects*, Minneapolis: Univocal, 2017.

16 Friedrich Kittler, *Gramophone, Film, Typewriter*, Stanford CA: Stanford University Press, 1999.

17 Pier Paolo Pasolini, *Heretical Empiricism*, Washington, DC: New Academia Publishing, 2005.

to which a national language came very late, and until the '70s many subaltern and regional people did not speak a recognizable version of the dominant Italian. Many ended up speaking their *subaltern* language even in the cities to which they migrated for work.

Cinema functions like group psychoanalysis, normalizing intensities, making a hierarchy between language and the rest. The effects of classic Hollywood are not ideological and don't work primarily through language, even if it is a controlling level. Cinema is a mixed regime of signs. For Pasolini, cinema was also a mixed semiotics that starts with the image, with a kind of vision in which the machinic eye is embedded in objects.[18]

Hollywood-style cinema was important for what Pasolini called *neo-capitalism*, product of a second and final bourgeois revolution. If the first created the industrial worker, the second created the industrially produced consumer subject to match. Neo-capitalism needed new kinds of flexible subjects mobilized by a functional language devoid of meaning. It reversed the old semiotic hierarchies. Ideological superstructures (law, school, university) were no longer very important. Subjects were directly made by production and consumption systems.

Pasolini was loyal to the lumpen-proles who made themselves outside this emerging regime, excluded not just on linguistic but also existential grounds. Neo-capitalism remade them as new-model Italians and consumers, territorialized on a far more restricted and heteronormative model of the family. Neo-capitalism does not just require ideological submission but also directly manufactures the subjects it wants. It is a subjective economy, which draws on old familial forms of life and adds a new false tolerance—tolerant only of consumer choices. It destroys the old popular cultures and their sacred animist worlds. Pasolini's literature and cinema tried to reanimate the old animist culture in a new machinic form, a "machinic animism" (134).

Pasolini makes a strange bedfellow with materials drawn from

18 McKenzie Wark, "Pasolini: Sexting the World," *Public Seminar*, July 15, 2015, at publicseminar.com.

Italian workerist and autonomist theory. Antonio Negri certainly never forgave him for siding with the (working class) cops against the (bourgeois) students in a famous provocation.[19] But it has to be said, Pasolini had unique insight into the long arc of transformation in Italy. His provincial roots and his queerness gave him an existential ground for perceiving and creating affective life that the theorists did not have.

I don't know if we can still call this, after Pasolini, *neo-capitalism* given that it has been with us now for half a century, although in the larger scheme of things perhaps that is still rather new. For all their refusals of the language of base and superstructure, one way of reading Guattari and Lazzarato is as flattening the strata of natural-social organization, such that the top layers—the ideological—are omitted, but unfortunately so too are the deeper layers, the earthy substrata that was not foreign to Pasolini. One wishes sometimes for a more vulgar-Marxist note, or perhaps more of the Guattari of *Three Ecologies*.[20]

Still, the neo-capitalism concept does touch on certain key features, to do with how subjectivity is *machined* rather than merely *hailed* into existence via language, as in Žižek. Lazzarato draws attention to the vacant language of org charts, graphs, budgets—one might add PowerPoints. Hierarchy is really organized more through the asignifying aspects of such procedures. Or take the call center, where the latest systems do not even require that the worker actually speak. She or he can just click on prerecorded phrases to step the caller through the sales routine.[21] The software of course includes rating, ranking, classifying and timing functions.

In a useful insight, Lazzarato claims that what is managed now is not really labor so much as *processes*, of which labor is just a component. Management is not really about "human resources," just resources for machinic enslavement, cordoned off in subroutines that

19 See Antonio Negri, 'On Pasolini', in *Animal Shelter*, No. 3, 2013.

20 Félix Guattari, *The Three Ecologies*, London: Bloomsbury Academic, 2008; McKenzie Wark, "Four Cheers for Vulgar Marxism!!!!," *Public Seminar*, April 25, 2014, at publicseminar.com.

21 Some details here are from a conference paper by Mashinka Firunts.

are controlled and which have no reciprocal capacity to effect control. Lazzarato:

> Sociology and industrial psychology seem to be incapable of grasping conceptually the qualitative leap that has occurred in the move from "work" to "process," from subjection to enslavement. Those high on the hierarchy no longer deal with work but with "process" which integrates labor as "one" of its parts. (119)

Against those versions of Marxism that assign all value and creativity to living labor against dead labor, such as Virno, Lazzarato is closer to Haraway in seeing only hybrids of dead and living labor.

The great deterritorializing molecular flood is money, the general equivalent, but it can't function on its own. Its asignifying functions have to be infused with meaning from without by molar, interpretive interpellating functions. Sometimes this subjective production can be progressive. Signifying semiotics can produce things like the worker's movement. The worker deterritorialized in production could be reterritorialized in different directions, either radical or reactionary.

But the party-and-union model of the labor movement, based on territorializing worker subjectivity on the dignity of labor, may have run its course. New subjective modes might have to be created. Lazzarato spends some time on a strike by part-time culture workers, whose conditions of labor and life were being determined for them, without their input, by researchers, experts, the media and political spheres. Their counter slogan: "we are the experts."

The strike fits a general pattern of a politics that challenges the delegation of knowledge and speech to experts and the exclusion of the governed. The anti-GMO campaign noted by Stengers might be another European example. Recent American examples here would include Occupy Wall Street, Occupy Sandy, Strike Debt and Black Lives Matter.[22] These movements refused to let a "problem" be defined by others, rather than by the people affected. In order to

---

22 See L. A. Kauffman, *Direct Action*, London: Verso Books, 2017.

exist politically one has to refuse the homogenous space of acceptable differences and force a cleavage which in turn allows a new kind of subjectivity to form.

Being based on the French situation, Lazzarato spends quite a bit of energy on psychoanalysis as a kind of pastoral power which reconciles the subject with dominant modes of being a subject in a family. In the United States a mediatized version of the old religious pastoral care is probably more salient here. In either case: "There is nothing natural about the subject-function in communications and language. On the contrary, it must be constructed and imposed" (162). And can be challenged.

The latter part of the book is a fairly sweeping critique of rival positions, although I doubt those critiqued would recognize themselves as presented here. Lazzarato refuses the language of *performativity*, which he finds at work in Virno, Butler and Marazzi, for whom language is still something of a transcendent and homogeneous plane.[23] Deleuze and Guattari's adventures in anthropology had already shown that this linguistic plane is not a given but an historical and political construct.

Lazzarato thinks there is too much emphasis on the conventional function of language in reproducing social obligations. He focuses on the idea—borrowed from Austin—of the *illocutory act* which institutes an obligation.[24] This line of thought tends to concentrate on formalized and institutional settings where the speech act does not really involve or commit the subject to the truth of the statement. That would be a matter of *parrhesia*, or a rupture with dominant signification. Lazzarato draws on, and extends, Bakhtin's pragmatics of the situation of speech. For Bakhtin, the dialogic is not reducible to language, which is supplementary to the situation. The performative is just one element of a heterogeneous situation.

Enunciation is accomplished in a situation where the world can

23 Christian Marazzi, *Capital and Language*, Los Angeles: Semiotext(e), 2008.

24 J. L. Austin, *How to Do Things with Words*, Cambridge MA: Harvard University Press, 1975.

be a problem (Bakhtin) not just a convention (Austin). Lazzarato wants to stress the micropolitics, or situation, of enunciation, as more than an intersubjective relation between speakers. In Bakhtin the listener is not put in a subordinate position by the performativity of the speech act, but it is possible to go further and see enunciation not as performative at all, but as *strategic*. Enunciation contains pre-individual voices, gesture, expression. Hence revolt is firstly asignifying, invoking a new existential field of reference.

Contra Althusser's attempt to revive a science of history, Guattari and Lazzarato's corner of the Marx-field is an *aesthetic paradigm*.

> The enunciation of the relation to the self and the existential territories that support them always depends on a *détournement* of narrative whose primary function is not to produce rational, cognitive, or scientific explanations, but to generate complex refrains ("mythico-conceptual, phantasmatic, religious, novelistic") which give consistency to the emergence of new existential territories. (201)

There is no science of history, but there might be an art. An art of the pragmatics of the relation between the discursive and existential, or the actual and the virtual, the possible and the real.

It would be a topical art, perhaps not unrelated to what Fredric Jameson called *cognitive mapping*.[25] Or in this case perhaps it should be called *affective mapping*: a cartography not just of feelings but of their forces. It would start from neo-capitalism's failure to produce subjects to match its products, inaugurating the long slide in soft fascism and depression, with all the "pathology of subjectivity," its racism, misogyny and intolerance of disability (217).

Neo-capitalism seems hell-bent on a kind of *anti-production* that intentionally multiplies stupidity. "Only a rupture with the mode of subjectivation can secrete an existential crystallization productive of new references, and new self-positionings, which, in their turn, open the possibility for constructing new languages, new knowledges, new

25 Alberto Toscano and Jeff Kinkle, *Cartographies of the Absolute*, Winchester, UK: Zero Books, 2015.

aesthetic practices, and new forms of life" (223). It would be instructive to compare this, with its uncompromising modernism, not just with Pasolini but with, say, Raymond Williams, for whom the wellspring of another life was something that ran deep rather than that was current.[26]

There is certainly merit in the move towards understanding subjectivity as something produced by machinic operations rather than through a hailing, in language, via a superstructure. It is just a pity the actual machines do not become more concrete in Lazzarato. Some contact with the work of, say, Galloway or Chun might help here. The focus on the enunciation in the middle has a lot to say about the subject, but much less so about the object, which remains much more vaguely characterized. The molecular turns out to be rather too metaphorical. The *metabolic rift* via which actual molecules, containing carbon, or nitrogen, or other global flows currently in states of rift—none of this ever appears.

Even on the side of the subject, there is not enough on specific property forms and the kinds of subjects they make—for example class subjects of new regimes of ownership and non-ownership. We are stuck with a very static model of capital versus labor, where the modes of labor organization appear as outmoded, but the terms *capital* and *labor* themselves appear as ahistorical and eternal.

The emphasis on desire is a useful critique of the emphasis in Boutang on the cognitive as driver of this stage of commodification, even if it falls short of Préciado's bracing account of the molecular redesign of flesh. But it is not an effective way of addressing the centrality of *information*, or the way particular historical arrangements of the machinic make information a control layer over both objects and subjects, and indeed as what produces them and assigns them their values and rewards. In all these regards, Lazzarato has offered a vital and useful update on Guattari, showing his enduring value, but also his limitations.

---

26 Raymond Willams, *Culture and Society*, New York: Columbia University Press, 1983.

6.

Franco "Bifo" Berardi: Soul as Commodity

I once interviewed Franco "Bifo" Berardi before a live audience, and via closed-circuit TV with the overflow audience in the bar next door. It was exhilarating and exhausting. Bifo is such an energetic font of both good humor and sharp analysis. Then I found out it was his second event for the day. How he keeps it up, I'll never know.

Where Mario Tronti and Antonio Negri were born in the '30s, Berardi (1948) belongs, with Virno (1952) and Silvia Federici (1942), to a second wave of Italian Marxist thinkers who grew out of the workerist current that struck out on its own path, diverging from the official Gramscian postures of the Communist Party of Italy, not to mention latter-day revivals of Gramsci, as in Mouffe. The field of Italian Marxism has its own tangled genealogy, far beyond my competence. My interest is more in what can be made of it today. There's been a spate of translations of Berardi's work into English. I want to concentrate on *The Soul at Work: From Alienation to Automony*, as it has a useful sketch of how workerist and later autonomist thought diverges from other quadrants of the Marx-field.[1]

Berardi's objective is to account for the distinctive contours of what he calls *semiocapitalism*, which is close cousin to what Boutang calls cognitive capitalism, and which "takes mind, language and creativity as its primary tools for the production of value" (21). He does it through a sort of activist history of the uses of the category of *alienation*. In Marx, alienation is about the split between life and labor,

1 Franco "Bifo" Berardi, *The Soul at Work: From Alienation to Automony*, Los Angeles: Semiotext(e), 2009.

where labor is alienated from the life of the worker. The innovation of the Italian workerists was a reversal of perspective on this. They saw the worker not as the passive object of alienation, but rather as an active subject of *refusal*. The worker's estrangement from capital is the basis for affirming another life. This led to some interesting ways of thinking about, and practicing the life of, that other troubling character, the intellectual.

To put things very schematically, there might be two versions of the intellectual from which Marxism both draws and diverges. One is the intellectual as bearer of universal reason, guarantor of the proper functioning of public affairs, detached from any particular culture or background. The other might be the romantic intellectual, expressing the spirit of a people. This might have nationalist overtones, or occasionally more radical ones, connected not to the national folk but the people more broadly.

There is a tension between the Enlightenment intellectual and the romantic concept of a people. In the Marxist conception, the intellectual has to descend from the history of thought into history itself, and become an agent of a universal mission, the abolition of classes. For Lenin, the task of the intellectual is leadership on behalf of the working class, giving voice and organizational form to a universal spirit to correct the economism and spontaneity of working-class struggles.

Gramsci understood the intellectual more broadly as the strata that might have connections to sedimentary layers of past social formations, or might be the organic expression of a rising class. With Sartre, the intellectual is bound to consciousness rather than production. The Sartrean intellectual chooses to engage in a universal project, but he may have been the last of that line, given that he lived long enough to see the rise of what Virno calls "mass intellectualism" (33) in the '60s.

The Italian workerists took a different tack, drawing on Marx's "Fragment on Machines" from the *Grundrisse*.[2] There, machines are

2 Karl Marx, "Fragment on Machines," in Robin MacKay and Armen Avanessian (eds.), *#Accerate: The Accelerationist Reader*, Falmouth: Urbanomic, 2014.

an unnatural phenomenon, organs of the human brain created by the human hand. (Unfortunately neither Marx nor the Italians quite see how the reverse is just as true: human hand and brain were probably always shaped by tech.) The intellectual is hence a force of production, even if Marx's language is still saturated in older, idealist models of the intellectual, as is clearly the case with his stopgap concept of the "general intellect."

Still, understanding intellect as a force of production is progress over the Enlightenment and romantic ideas about the intellectual that still lingered. Berardi:

> At the time of the communist revolutions, in the first part of the twentieth century, the Marxist-Leninist tradition ignored the concept of the general intellect, therefore conceiving the intellectual function as exteriority and as a political direction determined within the purely spiritual domain of philosophy. (34)

Of course very few people knew Marx's *Grundrisse* texts even existed at the time. But there was at least one powerful alternative to the party as intellectual leader guided by a dogmatic philosophy, and that was Bogdanov's Proletkult, which sought to replace the party as central control with practices of coordination between sites of labor, be they manual or intellectual.[3]

In any case, the Marxist-Leninist model and its dialectical-materialist philosophical dogmas were clearly in crisis by 1956. Three tendencies emerged as alternatives. One was the Italian workerist current (based on Marx's *Grundrisse*) already mentioned. Berardi puts it alongside two others. A second school was led by those influenced by the young Marx, whether read in Hegelian fashion via Marcuse or more in the spirit of Kierkegaard via Sartre. A third school was the Althusserians, with their structuralist reading of *Capital*.

For the second current, the young Marx's focus on alienation was a central preoccupation, even if it was not handled with the subtlety of Wendling's reading. Particularly common was a sort of Hegel-lite

3 David Rowley, *Millenarian Bolshevism 1900–1920*, London: Routledge, 2017.

reading in which the alienation of capitalist production shatters a prior wholeness, a generic human essence. Revolution then becomes an essentially restorative, even conservative action to restore a lost unity. For Sartre, there is no lost unity, as alienation is constitutive of the human condition. But for Marcuse, alienation is an historical phenomenon that can be overcome.

The Italian workerists freed themselves from both Sartre and Marcuse, although like both of them they were trying in their own way to carve out a space beyond the strictures of official dialectical-materialist philosophy.[4] For them, there is neither a human essence to be restored, nor an eternal human alienation. Berardi: "it is precisely thanks to the radical inhumanity of the worker's existence that a human collectivity can be founded, a community no longer dependent on capital" (44). Labor is not a natural condition, but an historical one. An estrangement *from* labor is the basis for a new society. Their policy was an "active estrangement" (46).

The first-generation workerists celebrated a working class that was a "rude pagan race" (47). Here they were, like Pasolini, products of the Italian situation with its rich layers of cultural sediment, including a premodern proletariat, even if they shared little else with him. Like Bogdanov, they hewed close to the worker point of view, but unlike him, they stressed labor's *antagonism* to capitalism, rather than its capacity to reorganize the whole via labor.[5]

The workerists' stress on worker antagonism to capital is contrary to Marcuse's intuition that the working class was being integrated into capital.[6] This led Marcuse to seek other agents of liberation, resulting in an exaltation of the student radical, particularly in the hands of people he influenced. For workerists such as Tronti, the worker's demand for higher wages was not necessarily a sign of integration,

4 See Christian Marazzi and Sylvère Lotringer (eds.), *Autonomia: Post-Political Politics,* Los Angeles: Semiotext(e), 2007.

5 Pier Paolo Pasolini, *Heretical Empiricism*, Washington, DC: New Academia Publishing, 2005; Zenovia Sochor, *Revolution and Culture,* Ithaca, NY: Cornell University Press, 1988, suggests that Bogdanov was one of Gramsci's sources for the theory of hegemony.

6 Herbert Marcuse, *One-Dimensional Man*, Boston: Beacon Press, 1991.

however.[7] It is all about how the wage struggle is conducted. The "political wage" demand, for example, exceeded the limits of worker economism. In any case, student radicalism would hardly prove an enduring phenomena either.

Another path away from alienation theory is Althusser, although the provenance of this is a bit more complicated.[8] After 1956, "official" Soviet-aligned Marxist thought began its own embrace of Hegel-lite theories as part of a cautious and partial repudiation of Stalinism. Althusser rather uniquely rejected this development, not in the name of old-fashioned dia-mat but via a rather novel replacement of it by a kind of "theoretical practice" that owed more to Spinoza and French philosophy of science than to Engels's and Plekhanov's old formalizations of Marxisant philosophy. Or as Berardi says, Althusser left the "Hegel field" (52).

For Berardi, what is significant in Althusser is his understanding of knowledge as a form of production. Althusser reintroduces the theme of the world as produced by labor, and mental labor as productive labor. Unlike the workerists, the question of science as productive labor is one that he does not ignore, even if he is in the end not able to give it the autonomy the Bogdanovites would. Just as Lenin thought the party's universalizing theory and practice was needed to correct the spontaneity of the workers; so Althusser thought the theoretical practice of philosophy was needed to correct the "spontaneous philosophy" of the scientists.[9]

The workerists wagered everything on the *refusal of work* as the sole agent of history. "The motor of this constant transformation is the dynamic of subtraction of lived time from the wage-relation" (59). Refusing work creates a time and place for activities that escape labor domination. In the era of the industrial worker, the split between labor (in the form of abstract labor) and life was very stark. Work itself offered little. Life was what was lived outside of dead time.

---

7 Mario Tronti, *Ouvriers et Capital*, Paris: Christian Bourgeois, 1977.

8 McKenzie Wark, "Althusserians Anonymous: The Relapse," *Public Seminar*, February 26, 2016, at publicseminar.org.

9 Louis Althusser, *Philosophy and the Spontaneous Philosophy of the Scientists*, London: Verso, 2013.

With the constant replacement of labor by "labor-saving" technique, science is inducted fully into capital accumulation. Berardi thinks this calls for a new paradigm for labor and life. Surplus labor is no longer the condition for general wealth. As Wendling notes, Marcuse had hedged his bets on the question of science and technology. At his most pessimistic, he thought that "The totality generated by computers has replaced Hegel's totality...The matrix is replacing the event" (73). The real has become rational and the rational real, but in a non-dialectical form, as a means of control.

The moment of 1968 put all of these late-Marxist theories to the test. For Berardi, it was a moment of alliance between mass intellectual labor and refusal of industrial labor. Students had become a mass, a form of intellectual labor absorbed into production.[10] It was the end of the intellectual as universal conscience and the beginnings of a full subsumption of intellectual labor into production, although one that might produce its own modes of refusal.

One such moment of refusal was 1977, that "last reawakening of consciousness" (114). Berardi, who was only twenty in 1968, is more a thinker shaped by the late '70s.[11] This was when Italian workerists, their descendants the autonomists, Berlin squatters and British punks all seemed to be acting on the same intuitions about the absorption of manual and intellectual labor into production, and the same desire to strike out for another life. "That 1977 moment therefore used the ideology of happiness as a powerful critical instrument against the Taylorist factory and the Fordist production cycle, but also against the social and disciplinary structure based on the factory model" (93).

After that—often neglected—high-water mark of refusal, the landscape changes. Berardi's whole body of work can be read as an attempt to understand how and why. After 1977 we see the spread of post-Fordist models of labor and of digital technologies that will make them possible. Before 1977, desire was located outside of capital; after, desire means self-realization through work.

The working-class community outside of the labor process has lost

---

10 Georges Perec, *Things: A Story of the Sixties*, Boston: David Godine, 2010, is an excellent guide to this moment.

11 Nanni Balestrini, *We Want Everything*, London: Verso, 2016.

many of its powers of self-organization.[12] "Communism was the form of universal consciousness produced by the working community" (84). In Italy, at least, it had "a common project, a shared mythology" (85). Labor today, at least certain kinds of advanced labor in the overdeveloped world, has a different character. Look around any metropolitan café at all the people on their laptops or tablets. The tools are the same, but the labor itself is varied and can even be imbued with the personality of the worker. Whatever its discontents, it is not the alienating factory work of another time—or place.

For Berardi, it is partly this different quality of labor, and partly the decay of communal spaces outside of it, that leads workers to invest emotional energy and desire in their work itself: "labor has regained a certain position in the imagination" (80). Identity based on a job role can replace pleasures formerly sought outside of it, as so eloquently summed up by the '60s Australian group the Easybeats in their hit "Monday I've Got Friday On My Mind."

Berardi is far from rapturous about this new kind of embrace of work. It may bespeak a failure of any other understanding of what "wealth" could be outside of accumulation. There is a "reduction of the erotic sphere" and "metropolitan life becomes so sad that we might as well sell it for money" (82–83). The attempt to find freedom, humanity and happiness can only be through that ambiguous term, "enterprise." I wonder what leverage one might get here by juxtaposing the commonplace *free enterprise* against a notion of *true enterprise*. What might it mean to have a real project of making the good life?

The historical distinction Berardi draws here between Fordist and post-Fordist work is illuminating but might be a bit too sharp. Not many metropolitan workers enjoy such conditions, in either sense. It might not be the case that all workers found Fordist labor alienating. Lyotard notoriously thought otherwise, and there is a magnificent scene in Elio Petri's *The Working Class Go to Heaven* (1971) that shows the hard, visceral engagement of worker and machine.[13]

---

12 A novel by the Italian writer's collective Wu Ming, *54*, London: Harcourt, 2006, gives a vivid account of that lost world.

13 Jean-François Lyotard, *Libidinal Economy*, Bloomington, IN: Indiana University Press, 1993.

Still, it seems an at least partially accurate delineation of the metropolitan present: where accelerated capital blocks the formation of community; where the cell phone makes possible endless recombinations of fragments of labor, making all of time potentially productive; and where it takes a whole pill cabinet of antidepressants, stimulants, antianxiety medications and even cocaine just to keep working through the cycles of panic and depression.

Conceptually, Berardi wants to rethink the tradition of alienation, drawing on both the young Marx (but without the lost whole) and the workerists (but without the faith in labor as an outside). It's a matter of thinking the shift from incommunicability to overcommunication in an era when the problem is not so much being separated from the product of one's labor as incessantly nagged by the products of other people's labor for our time and money.

Berardi:

> Within the postindustrial domain, we should talk of derealization rather than reification. The concept of alienation is then understood as: 1. A specific psychopathological category; 2. A painful division of self; 3. A feeling of anguish and frustration related to the inaccessible body of the other…It is the third meaning of the term alienation that best describes our present times: an era marked by the submission of the soul, in which animated, creative, linguistic, emotional corporeality is subsumed and incorporated by the production of value. (108)

Once workers' souls were at least partly left to their own devices. Fordist capitalism put body to work, but then post-Fordism caught up with the soul as well. Extracting the body from alienation through an affirmative alienation *from* labor was possible while the soul was created as a thing apart. *Semiocapitalism* puts the soul to work.[14]

Here Berardi performs a bit of self-criticism, in that like a lot of us influenced by Deleuze and Guattari, it seemed sometimes that the liberation of desire pointed in a direction outside of commodification,

14 Berardi, like Andrey Platonov before him, makes soul a useful and curious Marxist concept.

a direction not indicated by the communalist but also conformist cultures of working-class solidarity. But desire might be an illusion. "Yet we need to acknowledge that this very illusion is history, the city, falling in love, existence: it is the game we have been playing knowing it was a game" (117).

Perhaps the mistake was in seeing desire as a force rather than a field, and downplaying negative forms of desire. "Desire judges history, but who judges desire?" (118). Judging desire, or rather reformatting it, might be what "politics" amounts to in the twenty-first century. Desire experiences limits, but can the limit not always be another to push against, but rather a node of (com)passion? "Social recomposition is the process through which the relation to the other is linguistically, affectively, and politically elaborated, then transformed into a conscious collective, an autonomous aggregate, a group in fusion, constructive in its rebellion" (119).

There're ways to find this in Deleuze as well. Galloway thinks it is time to move away from the *expressive* legacy of Deleuze to a more *prophylactic* thought.[15] Berardi might almost agree, but rather by seeking out different resources within Deleuze (and Guattari). He retains the rejection of the pre-constituted subject. "Subjectivity does not pre-exist the process of its own production" (123). His interest shifts to the idea of the *chaoid*, a kind of modulator of communicative excess and chaotic unpredictability.[16]

How did sadness come to prevail? In post-Fordist production solidarity was throttled, labor became precarious and the soul was put to work. There was a dissolution of chaos-reducers, refrains, organizers of fields—*chaoids*—and the result is an exhausting cycle of panic and depression, where depression is a refusal of the field of communication and the stimulants to desire it offers, all of which connect to nothing but more labor and more commodities. "We are entering the civilization of emptiness" (146).

---

15 Alexander R. Galloway, *Laruelle: Against the Digital*, Minneapolis: University of Minnesota Press, 2014.

16 Gilles Deleuze and Félix Guattari, *What Is Philosophy?*, London: Verso Books, 1994, 204ff.

The rhetoric of desire is thus rather exhausted itself. Here Jean Baudrillard's critique of it turns out to be prescient.[17] He understood desire's in-folding into commodified acceleration. Desire turns out not to be an outside. There was a critique in advance here of the idea of the *multitude*, presented as if it was a boundless positive energy. It is rather the so-called black hole of the masses, who absorb all communication but refuse to respond.

Berardi speaks instead of libidinal parasites, and a "thermodynamics" of desire in which desire is actually quite limited—maybe imploding, and perhaps suffering what Dominic Pettman calls *peak libido*.[18] Berardi: "having abandoned a certain Spinozist triumphalism, we can admit that libidinal energy is a limited resource." Desire is an ambivalent field, not a divine force. "The schizo vision thinks that the proliferation of desire can endlessly erode all structures of control. The implosive vision sees proliferation as the diffusion of a derealizing virus" (160).

This is an era then of thano-politics (what I call *thanaticism*), where the soul becomes fully weaponized.[19] It is post-political to the extent that it is no longer possible to consciously and mythically organize information around a shared project. It is a time of "soul troubles" (209). Of war against collective intelligence. Power even turns against one of its own servants—the university.

If, as Berardi suggests, Michelangelo Antonioni was the filmmaker of an earlier era of alienation, then perhaps Olivier Assayas is the filmmaker of derealization. As Steven Shaviro says of Assayas's *Boarding Gate*, it is a film of relentless horizontality, of connection, none of it good.[20] His *Demonlover* prefigures what Berardi calls "a pathogenic separation between cognitive functions and material sociality" (109).

It is a bleak vision, which becomes even more so in Berardi's later book *Heroes*, which documents a lurid fascination with serial killers

17 Jean Baudrillard, *Seduction*, New York: Palgrave, 1991.

18 Dominic Pettman, *Love and Other Technologies*, New York: Fordham University Press, 2006.

19 McKenzie Wark, "Birth of Thanaticism," *Public Seminar*, April 3, 2014, at publicseminar.org.

20 Steven Shaviro, *Post Cinematic Affect*, Winchester, UK: Zero Books, 2010.

and other symptomatic news stories, not unlike Bernard Stiegler's little book *Acting Out*.[21] Berardi's call for a therapeutic (post-)politics could be connected to Stiegler's for the restoration of "long loops of desire" against the short circuits and synchronizations which paradoxically prevent the formation of a primary narcissism that might ward off a more damaging lack of autonomy.

Berardi still uses some of the language of the late-workerist-*cum*-autonomist writers. As I argued in the chapters on Lazzarato and Boutang, I don't find the invocation of the terms *immaterial* or the *cognitive* particularly helpful. Berardi's own account of the declension of the intellectual into the sphere of production would seem to indicate why one should push harder towards a fully material account of information.

21 Franco "Bifo" Berardi, *Heroes: Mass Murder and Suicide*, London: Verso, 2015; Bernard Stiegler, *Acting Out*, Stanford, CA: Stanford University Press, 2008.

7.

Angela McRobbie: Crafting Precarity

The fate of cultural studies in the United States appears to be twofold. On the one hand, it still generates moral panic. Right-wing nut-jobbers think that "cultural Marxism" is some insidious, decadent creed, probably created by Jews and Blacks to destroy America. On the other hand, it has finally become seamlessly commodified. Dick Hebdige, once known as the author of a famous book about subcultures, is now a character in a novel by Chris Kraus that has been produced for TV by the makers of the popular show *Transparent*.[1] These two modes of recuperation were, incidentally, what Hebdige thought was the fate of all subcultures.

Hebdige broke new ground by rescuing subcultures such as the British mods, rockers and punks from the clutches of criminologists who could only think of them under the heading of deviance, and who at their most open-minded wanted to send the social workers after them rather than the cops. For Hebdige, subculture was rather a matter of culture and aesthetics, a form of *resistance through rituals*.[2] This became a rather influential approach, not least in the art world, which is always on the lookout for new sources of aesthetic value, even if it means slumming it.

McRobbie thought this was fine as far as it went, but that Hebdige tended to see subculture as something that mostly young working-class

1 Chris Kraus, *I Love Dick*, Los Angeles: Semiotext(e), 2006.

2 Stuart Hall and Tony Jefferson (eds.), *Resistance Through Rituals*, London: Routledge, 2006.

men get up to.[3] What happens instead if one looks at the self-making of young working-class women as subculture? That too was fine as far as it went, but one has to ask whether the noise and resistance of late-twentieth-century British subcultures was a generalizable phenomenon. Maybe it was of its time and place. Maybe it was an artifact of a declining industrial working class crossing with the rise of broadcast-era consumer culture in the space of the city.

In her book *Be Creative* McRobbie updates the subculture story.[4] She traces the fallout from the clash of subculture with the culture industry through to a more recent obsession with the *precariat* and the *creative industries*.[5] Is there more than a mere change in terminology here? And what can be learned by tracing the paths of young working-class women through this more contemporary urban landscape?

Drawing on Stuart Hall, and others in the cultural studies field including Hebdige, Gilroy and Andrew Ross, McRobbie takes a close interest in the utopian possibilities of everyday culture, but subjects it to a critical scrutiny, attendant to how popular aspirations are coopted by the commodity form or channeled elsewhere by disciplinary power. The people make culture, but not in a context of their own choosing.

Firstly, McRobbie has to bring the story up to date. Hebdige was writing about a time when subcultures appeared as *noise*, interrupting the orderly repetitions of the mass culture industry. Mass industrial work at least afforded mass industrial leisure. Subculture was, among other things, a *displacement* of the aspirations of the working class, shifted from struggles at the sites of mass production to the sites of mass consumption.

That was the case in the '60s and '70s, and the pattern was at least partially recognizable through to the club culture of the '80s and beyond. But from the rise of New Labour in 1997 onwards, all that fell away. Elements of youth subculture got imported into the creative industries. The nighttime economy of club culture translated

3 Angela McRobbie, *The Aftermath of Feminism*, Thousand Oaks CA: Sage, 2008.

4 Angela McRobbie, *Be Creative*, Cambridge: Polity, 2016.

5 John Hartley, *Creative Industries*, Hoboken, NJ: Wiley-Blackwell, 2005.

into endless work days. A rapid capitalization of the cultural field led to a celebrity media sphere of a more individualistic kind, one that encouraged self-promotion and self-exploitation. With it came a more extensive detachment from community and class culture. The solution to social problems lay in getting out and getting on.

And what is the role of university in managing this? There is a certain irony here, as "the unexpected outcome of cultural studies is to have found itself canonized as a curriculum for a new creative economy" (9). Now McRobbie, who teaches at London's Goldsmiths College, encounters students who aspire to work in the creative industries, who are often young and childless, but who juggle endless part-time jobs while trying to get their degree. The university exists both as a form of credentialing, but also as a place for networking.

Those part-time jobs are a means to an end, to an idea of a creative life. Subculture used the space of leisure as one in which a creativity suppressed at and by work could flourish. Now the idea is that work itself can be the site of that expression. Work becomes a kind of romantic relationship. "Work has been reinvented to satisfy the needs and demands of a generation who, 'dis-embedded' from traditional attachments to family, kinship, community or region, now find that work must become a fulfilling mark of the self" (22).

Of course, all this independent, creative work ends up dependent on centrally owned and controlled infrastructure, from which a new kind of ruling class extracts the rent. Around it buzzes the old kind of petit bourgeois "ducking and diving," of trying one's hand at this and then that, rather than specializing in a trade or profession. Young people function as the crash test dummies for new styles of living this old kind of work, as passionate and involving. The older kind of petit bourgeois could not dream of a million Instagram followers.

McRobbie is sensitive to the ambivalence and ambiguity of all this. "What starts as an inner desire for rewarding work is retranslated into a set of techniques for conducting oneself in the uncertain world of creative labor" (37). From the point of view of the young worker, its about autonomy; from the point of view of the state, "it is a matter of managing a key sector of the youthful population by turning culture into an instrument of both competition and labor discipline" (38).

Marx had imagined that the petit bourgeois strata would become progressively proletarianized as big capital moved in and colonized its various market niches. McRobbie describes something like the opposite phenomena. Various strata of what was once a working class is made petit bourgeois. Capital no longer owes them even a factory or an office to work in. The absence of security is presented entirely as a good thing, as a lack of routine. The generalized urban economy, no longer of the culture industry (singular) but the creative industries (plural), gives the young, particularly young women, a feeling of going places. It presents the endless possibility of personal success.

While I am skeptical as to how useful a concept *neoliberalism* might actually be, it does help account for some aspects of how class is subjectively lived today. Following Foucault, McRobbie traces neoliberalism to the *ordoliberals*, German state functionaries and intellectuals who had kept their heads down during the Nazi years, and came up with a more palatable right-wing philosophy after it. One that, in an irony of history McRobbie doesn't mention, displaced the state socialism of those intellectuals who had rallied to the British state in the cause of defeating the Nazis.[6] The ordoliberals redefined the human not in terms of labor but as an entrepreneur of its own life force. It is a kind of market vitalism, which prescribes a narrow set of rules for human conduct, the sole objective of which is, in every sense, self-appreciation.

While political theorists may dream of such a neoliberal subject, what actual subjects end up thinking and feeling and doing may be a bit more complicated and interesting, and that is McRobbie's bailiwick. "I see passionate attachment to creative work as comprising 'lines of flight,' embedded family histories of previously blocked hopes and frustrations" (46). The class politics of the parent culture that is submerged in commodification used to reappear as subculture, but now (post-)subculture is no longer an injection of noise against the hegemonic order but the seeding of new information for

6 C. H. Waddington, *The Scientific Attitude*, Harmondsworth: Penguin, 1941. This was not the best popular book to come out of the engagement of progressive scientists in the war against Fascism, but it is the one Friedrich Hayek chose to attack in *The Road to Serfdom*.

it to commodify. Meanwhile, the industriousness sustaining the creative industries is provided by a "risk class" without permanent jobs. Creativity promises the reward of realized self; insecurity appears as part of the adventure.

This all seems to confirm the work Eve Chiapello and Luc Boltanski did on how the ruling class responded to the challenge to its hegemony in the '60s by resisting one line of attack yet incorporating the other. The line resisted was the *labor critique,* in the form of wildcat strikes and factory occupations. The line that was incorporated was the *artistic critique*, which spoke not of labor but of *alienation*. It turns out that extracting value out of labor could function just fine without rigid, externally imposed discipline and uniformity. McRobbie: "While the prevailing value system celebrates the growth of the creative economy and the rise of talent, the talented themselves are working long hours under the shadow of unemployment in a domain of intensive under-employment, and self-activated work" (153). McRobbie works this observation through a study of the work of Richard Florida, Richard Sennett and the Italian workerist school and its descendants, such as Virno, Berardi and Lazzarato.

McRobbie offers a less rosy view than that of Richard Florida, with his celebrations of the *creative class* that populates prosperous cities, for whom the old working-class districts become gentrified playgrounds.[7] McRobbie points out that Florida's sunny vision is the flip side of what for Loïc Wacquant is a decline of sociological explanation about how urban space actually functions.[8] The occupation of the city as a space for creative-class play takes place against a background of mass incarceration which criminalizes a whole other urban population. On the one hand, part of what was subculture can become the creative industries; but on the other, a part of it no longer gets the social-worker treatment but goes straight from school to prison.

Where Richard Florida celebrates the hipster version of the creative industry, Richard Sennett prefers a more traditional version

7 Richard Florida, *The Rise of the Creative Class*, New York: Basic Books, 2014.

8 Loïc Wacquant, *Punishing the Poor*, Durham, NC: Duke University Press, 2009.

of the value of ordinary work and craft labor.[9] As McRobbie notes, there's something patriarchal and conservative about some of Sennett's attraction to old guys working steadily with their tools, but there might yet be something to draw out of this counter-model to the embrace of the creative industries.

Sennett sees work as life-enhancing and not mere drudgery. Here he thinks about labor quite differently to Hannah Arendt. However, for Sennett, changes in work may have led to a corrosion on character. Perhaps this could be reversed by returning to older habits of cooperative labor with their ethic of the job well done. McRobbie thinks there might be value in putting creative work alongside supposedly "uncreative" craft work to counter the romance of creation, although one has to wonder if this is just another romance.

There are also tricky issues here of how any kind of labor might give rise to some form of intellectual property separable from the thing itself, which might at one and the same time yield an "author"—and owner—and on the other a means of controlling the market in a particular line. Unfortunately, McRobbie does not pursue this, perhaps because her example is fashion, where intellectual property intervenes mostly at the level of the brand and the trademark rather than the individual designs.

All the same, Sennett offer a way of thinking about craft labor as one of the rhythms of the city, which has a certain value in its impersonality. It is a less grandiose way of thinking work; less about genius, talent, inspiration and competition, to which one might add—less about intellectual property. "A craft approach means being able to work all the time with failure" (156). Craft skills are within the reach of most people. It's not an elite sensibility. Its reach is local. All well and good. "But the patient labor of craft is likely to remain a distant ideal for freelancers working on a piece-rate system and having to cut corners" (158).

Craft may have little place in the contemporary cities of the overdeveloped world, with their sundering of local ties, temporary social

---

9 Richard Sennett, *The Craftsman*, New Haven, CT: Yale University Press, 2009.

relations and relentless corporate culture of "teamwork." There might be some capacity for resistance (or—dare we hope—political innovation) embodied through memory and family history, but it may no longer take a subcultural form. Perhaps it is in the residues of a craft sensibility which show up in the creative industries. Sennett provides a "parent culture" view. Crafters and artists could do well to look it up, as it is their story.

McRobbie wonders too what would happen if the kinds of labor traditionally thought of as women's work got the same treatment in Sennett as his craftsmen.

> Where it may be fruitful to downgrade the dizzy expectations of artists and creative people so that they can sit alongside others, and benefit from the time-slow pace of a mode of working that gratifies on the basis of a job being done for its own sake, it proves more difficult to upgrade some stubbornly unrewarding jobs such as domestic cleaning. (160)

One might pause here to consider the loss or invisibility of familial or community connection to such an ethos of craft labor. Thus the neo-bohemians populating Chicago's Wicker Park in Richard Lloyd's study are not able to see who is no longer living among them. Meanwhile, the *digital artisans* Andrew Ross studied at New York's Razorfish advertising agency could be self-ironizing about their cool sweatshop and the cult-like commitment it extracted from its associates, but they had not much appreciation of how their laptop creations could end up as the decorations on merchandise made in actual sweatshops. In any case, things have moved on. Wicker Park and Razorfish are names from a forgotten era, even if it was only a decade ago.[10]

Rather than try to keep up with the ever changing fascination with cool neighborhoods and cool employers, McRobbie returns to a study Jacques Rancière did in the '70s, about nineteenth-century workers. In *Proletarian Nights*, Rancière looked to workers whose aspirations

---

10 Richard Lloyd, *Neo-Bohemia*, New York: Routledge, 2010; Andrew Ross, *No Collar*, New York: Basic Books, 2002.

were not limited to forming unions or cooperatives or political parties, or even to demanding the abolition of work.[11] These *deserters* from the class struggle wanted a different kind of work. They wanted independence, and they expressed that desire in things like poetry—of an often quite formal and traditional kind.

McRobbie connects this to the British cultural-studies tradition, which had shifted attention from the sphere of production to that of consumption in order to understand how the desires and ambitions of labor had sought expression there. Taken together, these parallel French and English approaches took an interest in nontraditional kinds of "politics," if that is still the word for it. The British approach, more cultural than capital-P political, took the disco or the kitchen table as significant sites. McRobbie:

> These communal, familial, collective or indeed institutional spaces permitted alternative working lives to be imagined. Cultural studies therefore anticipated a neo-Marxism open to difference and diversity, open to the equal stature of the family and the community alongside that of the workplace and the sphere of formal politics. (58)

But this popular culture of labor's aspirations and capacities could in turn be instrumentalized. In the British context, the significant changes happened under so-called New Labour. Creativity became a kind of labor reform, in which the artist would stand as a model for a new kind of human capital. McRobbie: "These were the Damian Hirst times" (42). Art and culture were put to work. This was a kind of transitional model, replaced in more recent times by the idea of tech-centric *innovation*.

The basic formula is not that different, however. The new-model worker is to aspire to apply creativity to achieving individual success and celebrity. In both its creative and innovative flavors, this is a model hostile to traditional or "elitist" versions of either culture or the social. It can sometimes have a vaguely inclusive rhetoric. It is meritocratic, but does not pause for too long to ask if winners really

11 Jacques Rancière, *Proletarian Nights*, London: Verso, 2012.

started from the same starting blocks as the losers. And of course, it never presents all this from the worker's perspective. Workers are supposed to go away. The labor movement is replaced by networks of demassified, autonomous free agents.

Ironically, cultural studies itself became a kind of textual material that could be reworked into this image. For example, Paul Willis on working-class youth creativity got repurposed in the language of "New Times" post-labor politics, initially sponsored by the Gramscian wing of whatever was left of the Communist Party. This in turn became language for New Labour. It would be churlish to hold against cultural studies what others did with it. McRobbie defends Stuart Hall as trying to cope with the rise of post-Fordism and its effects on consumer culture via a new popular politics. "Hall's expansive ideas for how the left could forge a new popular politics were taken up and deflected in unexpected right-wing directions" (68).

A characteristic of British culture that sets it apart a bit from the United States is that for a long time it had maintained a public education system that opened a pathway into the arts for talented and often disaffected working-class kids.[12] For McRobbie and others in cultural studies, this was the site of displaced antagonisms from the factory floor. Where that tradition ended however is probably with the artist-celebrity as champion of so-called neoliberal ideas of self-making, of which Tracey Emin and Damien Hirst would be avatars.

What the ordoliberals probably did not anticipate was that the artist would in some ways become the ideal type of neoliberal subject, who would engage in a knowing self-exploitation in pursuit of a dream job. McRobbie thinks there are three subtypes of the artist, although I don't find the categories too convincing. They are the socially engaged artist, the global artist and the artist-precariat, with the latter forming a kind of critical refusal from within in the ideal neoliberal subjectivity of the artist. McRobbie: "The rhizomatic tactics and strategies of such creative activities are totally incommensurate with the vocabularies of the toolkits and business studies modules and thus can be seen as a direct challenge to the 'entrepreneurial university'" (84).

---

12 Simon Frith and Howard Horne, *Art into Pop*, Methuen, London, 1988.

Where the modernist artist was the exception to the culture industry, the contemporary artist is the exemplar of the creative industries. The category of the creative industries is of interest not least because it blurs the line between fine art and applied art, or craft. Postmodern art's stylistic complications of the boundaries between the aesthetic and kitsch seem tame compared to the extended commodification of the production of information of all kinds.

McRobbie is more interested in the more "vulgar" kinds of creative industry and the young women drawn to them. There she finds enthusiastic career girls, performing elaborate body rituals that are coded by a kind of postfeminist masquerade. They perform so-called immaterial labor and emotional labor, or what McRobbie calls "passionate work" (89). They don't entirely disavow class or ethnicity or community. They just see a narrow path to a more passionate life that involves some compromises. Normative femininity is a way to cover over traditional working-class traits that may be disabling in the workplace. Feminism opened up a path of opportunity but one now reclaimed by a more traditional-seeming code of femininity.

"Capitalism makes a seductive offer to young women with the promise of pleasure in work, while at the same time this work is nowadays bound to be precarious" (105). These women tried to refuse work as a way to escape from monotonous jobs in favor of self-directed activity, but this then has become recuperated too. McRobbie: "the idea of 'romance' has been deflected away from the sphere of love and intimacy and instead projected into the idea of a fulfilling career" (91).

Compared to Italian workerist thinkers, where a rather masculinist approach to politics remained standard, McRobbie's cultural studies approach opens up some interesting questions where labor and gender combine. By contrast to the "Bologna school," the Birmingham school moved from the factory floor to everyday life and uncoupled different kinds of struggle. McRobbie:

> without a concept of "culture," the idea of "the street" can only connote a weaker space which is not the shop-floor and hence not primarily an expected location for class politics. In this thinking the idea of the

> factory floor still takes precedence even when the workforce is in flight from it. (95)

Where the workerists spoke of the *social factory*, cultural studies might speak of the *social kitchen*. A change of metaphor here might alter how we think of what became of both labor and culture in the era of the so-called creative industries.

The workerists still treat the classic class antagonism of capital and labor as central, whereas the culturalists treated the political and cultural levels of the social formation as equally substantive. In the spirit of E. P. Thompson and Raymond Williams, cultural studies saw culture as a popular landscape of resistance and protest.[13] The workerists thought there was a new kind of subjectless class politics to which post-Fordist production processes responded. "Yet lacking a strong concept of working-class culture these authors can only rest their case on the refusal of work" (97). Even if they were never quite clear what refusal meant. Meanwhile, the culturalists expanded Gramsci's conception of a popular culture (although after Gilroy no longer necessarily a national one) as a common resource.

McRobbie retrieves from the workerists the idea of the line of flight, the desire to escape, and mobility as response to labor. Of course not all workerists (and post-workerists) are enthusiasts for these lines of flight. Lazzarato and Berardi, for example, become quite pessimistic. McRobbie's question is whether young women get the same chance at the "immaterial" as young men. Is today's labor market just as (or more) gender segregated? Is there a return to a kind of neo-traditional sexism? Or, more broadly: "How then can we talk about the gender of post-Fordism?" (101).

McRobbie:

> Refusal is more of a desire and a yearning for rewarding work, something that is within sight and perhaps within reach through access to further and higher education. This "flight" also acquires gendered

13 Raymond Williams, *Culture and Society*; E. P. Thompson, *The Making of the English Working Class*, London: Penguin, 2013.

> characteristics. The impact of 1970s feminism made the idea of a career for young women completely acceptable. Unlike the autonomist Marxists, I do not make such fulsome claims for a new radical politics emerging from the "social factory," instead I see a field of ambivalence and tension, where lines of flight connect past parental struggles with the day-to-day experiences of their children in the modern work economy. (93)

Despite the utopian promise of passionate work as escape from traditional labor, it ends up being a desire that can in turn be exploited. Passion becomes a means of production, complete with precarity, long hours and low pay. "I pose the idea of passionate work being a distinctive mode of gender re-traditionalization…whereby the conservatism of post-feminism re-instates young women's aspirations for success within designated zones of activity such as creative labor" (110). Passionate work becomes self-exploitation, complete with its own codes of affect—a permanent appearance of enjoyment—and a bodily style of exuberant enthusiasm.

Creative work has become separated from ordinary labor, but does it follow as McRobbie thinks that it is thereby depoliticized? Maybe there's another kind of politics for something that is not exactly labor. It is the case that a wedge was driven between creative labor and other kinds, thereby weakening social-democratic politics. But perhaps the strategy is not then to bring the former back into the latter. McRobbie sometimes sounds as nostalgic as Sennett, if not exactly for the same image of the past. Rather than a neoliberal vocabulary of the entrepreneur, or the old social-democratic one of industrial labor, perhaps it is time to think of another one that might more accurately map onto the class formations of our time. Rather than reverse the neoliberal turn, let's take a new turn.

McRobbie encourages us to look to less masculine-coded practices for signs of possibility. She is interested in women crafters who make public women's traditional skills, such as the yarn bombers weaving public artworks that knit bicycles to lampposts. There's an ambivalence to these subcultures. In part, they look back to a rather traditional and idyllic culture of femininity. On the other hand, they sometimes draw from those pasts to create more self-consciously feminist practices in the present. As always with culture, there are tensions and ambiguities which can be fruitful and interesting. This subculture, as an example, is a sort of return to the craft critique of production of William Morris, without the paternalism.[14]

Perhaps it is not quite the same to be making the old things and to be making new information. Perhaps the latter seems so lacking in the history and culture of labor because it isn't exactly labor. The temporality of its production may not have much in common with the patient persistence of craft work. Its relation to the commodity form is rather different. It does not produce the thing to be sold as a piece of property, but rather creates an arrangement of information that is novel enough to count as intellectual property. It is so easily copied that other strategies have to come into play to extract value from its production, which is where creating the aura of special skill around particular creators comes into play. The networks within which information is made are partly local, and as yet nothing beats the city as a way of organizing it. But its networks also extend far beyond urban space. The infrastructure of information makes the physical and informational aspects appear quite separate, although there is nothing immaterial about it.

In short, maybe this relatively new kind of production is as unlike craft labor as it is unlike industrial labor. It comes into being only at a time when information can be private property, and yet information can be rapidly and fully copied and shared. It is a relatively new set of forces of production that make it possible—information technology. It is both shaped by, and exceeds, the relations of production extruded out of the property form to embrace it—intellectual property. Maybe it even produces quite distinct class relations, between producers and owners of information.

These aspects of the creative industries I find neglected both in British cultural studies and Franco-Italian workerist theory. One might however draw from McRobbie an attention to gender in how

---

14 E. P. Thompson, *William Morris: Romantic to Revolutionary*, Oakland: PM Press, 2011.

creative industries have evolved. If one looks at fashion as the archetypal form of *creativity* and tech as the archetypal form of *innovation*, one finds a very strong imposition of very conservative ideas about what is men's work and what is women's work—even if neither is exactly work anymore.

8.

Paul Gilroy: The Persistence of Race

Aimé Césaire called it: the so-called West is a decaying civilization.[1] In both the United States and Europe, where institutions are receding, a base level of race-talk and racial solidarity is revealed as metastasizing beneath them. In such dim times, I turn to the writings of Paul Gilroy as offering an antiracist vision that is transnational and cosmopolitan, but which draws on popular and vernacular forms of hybridity rather than elite ones.

In *Darker than Blue: On the Moral Economies of Black Atlantic Culture*, Gilroy offers a series of essays on the culture of what he has famously called the Black Atlantic as an alternative to race-talk but which is also outside of the various alternative nationalisms that flourish as a response.[2] It is not reducible to liberalism, and it also attempts to fend off incorporation into the culture industry. That might be an urgent project for this "age of rendition" (87). One in which in Butler's terms that which is grievable, or in Haraway's that which is killable, are respectively diminishing and expanding categories.

Gilroy is wary of responses to racism that borrow from it. He would probably strongly reject Chantal Mouffe's understanding of all politics as necessarily based on a tangible equality of participation in a shared substance, which necessarily excludes the other as unequal to us. Hence he is not any more inclined towards Black nationalism

---

1 Aimé Césaire, *Discourse on Colonialism*, New York: Monthly Review Press, 2011.

2 Paul Gilroy, *Darker than Blue*, Cambridge, MA: Harvard, 2010.

than towards any other. Instead, he builds upon the moral economies of the Black Atlantic, in which the struggle against slavery and racism pose the question of a transnational belonging, or what I would call the problem of species-being. Just as E. P. Thompson saw the English working class as self-making, Gilroy is interested in the coming-into-being of a people in struggle, but beyond Thompson's rather provincial national frame.[3]

This is in some respects an old-fashioned project. Gilroy: "After the Hegelian and Marxist imaginings of figures like W. E. B. Du Bois and C. L. R. James, the idea that the slaves' pursuit of human freedom could retain any broader philosophical, political, or commercial importance was seldom considered seriously" (5). Indeed what is timely in Gilroy is his insistence on the ongoing pertinence of just such questions, even if the forms of answering to their call need changing.[4]

The struggles against slavery and against colonialism are not always central to the self-understanding of human-rights talk, perhaps because they keep pointing past the point where human rights could be made compatible with liberalism. Antislavery took some of its moral energy from the chiliastic Christianity of St. Paul and aimed it towards a radical inclusiveness of the category of the human, beyond kith and kin.

Gilroy revises James Baldwin's critical judgement on *Uncle Tom's Cabin*.[5] While acknowledging the ways that sentimental stories can block the full import of feelings of shame, Gilroy wants to retrieve something of the popular moral economy the text created through its global networks of translation and production. "*Uncle Tom's Cabin* composed a cosmopolitan chapter in the moral history of our world" (66). Sure, it is problematic as a portrait of slave passivity and it treated suffering as redemptive, but it also treated Black characters as actually having humanity. Like Butler, Gilroy wants to find once again a structure of feeling that can acknowledge the suffering of others.

---

3 E. P. Thompson, *The Making of the English Working Class*.

4 C. L. R. James, *American Civilization*, London: Verso, 2016.

5 James Baldwin, *Notes of a Native Son*, Boston: Beacon Press, 2012, 13ff.

As in his earlier book *Against Race* (2000), Gilroy also makes a case for the antifascist strand of antiracist struggles for national liberation from colonial rule. That history tends to complicate stories that take identities as given and coherent, and innocently put-upon by some outside aggressor. Gilroy insists it cannot be assimilated to identity politics, no matter what current American academic reading lists might say. Gilroy: "That depressing pseudo-political gesture supplies an alibi for narcissistic quiescence and resignation to the world as it is" (66).

Restored to the story of both antifascism and antiracism here is the historical role of Ethiopia. Haile Selassie became emperor of this ancient state in 1930, and Italy began its second war against it in 1935, a war in which chemical weapons were used against civilian populations. It is worth remembering that the civil war in Spain is not the only skirmish that presages the return of world war. Spain might have galvanized the antifascist left worldwide, but Ethiopia played an analogous role for pan-African politics.

These of course are just gestures to complex and profane histories. Gilroy mentions them to ask about the role of antislavery and anticolonialism in the struggle for human rights.

> Taken together, those struggles contribute to a culture of freedom sourced from deep within the experience of object-hood. All of them resist the process by which a human being is reduced to a thing. For descendants of slaves, they summon the history of being locked away from literacy on pain of death, confined in a place where cognition—thinking—was not a special door to doubt, method, and modern being but rather a shortcut to the radical vulnerability of nonbeing and social death for a people whose infra-human status meant they could be disposed of with impunity. (72)

One might imagine that the challenge of a thought premised on vulnerability to nonbeing had finally arrived in Giorgio Agamben's work.[6] There the concentration camp replaces the city as the *topos*

6 Giorgio Agamben, *Homo Sacer*, Stanford, CA: Stanford University Press, 1998.

for political theory. But as Gilroy insists, the prehistory of the camps in colonial history is only ever a gesture in Agamben. Gilroy turns instead to Primo Levi, and his concept of *useful violence.*[7] In the camps, even the rationality of means, production targets or profits gets subordinated to something excessive. This suggests to Gilroy that racism has its own agency.

Why is violence useful to the perpetrator over and above compulsion and coercion toward some material aim? Strangely enough, it enables them to carry on murdering and torturing while minimizing emotional disturbance to themselves, as the victim is only *infrahuman* and calls for no respect as a fellow member of a species-being. In a less world-historical but more everyday key, this seems like a valid line of thought for explaining those photographs of the debasement of Iraqis from Abu Ghraib prison. It is also the conceptual, as well as emotional, heart of the very phrase Black Lives Matter.

Like Agamben, Hannah Arendt tries to sidestep the question of race.[8] For Arendt, when people appear outside the envelope of the national they appear as natural, provoking violence against their very humanity. But for Gilroy, Arendt mistakes the naked human for the natural one. The vulnerable figure is the racialized human, not the naturalized human. The racialized infrahuman body is made to perform the subordination that race theory assumes, but that their bodies don't seem to support without such acts of debasement. Gilroy: "Racial discourse can be thought as contributing to a system for making meaning that feeds the tendency to create exceptional spaces and populate them with vulnerable, infra-human beings" (85).

Antiracism as a project might exceed not only liberal but also more critical political theory. But it might have a tendency on the other hand to collapse into the cloying embrace of the commodity form. Gilroy: "African Americans were interpellated as consumers long before they acquired citizenship rights" (9). Jesse Owens, the track star who enraged Hitler, became a shill for Coca-Cola. I think the

---

7 Primo Levi, *The Drowned and the Saved*, New York: Vintage, 1989.

8 Hannah Arendt, *The Human Condition*, Chicago: University of Chicago Press, 1998.

tensions Gilroy identifies between a political and a consumer identity are on full display in the American TV show *Blackish*, about the family of an upwardly mobile Black advertising executive. The central character's father claims to have been a militant in the '60s, but was a member of the Bobcats, who he defends as "Panther adjacent." The family has to navigate upper-middle-class life, complete with questions about purchasing shoes and cars.

Blackish is alive to questions of getting to consume things you are not supposed to have, and to buying things as talismans of prestige denied in any civil register. It also acknowledges the role of Black consumption as rendering certain commodities cool by association and thus available for white buyers. Consumption can appear as a form of rebellion, but also of resignation. The product is a stand-in one can have for what one can't have.

What other vision of the good life does the commodity, big or small, occlude? As Berardi and others note in another context, the commodity as placebo might just lead to cascades of envy. Gilroy: "A lingering negativity betrays black citizens' desire to join in the carnival of American plenitude as full participants in ways that racism used to deny" (21).

For Gilroy, the car is the ur-commodity of the relation of Black culture to consumption, and one which complicates any attempt to align African-Americans with an anticolonial project, given the intense connection between American neo-imperial projects and access to oil. But he offers a nuanced reading of the role the car played and continues to play in the African-American imaginary, from Ralph Ellison and Richard Wright to bell hooks and Cornel West. Ellison already understood the tension between African-American self-making and freedom through consumption that is in the end alienating. Still, the car could figure in the place of the train as a powerful figure for flight, restlessness and mobility as responses to racial terror, forced labor and confinement.

Car culture privatizes freedom and becomes a new instrument of segregation. "For much of the twentieth century, the private automobile, and the social order it supported, constituted something like an index of hegemony" (23). Gilroy connects the rise of the car to a loss of Blackness as resistance, solidarity, and its replacement with a lifestyle code. The infrastructure of the car puts technology right at the heart of everyday life.

The highway offers a kind of serial existence devoid of civil contact, and the default instance of being separate but equal, unless one is pulled over for the crime of Driving While Black. It turns out that having the same stuff does not promote much community, and one ends up acquiring stuff instead of rights. The car made white flight possible and still reinforces a geography of segregation. Perhaps it is no accident that Henry Ford was an enthusiast for Hitler. Fordism and fascism might be quite intimately connected.

Still, the car figures as a lot of things in African-American culture, from Jack Johnson behind the wheel of a fine machine with a white woman by his side, to Malcolm X working in a Ford factory. The car replaced the train in popular poetics, and its influence as a figure extends far beyond the American context. The car generalized the segregation of the colonial city. The car itself puts its occupants in a bubble, complete with its own sonic environment. The car ends up as "a kind of giant armored bed on wheels that can shout the driver's dwindling claims upon the world into dead public space at ever increasing volume" (48).

In African-American popular music, the erotics of the car is a whole subgenre. One thinks here of: Robert Johnson, "Terraplane Blues"; Ike Turner, "Rocket 88"; Chuck Berry, "No Particular Place to Go"; Jimi Hendrix, "Crosstown Traffic"; Prince, "Little Red Corvette"; and TLC, "Scrubs." Gilroy points to Williams DeVaughn, "Be Thankful For What You've Got" as a rare song that celebrates not owning a car, and Albert King, "Cadillac Assembly Line," which speaks not of the erotics of consumption but the labor of production. To which we might add the Detroit blues of Joe L. Carter, "Please Mr. Foreman."

The latter includes the lines "I don't mind working, but I do mind dying," from which comes the title of a famous account of radical Black workers: *Detroit: I Do Mind Dying*.[9] One could usefully

9 Marvin Surkin and Dan Georgaka, *Detroit: I Do Mind Dying*, 3rd edition, Chicago: Haymarket Books, 2012.

connect Gilroy on car consumption to this text on their production. Black workers were central to "Fordism" in many ways. Henry Ford famously used Black workers as strike breakers, but the war brought many up out of rural work to factory work, and eventually into the United Auto Workers union. Ford and GM moved key production out of the Detroit area, but Chrysler was still dependent on key production facilities there in the late '60s, where radical Black workers challenged both the company and the union with a series of wildcat strikes and a range of community actions, including resistance to Detroit's aggressive policing.

By the late '60s, the car companies were struggling against cheaper and better imports. They claimed to be meeting the challenge with automation, but Black workers called it *N---ermation*. Really it was the same old dirty, dangerous, authoritarian workplace and the time-old speedup. And needless to say Black workers were among those still stuck with the most dangerous and low-paid jobs. As were Arab workers, latest in a wave of migrants caught up in divide-and-rule tactics by management and even the unions.

The connection between race and production hardly appears in Gilroy. I'm skeptical about his claim that "cars fudge any residual distinctions between material and semiotic, base and superstructure" (30). It might make more sense to think of cars à la Lazzarato as connected to an infrastructure that is both material and semiotic, which is deeply embedded in a global geography of production and distribution, shaping cities to its affordances. As Pasolini had noted in the '60s, the production lines of neo-capitalism stamp out subjects as well as objects. What I find most promising in this part of Gilroy's work is the opportunity to think about how race and infrastructure interact, and always on a global scale.

Fast-forward to the present: one could think then about the role of an image like Jay Z behind the wheel of a Maybach in driving global production and consumption chains. He may not sell many Maybachs, as practically nobody—Black or white—can afford them. But he might sell quite a few hats. The globalization of Black culture is oriented to American standards.

What would a popular form of hybridizing Black culture not

entirely oriented to consumption look like? Gilroy offers two examples: Bob Marley and Jimi Hendrix. Before he was famous, Marley was a nomadic migrant worker, traveling across the leaky borders of both the underdeveloped and overdeveloped worlds. And to this day, "His recordings have been found in the pockets of unidentified African bodies washed up upon the beaches of Europe" (88).

Gilroy: "What answers does the mixed-race person give to the apostles of purity, who can be found in all communities?" (103) Marley borrowed from Jamaican rude boys, from Curtis Mayfield, but also from Black Power: "I Shot the Sheriff," as a famous Marley song has it—but not the deputy. For Gilroy, Marley is a version of Blackness that can include, but is not reducible to, African-American culture. It borrows from the diasporic cult of Ethiopia but makes it more a symbolic than an actual homeland. From the Rastafarians it also takes a view of wage work not as self-mastery but as an extension of slavery. From the discovery of swinging London it evolves into the "Kinky Reggae" of the "Midnight Ravers."

Where Marley had been an itinerant worker, Hendrix was a former soldier, who swapped the "Machine Gun" for the electric guitar, itself also bound up in curious ways with military technology. He produced an *Afrofuturist* sound that was, as Caetano Veloso put it, "half blues, half Stockhausen."[10] Gilroy:

> Hendrix's career tells us that by this point, black music could produce its own public world: a social corona that could nourish or host an alternative sensibility, a structure of feeling that might function to make wrongs and injustices more bearable in the short term but could also promote a sense of different possibilities, providing healing glimpses of an alternative moral, artistic, and political order. (147)

For Gilroy there is something utopian in such flickering of diasporic Black culture. "These musical traditions do not always fit neatly into the stories of ethnic resilience, heroic masculinity,

---

10 Caetano Veloso, *Tropical Truth*, Cambridge MA: DaCapo Press, 2003, 168.

national liberation, racial ascent, and vindication that would serve the immediate political interests of its creators" (101). They touch on the affective registers of an unequal yet interdependent world. "Purity becomes impossible, and hybridity ceases to be the exclusive preoccupation of some imaginary postcolonial elite. Instead, it becomes a routine principle of unruly multi-culture" (151). Perhaps this could even be an intimation of Karatani's fourth mode of exchange, the Kingdom of Ends.

Yet there is a mournful note in Gilroy's writing. "The countercultural voice of black Atlantic popular music has faded out. Song and dance have lost their preeminent positions in the ritual and interpretive processes that both grounded and bounded communal life" (121). Perhaps it is important to accept its passing in order to imagine something else in its place. It was, after all, an art that heightened awareness of loss and kept open some redress other than consumption. "A virtuous rapport with the presence of death was one key characteristic of the tradition of music making towards freedom which is now coming to an end, as the freedom to consume without limits promises the satisfaction of all desires" (126).

Gilroy really does think there has been what Adorno would call a "regression of listening" (129). Other writers might disagree. Kodwo Eshun makes a case for the digital turn in Afrofuturism. Rachel Kaadzi Ghansah writes compellingly about Kendrick Lamar and the fan culture of Beyoncé.[11] As to whether they are convincing, it is not my place to say. Certainly, the changing global infrastructure within which popular cultures flourish or not is a rather different environment now to what it was in what one might call the late-analog era.

What would a popular, affective, diasporic culture of hybridity be like now? Would it be elsewhere than in popular music? Might it dispense with even the alternate versions of masculine stardom? It still seems an urgent question. For Gilroy, it is about the problem of approaching a workable version of species-being. In his reading,

11 Kodwo Eshun, *More Brilliant than the Sun*, 2nd edition, London: Verso, 2016; Rachel Kaadzi Ghansah, 'When the Lights Shut Off', *Los Angeles Review of Books*, 31st January 2013, at lareviewofbooks.org.

Frantz Fanon is not a writer who would easily assimilate into the default antihumanism of the American academy. In trying to conceptualize species-being without race, Fanon refuses to see cultural differences as absolute, eternal or insurmountable.[12]

In Gilroy's Fanon, racism exacts a cost from both victims and perpetrators in that a common humanity is amputated and authentic interaction becomes impossible. He refuses any easy position of innocence. The perpetrator and victim roles are, as in Baudelaire, exchangeable. Gilroy stresses the continuity in Fanon of the antifascism of the war years and the anticolonialism that gained momentum after it. There is a utopian moment that gestures toward universality here, but in the negative. There need be no idealized core to a concept of species-being. It is rather a decision to accept the relativism of cultures vis-à-vis each other. Indeed, it has to pull away the prop of an essential and restrictive claim to humanity made by any race as a component of the useful violence that produces a hierarchy of difference.

12 Frantz Fanon, *Towards the African Revolution*, New York: Grove Press, 1969.

9.

Slavoj Žižek: Absolute Recoil

Whenever Marxists lift their attention from vulgar matters and start creating theories of the *subject*, it is always the bourgeois subject that seems to need theorizing. Perhaps there is no other kind.

Althusser illustrated his theory of the subject with an anecdote about being hailed in the street by a cop: "Hey you!" In recognizing (or rather misrecognizing) oneself when being hailed as the subject addressed by power, one becomes the subject of an *ideology*.[1] But what if one takes this anecdote seriously and asks about what else might happen in the encounter with a cop in the street?

As I write, people in the town of Ferguson near St. Louis are still taking to the streets and refusing to be "good subjects" over the shooting by a cop of an unarmed Black youth.[2] For people of color, "Hey you!" might mean something quite different. It might mean that it does not matter whether you are guilty or not, or whether you think you are guilty or not. A cop has seen you and he automatically "knows" you are guilty.

A person of color in today's United States might be less worried about the hail of address and more about the hail of bullets. There is no neat partition between the ideological and repressive state apparatuses. The police rather selectively turn the ideological face toward property owners, but it is the repressive boot that many people more

1 Louis Althusser, *On Ideology*, London: Verso, 2008.

2 Keenga-Yamahtha Taylor, *From #BlackLivesMatter to Black Liberation*, Chicago: Haymarket Books, 2016.

regularly get to see. Moreover, it matters which street you happen to be on. There is no universal abstract "street"—as Butler at least suspects. A street has qualities, affordances, ambiances—a *psychogeography*—and much else besides.[3]

Surely Althusser might have known this. He was writing just after the peak of the Algerian war, when the Paris police were battling Algerian freedom fighters, when Paris regularly had curfews, and Algerians were ending up dead in the Seine with their hands handcuffed behind their backs. And surely his "Hey you!" anecdote owes more than a little to Sartre, who had used a similar anecdote about cops and the street to illustrate what a *situation* is.[4] If I go out after curfew, I exercise my freedom, but I don't know the exact contours of freedom's limit. The cops might be there to challenge me, or they might not. Not only does a street have qualities, it can be a variable situation. Sartre, who in other respects probably started the Marxist obsession with the bourgeois subject, at least knew a little bit about streets.

But none of these are objections that occur to Slavoj Žižek in his commentary on Althusser in *Absolute Recoil*.[5] The sort of *street Marxism* that passes from Sartre to Debord and Lefebvre does not show up in Althusser or Žižek.[6] For them, the anecdote about what is clearly the *bourgeois subject* being hailed by the police grounds a theory of the *universal subject*—which is to say, the bourgeois subject. In Žižek's reading, Althusser's anecdote does deal with the relation between ideology and repression, but in the following manner: first, force can be shown, so as not to have to be used; secondly, force does not even have to be shown, so as not to have to be used. Žižek: "First, one makes a show of force so as not to have to use it; then, one does not make a show of force so as not to have to use it. We are effectively dealing here with a kind of negation of the negation" (53).

---

3 On psychogeography: McKenzie Wark, *The Beach Beneath the Street*, London: Verso, 2015.

4 Jean-Paul Sartre, *Being and Nothingness*, New York: Washington Square Press, 1993.

5 Slavoj Žižek, *Absolute Recoil*, London: Verso, 2015.

6 Andy Merrifield, *Metromarxism*, London: Routledge, 2002.

The first is the real, the second is the symbolic. And so even with the non-showing of force, force is still present as that "little piece of the real" (54) that still inheres in the symbolic. Žižek's reading of Althusser is a fun one—if one is a bourgeois subject. For Žižek, what is elided in Althusser's theory is the *gap* in knowledge that requires *supplement* with belief. In Althusser the ideological field constructs subject positions, while a science does not. In Žižek, it is ideology all the way down.

Žižek will then use the cop anecdote to found an allegedly radical materialism, one not just about the priority of the material, but the "immanent materiality of the ideal order itself" (55). Note, however, that the prior level of the material, that of a "street Marxism," here *does not occur at all.* We move immediately to the ethereal real of the bourgeois subject. Our topic is then not going to be the unreasonable use of direct violence against Black bodies by cops who seem to get their armaments out of Marvel comics. Which is akin to what Gilroy calls the *necessary violence* through which race is enforced as a distinction between bodies to be treated as human and those not. Rather, our topic is going to be the unreasonable taint at the heart of reason itself, the impossibility of a knowledge that does not traverse non-knowledge. Any actual materiality can only ever be mentioned in passing in Žižek: his subject is *the* subject, which is everywhere.

Žižek:

> Hegel's point is that the endless postponement of the arrival of a fully moral universe is not just an effect of the gap between the purity of the Ideal and the empirical circumstances which prevent its full actualization, it is located in this Ideal itself, inscribing a contradiction (a self-sabotaging desire) into its very heart. (56)

Or so it might be, for those for whom irrational violence does not arrive first from without.

In Althusser, external obedience is the beginnings of ideology.[7] For Žižek, of course, it all "functions in a much more twisted way" (62).

7 Rather like faith in Pascal.

For Žižek, the tendency to cheat, lie, to "distort" language, is not a secondary effect but is at the core of language itself. Hence a certain internal difficulty in those regimens for producing good bourgeois subjects in which one goes through the rituals, the external manifestations, and in the process becomes a believer.

The bourgeois subject who hears the "Hey you!" in the street feels both innocence but also a Kafkaesque guilt upon being hailed.

> What remains "unthought" in Althusser's theory of interpellation is thus the fact that, prior to ideological recognition, we have an intermediate moment of obscene, impenetrable interpellation without identification, a kind of vanishing mediator that has to become invisible if the subject is to achieve symbolic identity. (64)

Or in short, who is the bourgeois subject before it becomes the bourgeois subject, (mis)recognizing itself as hailed?

But why should that even be our question? Why not ask: Who is the Black man hailed by the police in today's America? What if there is no universal act of "enhailment" into the space of ideology? Who even gets to be a subject? Who rather gets a bullet in the back? Who is not even worth addressing before being attacked? Who is killable (Haraway) and not greivable (Butler)? Who is infrahuman (Gilroy)?

Thus, we can answer the following Žižekian question, but perhaps not in the way he intended. Žižek:

> What would a materialism look like which fully took into account this traumatic core of subjectivity irreducible to natural processes? In other words, what would a materialism look like which fully assumed the main result of transcendental idealism: the gap in the natural order signaled by the emergence of subjectivity? (72)

It would give us a definition of the bourgeois: those for whom there appears to be a gap in the natural order.

The truth of Althusser's theory of the bourgeois subject is to be found in Alain Badiou's reversal. For Althusser, subjectivity is ideological; for Badiou, truth is subjective. This is the foundation of Badiou's *bourgeois communism.* Žižek's position will end up close to this, but not before subjecting Badiou to the strictures of a more orthodox Lacanian critique. What the two of them together—Badižek—oppose is "democratic materialism." Žižek:

> The predominant philosophical struggle occurs today within materialism, between democratic and dialectical materialism—and what characterizes dialectical materialism is precisely that it incorporates the idealist legacy, against vulgar democratic materialism in all its guises, from scientific naturalism to the post-Deleuzian assertion of spiritualized "vibrant" matter. Dialectical materialism is, first, a materialism without matter...*it is a materialism with an Idea.* (73)

Now, I have my differences with the post-Deleuzians on precisely their proclivities towards forms of vitalism (hence my interest in strong critics of vitalism such as the neglected Joseph Needham, an early inspiration for Haraway).[8] But here I must close ranks with the post-Deleuzians against Badižek on this. Žižek: "materialism's problem is how to explain the rise of an eternal Idea out of the activity of people caught in a finite historical situation" (73). Well no, that is not materialism's problem. That is *Badiou's* problem. The way he finesses this is the mystified notion of the *event* as a kind of non-dialectical, contingent starting point of the dialectic.

If for Althusser the subject is the one interpellated by the "Hey you!" of the ideological state apparatus, in Badiou the subject is the one who *says yes to the event.* The subject is curiously not that which has free choice, but is the product of a free choice, a choice of *fidelity* to an event. But who exactly gets to be a subject of an event? On this Badiou has changed his mind. In *Being and Event*, only those who name and love the event are its subjects. Later, in *Logic of Worlds*, the event includes other kinds of subjects besides those who affirm it, even though it still excludes the neutral observer.[9] Now there is the

8 McKenzie Wark, "Joseph Needham, the Great Amphibian," *Public Seminar*, September 5, 2014, at publicseminar.org.

9 Alain Badiou, *Being and Event*, London: Continuum, 2007; Badiou, *Logic of Worlds*, London: Continuum, 2009.

faithful subject, the reactive subject, the obscure subject and "the resurrection." The event localizes the void in the subjects who not only affirm it but acknowledge it.

Žižek:

> We thus have three (logically, if not temporally) consecutive moments: the primordial unlocalizable void of multiplicity; the event as the localization of a previously unlocalizable void; and the process of subjectivization which emerges out of the free decision to choose fidelity to the event. (77)

One is reminded of Sartre, perhaps the great thinker of the bourgeois subject, for whom the world *just is*, made by nobody, maintained by nobody, just waiting for the bourgeois subject to arrive to give it all meaning. That same Sartre who, in his other famous anecdotes, had the nerve to accuse the *woman* and the *waiter* of living in *bad faith*. Bourgeois subjects tend not to know who makes the world for them, and to be rather judgy about those who do.

But if it takes a *special* event to make a subject, what about those of us wannabe bourgeois subjects who live in boring times? Even better! Those are the times of the *anticipatory* subject who holds open a place for a political subject to come—the philosophical subject! The philosopher gets to be the proto-bourgeois subject. Žižek: "the subject is prior to the process of subjectivization: this process fills in the void (the empty form) that is the pure subject" (80). You won't get to be Lenin (and still less Bogdanov) but—even better!—you get to be Plekhanov.[10]

The subject is thus not the unstable, provisional, plural thing that it might be for "democratic" materialisms, be they Deleuzian or not. For Žižek's kind of self-described dialectical materialism, the subject is first and last: first the empty frame, the pure form, and then the full subject that chooses to affirm the event in some manner.

This is unfortunate, as in Žižek the question never really gets asked as to what produces the subject other than the pure empty frame. If there was a productive side to the Deleuzian or democratic

---

10 G. V. Plekhanov, *Fundamental Problems of Marxism*, New York: International Publishers, 1992.

materialism, it is in writers such as Lazzarato or Préciado, who really inquire into the *apparatus* that produces subjects and their corresponding objects. These books seem to me closer to the Marxist tradition in asking after the means of production—in this case not of the commodity but of the corresponding subjects that might produce and consume them.

Another point on which one might choose to side (with some reservations) with the Deleuzians is in their refusal of *a priori* hierarchies of the human and the nonhuman. Oddly enough, here Žižek joins hands with those like Ray Brassier who want to celebrate a kind of scientific rationality which can only be a firstly human (but then possibly post-human) attribute.[11] Weirdly, the marking off of the human is here going to be for quite opposite qualities, in the one case for a rationality that can supersede the human (Brassier), the other for a rationality that is always and necessarily traversed by some merely human and subjective irrationality (Žižek). And, as is all too clear from Althusser's interpellation scene, or Badiou's insistence on the rarity of the event that makes the subject, only certain humans ever seem to get to be fully human—even if these are philosophers who claim to speak in the name of a universality.

As Žižek notes (apropos Badiou), animals merely follow their tasks, they do not reflect upon them. Humans, however, have the magical capacity to decide to follow or more often not follow the event. Žižek: "the human being is a lazy animal" (83). The subject gets bored, depressed, melancholic. Here he touches for a moment on a lively contemporary theme. This depressive subjectivity has its uses, as it is also a way of evading interpellation. In the overdeveloped world, the worker is supposed to be *on* all the time, constantly innovating and disrupting itself. As Berardi notes (in a Deleuzian mode), depression is now a common form of resistance, even if not actively chosen to be such.

Predictably enough, Žižek does not really inquire very far into the production of the subject today. Instead, we get that old Žižekian

11 Ray Brassier, *Nihil Unbound: Enlightenment and Extinction*, New York: Palgrave, 2010.

chestnut, Chesterton, and his charmingly everyday defenses of religious orthodoxy, and this time without the twist.[12] For Chesterton, the lawbreaker is boring, whereas the police are interesting. Promiscuity is boring, marriage is a "true adventure" (87). Heresy is boring, orthodoxy—be it Catholic or Lacanian—is supposedly a hoot. Here for once Žižek is not kidding.

And thus, the non-evental time when nothing revolutionary is happening turns out not to be a problem either: "the properly Hegelian approach posits the anticipatory 'empty' subject as the universal model, as the zero-level of subjectivity—it is only in the void of anticipation that the universal form of subjectivity appears as such" (87). One just faithfully repeats the philosophical procedure over and over, awaiting an event that comes from without—even if it gets a little boring.

It may well be that the one thing that is not obvious about a philosophy is what it actually does. But what could not be clearer about Žižek is the way he legitimates the existence of a philosophically inclined bourgeois subject in an era which probably no longer has or needs either a bourgeoisie or subjects. The ruling class is of another order now, and the machines that manage bodies and produce objects may no longer exactly produce subjects to correspond to them, even on the rather generous understanding of "subject" as the Deleuzians comprehend the term.

What could be better in such an age than to be a kind of Jesuitical-Lacanian sage? Awaiting the great event which one secretly hopes and even knows *will not happen*, producing the purely philosophical subject that only has to prepare the way. Taking an interest only in those things that speak to such a mode of thinking. Let's talk about Wagner and Heidegger and Beckett—just like the bourgeois intellectuals of old! Let's not sully ourselves with any knowledge of how the world actually works. And in our leisure time—pulp fiction, and *Pulp Fiction*. All with the charming and seemingly daring alibi that this is a "dialectical materialism." No wonder it has been popular, even if—like the actual Soviet dia-mat of old—the charm is wearing thin.

12 If one must, read G. K. Chesterton, *The Man Who Was Thursday*, London: Penguin, 2012.

Hence, it is illuminating to have comrade Žižek write about *Molecular Red*, a book I wrote very much to carve out a space in the Marx-field that does not pass through dia-mat.[13] I think his comments highlight two quadrants of the Marx-field where theory can choose to gravitate at the moment: the high zone of bourgeois philosophy, or the low zone of something else, as yet unknown. It is less about the wrong or right quadrant, and more about what kinds of thing each zone of the Marx-field allows one to do. So let me explain, via the contrast with Žižek's high zone, why I prefer a low one.

Perhaps the central concept in Marx for our time is *metabolic rift*. He understood from Justus von Liebig that even mid-nineteenth-century capitalism was sending molecular flows out of joint.[14] Liebig's agricultural science was pointing to deficits of nitrogen and potassium that happen when modern farming feeds an urban population, whose shit and piss end up washing out to sea via that great nineteenth-century infrastructure, the sewer network of central London, constructed under the supervision of Joseph William Bazalgette.[15]

There's an ambiguity in metabolic rift, however. It is tempting to read into it a diversion—rift—from some state of nature whose governing metaphor is harmony and order—metabolism. As if nature were like some self-correcting free market that tended to equilibrium. In this popular image, ecology is a state of balance, harmony and order from which "we" have departed and to which we have to return.

Sometimes, this metaphor is given a feminist coloration, as if ecology meant feminine virtues that had been discarded. Haraway long ago warned us of the limits of this tendency, which locks ecofeminism into some questionable assumptions about what is essentially feminine, such as nature, nurture, harmony, etc. Which sounds great

---

13 McKenzie Wark, *Molecular Red*, London: Verso, 2015; Slavoj Žižek, "Ecology Against Mother Nature," Verso blog, May 26, 2015.

14 Karl Marx, *Capital*, vol. 3, London: Penguin, 1993 878ff; John Bellamy Foster, *Marx's Ecology: Materialism and Nature*, New York: Monthly Review Press, 2000.

15 On the psychogeography of which see Bradley Garrett (ed.), *Subterranean London*, New York: Prestel, 2014.

until you notice the things it excludes: woman equals nature but not reason, and so on.

As Žižek puts it in his piece on my book, using his characteristic language: "One is tempted to add that, if there is one good thing about capitalism, it is that under it, Mother Earth no longer exists." Or as I put it in *Molecular Red*: it is not just that as Nietzsche says "God is dead," it is also that the Goddess is dead. There is neither Father Spirit nor Mother Earth. This whole metaphorical cosmology is no more. And in a double sense: these *metaphors* no longer apply; but neither is there a stable world to which this could apply. And as we shall see, the means by which we know this is not a stable world are extra-philosophical.

One of the figures for a realization of this passing is the Anthropocene. But one has to read this figure correctly to understand its significance. The Anthropocene does not mean the centrality of the "Anthropos." It is *not* an anthropocentrism. It is not the figure of the replacement of God and Goddess with Man ruling the world with Reason. It is something quite different. What marks the turning, the break into another kind of time, is that the earth is not marked by human intention but by *unintended* effects of collective human labor. The Anthropocene is the figure for a series of metabolic rifts destabilizing the world—of which climate change is just one—as unconscious and unintended effects, a kind of latent destiny.

Call it the *Capitaloscene* if you want, as Haraway and Jason Moore do, as it is indeed the case that metabolic rift is vastly accelerated when capitalism emerges.[16] But bear in mind two things: it is not the case that capital interrupts a prior world of harmony and order. Nature is not always stable, and collective human labor has always had transforming effects. Humans drove many species to extinction long before capitalism was even a thing. Also: the abolition of capital would not automatically solve all our problems. It is not enough to *negate* capital. That leaves unanswered the question of how to provide

16 Donna Haraway, *Staying with the Trouble*, Durham, NC: Duke University Press, 2016; Jason W. Moore, *Capitalism in the Web of Life*, London: Verso, 2015.

energy and shelter and food for seven billion people without *completely* destabilizing planetary metabolic systems.

So Žižek and I agree that the metaphorical language of return to a "natural" order is unhelpful. Žižek: "Wark's key achievement is to reject this path: there never was such a balance...the idea of Nature as a big Mother is just another image of the divine big Other." He also offers an interesting gloss on the Anthropocene:

> humanity became aware of its self-limitation as a species precisely when it became so strong that it influenced the balance of all life on earth. It was able to dream of being a Subject only until its influence on nature (earth) was no longer marginal, i.e. only against the background of a stable nature.

Which is another way of saying that the Anthropocene is not about Man, but rather the impossibility of Man. Note, however, that Žižek elides the question of how "humanity became aware."

Žižek gives three accounts of why the Anthropocene puts an end to the figures of nature as a homeostatic market-ecology of natural order. The first recodes my thinking into his language, and the second and third add his characteristic worldview to it. Žižek:

> Firstly, we never encounter nature-in-itself: the nature we encounter is always-already caught in *antagonistic* interaction with collective human labor. But secondly, the *gap* separating human labor from intractable nature (all that resists our grasp) is irreducible. Nature is not an abstract "in-itself" but primarily the resisting counterforce that we encounter in our labor...[Thirdly,] nature is *already* in-itself disturbed, out of joint. (emphasis added)

Firstly, in *Molecular Red* I follow Bogdanov in limiting the concept of nature to *that which labor encounters.*[17] But this may or may not be an *antagonistic* relation. Bogdanov thinks that such metaphors tend

17 Alexander Bogdanov, *The Philosophy of Living Experience*, Leiden: Brill, 2015.

to come from our own specific labor practices. Intellectuals think in terms of arguments for and against, and hence are inclined to a figure like antagonism as a basic metaphor. But there may be others, as not all labor takes such a form.

Secondly, Žižek characteristically emphasizes the *gap* separating labor and nature, which then becomes always essentially the same kind of gap—an *irreducible* one. Philosophy revs its engines here, anticipating an open road, based on a concept not amenable to empirical inquiry.

Thirdly, Žižek does want to say a bit more about nature *already*, by way of a gloss of a passage of mine that includes this: "What if there is only an unstable nature…?" But with the question mark removed, we have rather overstepped the bounds of what I think philosophy can say about nature without deferring to the natural sciences.

Žižek characteristically shifts attention from object to subject: "The rift between labor and intractable nature should be supplemented not only by a rift within nature itself, which makes it forever unstable, but also by a rift emerging from within humanity itself." Žižek here reinstates his famous gaps, voids and splits as a kind of philosophical constant, covering the whole field of object, subject and also object-subject relation. Labor's encounter with nature, which for me is only ever collective and historical, becomes the abstract universal gap between two gaps. Here is that difference that is always the same that so bothered the Deleuzians, even if it is a problem they too could not quite solve.

Rather than the constant of the gaps, I would rather emphasize the historically contingent form of the *relations* that cross those supposed gaps, and which may actually be what produce them in the first place as a kind of residue. The labor-nature relation is not reducible to a subject-object relation structured as an eternal antagonism. The hunter-gatherer's relation to a "nature" is not the same as the farmer's or the industrial worker's, or the intellectual's or the climate scientist's.

For instance: How do we even know about a metabolic rift such as climate change? Well, it takes a truly vast infrastructure, including apparatuses such as satellites and computers, global scientific organization and so forth. In short, it is a knowledge that can only be produced via the evolution of science and technology at a certain stage.[18] This organization of labor and nature produces an understanding of nature that is at one and the same time a science but which is also limited by the very form of the labor and apparatus that makes it.

As I see it, following Bogdanov, particular labors produce particular metaphors of the labor-nature relation. Indeed, following Haraway, we can even put some pressure on these categories of labor and nature themselves. Maybe "labor" is also too presumptive, too exclusionary. Maybe there are kinds of action in the world that are neither productive nor reproductive, kinds of "queer action," if you will. Indigenous worldviews might not be reducible to "labor," either. These might produce quite other metaphorical ranges.[19]

So if particular labors (and non-labors) in the world produce particular metaphorical understandings of nature (sometimes even as something other than a nature) then how are different actions in the world to relate to each other? This is where Žižek and I diverge most, and the slight recoding of *Molecular Red* that Žižek offers in his remarks start to matter.

Žižek: "Wark's unsurpassable horizon remains what he calls 'shared life,' and every autonomization of any of its moments amounts to a fetishizing alienation." Žižek would rather think of such moments as what Badiou calls an event, "the highest expression of the power of negativity." Faced with the cut that a particular labor makes with shared life, his solution is the "molar" one of *philosophical* abstraction: "the reduction of the complexity of the situation to the 'essential,' to its key feature," which for Hegel is "the infinite power of Understanding." Philosophy is that which has the capacity to reduce differences to the same.

Žižek: "We are not talking here just of ideal forms or patterns, but of the Real. The void of subjectivity is the Real which is obfuscated by the wealth of 'inner life'; class antagonism is the Real which is obfuscated by the multiplicity of social conflicts." Notice here that

18 Paul Edwards, *A Vast Machine*, Cambridge: MA, MIT Press, 2013.

19 Eduardo Viveiros de Castro, *Cannibal Metaphysics*, Minnesota: Univocal, 2014; Karen Barad, *Meeting the Universe Halfway*, Durham, NC: Duke University Press, 2007.

the gap between labor and nature disappears. The void of *subjectivity itself* becomes the real. Where earlier antagonism refers to the labor-nature relation, here that is forgotten, and only one antagonism matters: class antagonism. High theory then sets itself up as the discourse of what is essential—these eternal, unknowable gaps. The more pressing problem of nature starts to fall away.

This is where I think it is better to follow Bogdanov on another path altogether, which I call low theory, after Stuart Hall and Jack Halberstam, for whom theory is not the destination but the detour (or *dérive*) on the way to somewhere else.[20] Bogdanov was centrally concerned with the question of how to overcome the alienation of particular labors, and hence of their particular knowledge, from each other. He thinks there have been broadly three historical modes of organizing labor: *authority*, *exchange* and comradely or *cooperative* labor. Theologies, philosophies and even popular ideologies can be sophisticated mixes or crazy incompatible admixtures of all three.

From this point of view, Žižek borrows from philosophy a certain authority-gesture, where causal chains stop at a peak term beyond which there can be no questioning. Only that last term is no longer the God or the Goddess, and still less Man, but the Void. Everything ascends and descends from this key term, to which the philosopher alone is the guardian of the portal.[21] The Subject, the Object, even the Subject's encounter with the Object are always antagonisms riven by the self-same impossibility. The philosopher's self-appointed task is to show how any and all labors encounter the same limit of which the philosopher is the keeper of its essential names. This is high theory at its finest.

In these times, it is a discourse in search of a role. If one accepts that God and His mythological sidekicks are dead, then who needs their intellectual keepers? Metabolic rift, as Žižek acknowledges, happens at a molecular level: flows of nitrogen or carbon are out of whack.

---

20 Judith (aka Jack) Halberstam, *Queer Art of Failure*, Durham, NC: Duke University Press, 2011.

21 Alexander R. Galloway, Eugene Thacker and McKenzie Wark, *Excommunication: Three Inquiries in Media and Mediation*, Chicago: University of Chicago Press, 2013.

These flows are as imperceptible to molar "big politics" as they are to everyday life. Žižek: "It can only be accessed through 'high' theory—in a kind of self-inverted twist, it is only through the highest that we get to the lowest."

I am always suspicious of this phrase "it can only." Is this not the classic move of authority-discourse? Of the cop? It simply asserts its role as the alpha and omega of thought. The bourgeois subject knows itself to be hailed by the cop because it is its own kind of (spiritual) cop.

The Bogdanovite response would be as follows: rather than subordinate the particular labors that produce knowledge of things like metabolic rift to the authority of a first philosophy, let's take a step back. Such philosophies are themselves products of a form of labor—usually of intellectual labor—of a contemplative kind. Forms of labor produce metaphoric extensions of themselves which understand the world on the model of their own actions.

So: rather than subordinate all labors, particularly new and advanced kinds, to the metaphorical extensions of one particular labor, particularly an obsolete, authority-based one, let's do something different. Let's practice a *low theory* that looks for ways of extending metaphors out of all particular labors, and experimentally test these out as ways of understanding the big picture. A fine example is right here before us: as Wendling shows, Marx got some of his most "productive" metaphors out of scientific materialism, but he held them in a certain tension with other metaphors from more traditional philosophical authorities. For instance, Marx got metabolic rift as a metaphorical extension out of the life sciences and agricultural chemistry of his time, and it still works pretty well. It does not need recoding back into a timeless set of premodern concepts built on timeless voids.

Žižek tries to grapple with this problem of advanced scientific labor in the concluding paragraphs of his piece, where he tries to absorb my category of the *inhuman apparatus*. Building on Haraway, Paul Edwards and Karen Barad, I constructed in *Molecular Red* a Marxist approach to science which does not try to legislate for it, or fetishize its theories, or recover the totality from its alienated and specific forms. In short, I do not want to subordinate scientific labor to a philosophical one. Rather, I think a Marxist approach to any particular science has to ask: How is it produced?

We know that the *relations* of production within which science occurs can act as a fetter: it is subordinated to commercial or military imperatives. But an even more vulgar-Marxist view might ask what its *forces* of production are: What kinds of labor and apparatus go into making it? Hence from Karen Barad I take the question of scientific apparatus, that cyborg mix of flesh and tech that is generally to be found in the basement of a research institution. And from Paul Edwards I take the particular example of the apparatus that made climate science possible as a sensory apparatus.[22]

Here I was responding to Meillassoux, and speculative realism more generally. Briefly: There could indeed be objects of knowledge that preexist any subject that is its correlate. But what Meillassoux (like Žižek) omits is the apparatus via which such nonhuman things are mediated. What is the means of production of a knowledge of the nonhuman? How is the nonhuman mediated to a human which is not its correlate? The most interesting answer, I think, is the apparatus. The apparatus is the *inhuman* that mediates the *nonhuman* to the *human*, each of which is at least in part coproduced by this very relation.

Žižek: "The truly weird element in the triad of humans, the reality they confront, and the apparatuses they use to penetrate reality is thus not an intractable external reality, but the apparatuses which mediate between the two extremes." The inhuman nature of the apparatus is indeed a curious thing. But I would not say it "penetrates" reality, as that metaphor steers us back to Mother Nature hiding her secrets from Father Science. Is that not the very language we were trying to shed? Nor would I say that the human and the nonhuman are extremes mediated by an apparatus. Rather, I would stress the way the terms are at least in part produced by this relation, by the apparatus itself as historical product rather than philosophical given.

The *apparatus*—the force of production of knowledge itself—is always historical. The satellites and computers that make climate

22 Barad, *Meeting the Universe Halfway*; Edwards, *A Vast Machine*.

science possible arise out of a particular Cold War history in which scientific and technical labor are embedded. And yet they enable the production of new knowledge about nature. Just as Marx paid attention to the soil science of his time and produced the concept of it—metabolic rift—we can now extend and perhaps modify that metaphor in the light of climate science, which shows carbon to be subject to a global metabolic rift.

These are at least two general zones to the Marx-field, then: Either high theory, which *subordinates* labor and science to metaphors from its own past. Or low theory, which experimentally *plays* between metaphorical extensions from various forms of labor and science as they relate to the world right now. I choose the second zone, as it seems to me that the key problems to be thought arise out of the particular historical form in which labor encounters nature in our time, summed up in the figure of the Anthropocene.

In the little world Žižek and I share, of Marxist theory and its sources, I think the resources most useful here involve a rejection of Leninist dialectical materialism and choosing the other fork in that historical road—Bogdanov's *tektology*, or low theory. On this path, labor and science come first, and concepts are derived as a second-order practice to coordinate those separate labors. If this path has one small merit, it is that one's concept of what labor is, and of what nature is, can be more or less up to date.

One's thought can then follow the agenda science and labor set, rather than recoding that agenda through one that high theory generates internally, an agenda in which, curiously, nature keeps dropping out. Not least because it is such an historically variable term, changing with each epoch of labor and science, since it is, in the end, just a placeholder term for that which labor encounters. Žižek's high theory Marxism of the bourgeois subject has little to say about the times, not least because the bourgeois subject is itself a residual one. The textual field which produced it has lost cultural space to other forms of subject production, as Lazzarato, Berardi, Préciado and others have shown. Žižek may however be of interest as the last form in which the bourgeois subject sings of itself—in the negative, as destined for the Void.

10.

Jodi Dean: Decline in Symbolic Efficiency

It seems I got the title for my book *The Spectacle of Disintegration* from reading Jodi Dean. I read her book *Blog Theory: Feedback and Capture in the Circuits of Drive* in manuscript.[1] On rereading it, I find this: "disintegrating spectacles allow for ever more advanced forms of monitoring and surveillance" (39). And "Debord's claim that, in the society of the spectacle 'the uses of media guarantee a kind of eternity of noisy insignificance' applies better to communicative capitalism as a disintegrated, networked, spectacular circuit" (112). I think I mean something similar by *spectacle of disintegration* to what Dean calls *communicative capitalism*, even though we read Debord a bit differently, but more on that later.

How can we even write books in the era of Snapchat and Twitter? Perhaps the book could be something like the tactic of slowing down the pace of work. Still, books are a problem for the era of communicative capitalism, which resists recombination into longer threads of argument. The contours of Dean's argument are of a piece with this media strategy.

Dean offers "an avowedly political assessment of the present" rather than a technical one (3). The political is a term greatly expanded in scope and connotation across a half-century of political theory. In the hands of Mouffe, Butler, Brown or even Virno, it becomes not just relatively autonomous from the technical-economic but even primary. In Dean, it then becomes the language within which to critique the seeming naturalness and inevitability of the technical. But perhaps

1 Jodi Dean, *Blog Theory*, Cambridge: Polity, 2010.

this now calls for a kind of "dialectical" compliment, a critical scrutiny of the expanded category of the political, perhaps even from the point of view of *techne* itself. We intellectuals do love the political, perhaps on the curious assumption that it is the same kind of discourse as our own.

If industrial capitalism exploited labor, communicative capitalism exploits communication. It is where "reflexivity captures creativity" (4). Iterative loops of communication have not really led to a realization of democratic ideals of access, inclusion, participation. On the contrary, ours is an era of capture, of desire caught in a net and reduced to mere drive.

Dean draws her concepts mostly from Žižek. In the previous chapter, I argued that his late work offers little for a twenty-first-century critical agenda. But if anyone has made a case for the utility of Žižek, it is Jodi Dean. So let's approach Žižek then in an instrumental way, and see what use Dean puts him to as a tool. For both Dean and Žižek, "Ideology is what we do, even when we know better" (5). It is not a theory of false consciousness or even of the interpellation of the subject. In this approach to ideology—closer to Sloterdijk's enlightened false consciousness—it is about the gap between thought and action rather than thinking the "wrong" thing.[2]

The key motif in Dean's thought here is the *decline in symbolic efficiency*, also known as the collapse of the Big Other. These Lacanian phrases point to a growing impossibility of anchoring meaning or of totalizing it. Nobody is able to speak from a position that secures the sliding, proliferating chains of signification. One could question this thesis on both historical and sociological grounds. Perhaps the stability of meaning is only ever secured by force. When I studied Vaneigem's account of heresies in *Excommunication*, or Andrey Platonov's account of popular speech under Stalinism in *Molecular Red*, these looked to me like the decline in symbolic efficiency already, and in both cases consistency was only secured by force.[3]

---

2 Peter Sloterdijk, *Critique of Cynical Reason*, Minneapolis: University of Minnesota Press, 1988.

3 Alexander R. Galloway, Eugene Thacker and McKenzie Wark, *Excommunication: Three Inquiries in Media and Mediation*, Chicago: University

Moving from an historical to a sociological axis, one might then look for where force is applied. In the United States that might include the red purge, the imprisonment and assassination of Black power and the now global campaign to murder the ideological enemies of the United States via death-by-drone. Perhaps there's no Master's discourse at all without force. The same would apply on a more day-to-day scale with domestic violence and police murder.

There might certainly be particular instances of the decline in symbolic efficiency, when the function of the Master signifier is suspended, when there is no outside authority to tell us what to do, what to desire, what to believe, and where the result isn't freedom but rather a kind of suffocation. Dean gives the example of *Second Life*, where people are free to have their avatars do anything—and they end up having them build real estate, shop and do weird sex stuff. Tumblr might be another example, where being free from the Master signifier seems to mean putting together random collages of pictures and greeting-card quotations.

The Master signifier depends on virtuality. It is not just another sign in a chain of signs, but a potential for signification as such, a way to project across the gap between fantasy and the real. Interestingly, where for Virno the virtual ends up sustaining history as a theological premise, here the virtual is theology as historical premise, as that which declines, taking the possibility of desire with it from the world.[4]

Without the Master signifier, there's no reason to stay with anything. Bonds can be dissolved at no cost. There's a dissolution of the link between fantasy and reality; there's the foreclosure of the symbolic. It is the gaps in the symbolic that allow access to the real, but those gaps are foreclosed, resulting in non-desire, non-meaning, and in the saturation in enjoyment. We are caught in short, recursive loops that attempt to directly provide enjoyment, but which just repeat over and over again its impossibility.[5]

---

of Chicago Press, 2013; McKenzie Wark, *Molecular Red*, London: Verso, 2015.

4 Paolo Virno, *Déjà Vu and the End of History*, London: Verso, 2015.

5 Bernard Stiegler, *What Makes Life Worth Living: On Pharmacology*, Cambridge: Polity, 2013.

This kind of recursive or reflexive loop in which the subject is trapped applies also to the world of objects in communicative capitalism. Dean mentions climate change, but the Anthropocene more generally, or what Marx called *metabolic rift*, might be symptoms of such loops in operation, in which positive feedback dominates, with the result that more is more. The capture of both objects and subjects just keeps deepening and expanding. Dean: "More circuits, more loops, more spoils for the first, strongest, richest, fastest, biggest" (13).

How the hell did it come to this? Dean builds on the work of our mutual friend Fred Turner, whose *From Counterculture to Cyberculture* tracks the construction of what Richard Barbrook calls the *Californian Ideology*.[6] How did computing and information science, which were tools of control and hierarchy, become tools of collaboration and flexibility? Here I read Fred's book a little differently to Dean. What I see there is a kind of social and technical field that was always open to different kinds of research and different kinds of results. The wartime laboratory experience in science and engineering was strikingly collaborative, expanding and developing what JD Bernal thought of as the communist practice of real science, and what for Richard Stallman (a red diaper baby) was the commons of hacker practice.[7]

Of course, what the military wanted from such experimental practices was a tool kit for command, control, communication and information (aka C^3I). But even there, flexibility and openness was always one of the objectives. The Air Force's missile program might have imagined what Paul Edwards calls a closed world of cybernetic control, but the Army wanted tools that could work in the fog and friction of war as flexible, open, adaptive networks.[8] The technol-

6 Fred Turner, *From Counterculture to Cyberculture*, Chicago: University of Chicago Press, 2008; Richard Barbrook with Andy Cameron, *The Internet Revolution*, Amsterdam: Institute of Network Cultures, 2015.

7 JD Bernal, *The Social Function of Science*, Cambridge, MA: MIT Press, 1967; Richard Stallman, *Free Software, Free Society*, Boston: GNU Press, 2002. When left more or less to themselves to pursue research as free collaboration in laboratories, both experienced science as a kind of "communism."

8 Paul Edwards, *The Closed World: Computers and the Politics of Discourse in*

ogy that descended from such academic and military origins was always hybrid and multiform, adaptable in different ways to different kinds of economies, politics and culture, although certainly not infinitely so.[9]

What I find missing in Dean is the sense of a struggle over how tech and flesh were to coadapt to each other. Let's not forget the damage done to the conversation about the politics of technology by the Cold War purge, in which not only artists and writers were blacklisted, but scientists and engineers as well. Iris Chang's account of the fate of Tsien Hsue-Shen in *Thread of the Silkworm* is only the most absurdist of such stories.[10] This pioneering rocket scientist lost his security clearances for having social ties to people who, unbeknownst to him, were communists. And so he was deported—to communist China! There he actually became what he never was in America—a highly skilled scientist working for the "communist cause." This is just the craziest of thousands of such stories. Those who find the tech world "apolitical" might inquire as to how it was made so thoroughly so.

Hence the Californian Ideology is a product of particular histories, one piece of which is documented so well in Turner—but there are other histories. The belief that tech will save the world, that institutions are to be tolerated but not engaged, that rough consensus and running code are all that matter—this is not the only ideology of the tech world. That it became an unusually predominant one is not some naturally occurring phenomena—even though both Californian ideologists and Dean both tend to think it is. Rather, it is the product of particular struggles in which such an ideology got a powerful assist, firstly from state repression of certain alternatives, and then by corporate patronage of the more business-friendly versions of it.

Dean write about "geeks" (23, 25) as if they were some kind of freemasonry, pretending to be apolitical, but with quiet influence. One might usefully look here to a deeper history of the kind of power the

---

Cold War America, Cambridge, MA: MIT Press, 1997.

9 Antoine Bousquet, *The Scientific Way of Warfare*, New York: Columbia University Press, 2009.

10 Iris Chang, *Thread of the Silkworm*, New York: Basic Books, 1996.

sciences and engineers have had, one not quite covered even by the ever expanding sense of the "political" now employed. The counter-literature here might include what for me is Bruno Latour's best work: his historical study of Pasteur, and of a kind of spatially and temporally concentrating power of the laboratory.[11]

As Latour shows, Pasteur's actual political-politics were fairly conventional and not very interesting, but the way the lab was able to become a form of power is a quite different story. Can we—why not?—even think of this as a class power, which has accrued over time its own field of heterogeneous interests, and which stands in relation to the commodity form as neither capital nor labor even if—like all other classes—it is forced into one or other of those relations?

For Dean the geek, or in my terms the *hacker class*, is a displaced mediator, something that is pushed aside.[12] But by what? The formal category of mediator covers over the existence of a kind of struggle that is neither purely political nor a "natural" result of tech evolution. We still lack a sense of the struggles over the information vector of the late twentieth century, with their partial victories and eventual defeats.

Dean's book is called *Blog Theory*, and in some ways its strength is its relation—only occasionally signaled—to her own practice as a blogger. There was a time when I read Dean's *I Cite* blog religiously, alongside blogs by Nina Power, Mark Fisher (*k-punk*), Lars Iyer (*Spurious*) and a handful of others who really pioneered a kind of theory-writing in blog form, alongside the new kinds of more (post-) literary practices of Kate Zambreno and friends. I myself had been involved in an earlier version of such practices, using the primitive internet vector of the listserv.[13] Like Dean, my thinking tends to extrapolate metaphors out of such practices.

Blogging also looks like a displaced mediator, a step on the way to the mega-socialized media forms such as Facebook, or as Lidia

---

11 Bruno Latour, *The Pasteurization of France*, Cambridge, MA: Harvard University Press, 1988.

12 McKenzie Wark, *A Hacker Manifesto*, Cambridge, MA: Harvard University Press, 2004.

13 Josephine Bosma et al. (eds.) *Readme!: ASCII Culture and the Revenge of Knowledge*, New York: Autonomedia, 1999.

Yuknavitch calls it—Facehooker. Dean: "Blogging's settings...include the decline of symbolic efficiency, the recursive loops of universalized reflexivity, the extreme inequalities that reflexive networks produce, and the operation of displaced mediators at points of critical transition" (29). Tumblr already existed in 2010 when Dean wrote *Blog Theory*, but was not quite as perfect an illustration of Dean's conceptual framework as it is now.

Such media vectors become short loops that lock the subject into repeated attempts at enjoyment, where enjoyment is no longer the lost object of desire but the object of loss itself. All drive is death drive. These reflexive, iterative loops are where we are stuck. Communicative action is not enlightenment. "What idealists from the Enlightenment through critical and democratic theory, to contemporary techno-utopians theorize as the very form of freedom is actually a mechanism for the generation of extreme inequality and capture" (30). This is not even, as in Azuma, a return to a kind of human-animal. "The notion of drive counters this immanent naturalism by highlighting the inhuman at the heart of the human" (31). The all-too-human ability to stick on minor differences and futile distractions drives the human ever further away from its own impossibility.

Communicative capitalism relies on repetition, on suspending narrative, identity and norms. Framed in those terms, the problem then is to create the possibility of breaking out of the endless short loops of drive. But if anything, the tendency is in the other direction. After blogging came Facebook, Twitter, Instagram and Snapchat, driving even further into repetition. The culture industries gave way to what I call the *vulture industries.*[14] Dean identified the tendency already with blogs. They no longer fill a desire for a way to communicate. Desire is a desire *for a desire*—that absent thing—whereas a *drive* is a repetition not of the desire but of the moment of failure to reach it. The virtual dimension disappears.

Blogs had their counterpoint in search engines, as that which knows our desires even when we don't. With the search engine, one

---

14 McKenzie Wark, *Telesthesia: Communication, Culture and Class*, Cambridge: Polity Press, 2012.

trusts the algorithm; with blogs, one trusts one's "networks." Two kinds of affective response dominate in relation to both. One is hysterical: That's not it! There must be more! The other is paranoid: someone must be stealing all the data. As it turned out, the former drove people to search and search, blog and blog, all the better for actual agencies—both state and corporate—to indeed steal it all. Here I would stress the asymmetry and struggle over information as a crucial feature of communicative capitalism—which may no longer even be a capitalism, but something worse. A mode of production based on asymmetries of information, because it turns out that the ruling class of our time—I call them the *vectoralist class*—really is stealing our data and metadata.

The blog for Dean is not a journal or journalism nor a literary form. It may be something like the letter writing of a premodern era, which was meant to be circulated beyond the named addressee. It is a sort of *technique of the self*, one that installs a gaze that shapes the writer.[15] But there's an ambiguity as to who the writer is visible to. For Dean, this gaze is not that of the Big Other, but of that other creature of Lacan-speak, the *objet petit a*. In this version, there is an asymmetry: we are entrapped in a kind of visibility. I see from my point of view but am seen from all points of view. It is as if I am seen by an alien object—the *objet petit a*—rather than another person. I receive no messages back specific to me and my identity. Ego formation is blocked.

Dean:

> Blogging is a technology uncoupled from the illusion of a core, true, essential and singular self…In communicative capitalism, the gaze to which one makes oneself visible is a point hidden in an opaque and heterogeneous network. It is not the gaze of the symbolic other of our ego ideal but the more disturbing traumatic gaze of a gap or excess, *objet petit a*. (56)

15 Michel Foucault, *The Use of Pleasure*, New York: Vintage, 1990.

Hence I never quite know who I am, even though I take endless online quizzes to try to find out. Which punk-rock goddess are you? It turns out I am Kim Gordon, although sometimes I am Patti Smith.

The decline in symbolic efficiency is a convergence of the imaginary and the real. It is a world of imaginary identities sustained by the promise of enjoyment rather than a world of symbolic identities residing in the gap where desire desires to desire. Unanchored from the symbolic, and its impossible relation to the Big Other, I become too labile and unstable. It is a world of selves with boundary issues, over-sharing, but also troubled by any signs of the success of others, tripping circuits of envy and schadenfreude. It is not a world of law and transgression but repetition and drive. No more lost object of desire, it is all loss itself as object. Blocked desires proliferate as partial drives making quickie loops, disappearing into the nets.

Of courses there are those who would celebrate this kind of (post-) subjectivity. It could have been a step towards Guattari's planet of *three billion perverts*, all coupling and breaking in desiring machines of wildly proliferating sorts.[16] Dean explores instead the way the decline in symbolic efficiency was framed by Agamben as *whatever being.*[17] Dean: "whatever being points to new modes of community and new forms of personality anticipated by the dissolution of inscriptions of identity through citizenship, ethnicity, and other modern markers of belonging" (66). For Agamben, some of this is a good thing, in the dissolution of national identities, for example. His strategy—reminiscent of Baudrillard's fatal strategy—is to push whatever being to its limits.[18]

As every blogger knows, this media is not about reading and interpreting, but about circulating the signs. *TL;DR*, or "too long, didn't read," is the most common response. For Dean, the "whatever" in whatever being is a kind of insolence, a minimal acknowledgement that communication has taken place with no attempt to understand it.

16 Félix Guattari, "Three Billion Perverts on the Stand," in Gary Genosko (ed.), *The Guattari Reader*, Cambridge, MA: Blackwell, 1996, chapter 16.

17 Giorgio Agamben, *The Coming Community*, Minneapolis: Minnesota University Press, 1993.

18 Jean Baudrillard, *Fatal Strategies*, Los Angeles: Semiotext(e), 2008.

Agamben thinks there might be a way to take back the positive properties of being in language that communicative capitalism expropriates. He looks forward to a planetary refusal of identity, a kind of singularity without identity, perhaps other ways of belonging. Dean: "the beings who would so belong are not subjects in the sense that European philosophy or psychoanalysis might theorize" (82), To which we card-carrying Deleuzians (even a lapsed one like me) might respond: so much the worse for psychoanalysis and philosophy!

Dean, like Mouffe, is a thinker of *antagonism*, but Dean is disturbed by the apparent *lack* of antagonism of whatever being. But is it apolitical, or just a phenomenon in which differences work out differently, without dialectic? Dean: "I can locate here neither a politics I admire nor any sort of struggle at all. What could motivate whatever beings?" (83). They don't lack anything. But maybe that's the point. Of course, whatever being does not evade the state in the way Agamben might have hoped. The capture of metadata by the agencies and companies of the vectoralist class enables a recording that does not presuppose classification or identity.[19] The back hole of the masses has been conquered by the algorithm. Their silence speaks volumes.

Agamben (like Azuma) thinks the extreme alienation of language in spectacle could have a kind of ironic coda, where that very alienation becomes something positive, a being after identity. He actually has a positive way of thinking what for Žižek and Dean is drive. Are whatever beings really passive, or just a bit slippery? Why is passivity a bad thing anyway? Maybe there was always something a bit backward-looking about Lacan.

In *The Freudian Robot*, Lydia Liu reads Lacan as reacting against the information science of the postwar years. This was a period in which questions of texts and meanings were sidestepped by new ways of analyzing information mathematically, as a field of statistical probability.[20] It is time to rethink strategy on the terrain of information rather than that of meaning. Dean does not: "What's lost? The ability

19 McKenzie Wark, "Metadata Punk," in Tomislav Medak and Marcell Mars (eds.), *Public Library*, Zagreb: Svibanj, 2015.

20 Lydia Liu, *The Freudian Robot*, Chicago: University of Chicago Press, 2011.

to distinguish between contestatory and hegemonic speech. Irony. Tonality. Normativity" (89).

But were these ever more than illusions intellectuals entertained about what was going on in communication? Here I find reading Platonov salutary, as his accounts of the language of early Soviet times is really more one of frequency and repetition rather than a politics of ideology or propaganda.[21] I don't think the road to strategy necessarily always passes through critique, or through a politics of the subject as formed in the symbolic register. Perhaps the flux between the imaginary and the real is where the human resides most of the time anyway. It is not as if the symbolic has reliably been our friend.

Dean mentions Friedrich Kittler's cunning reworking of Lacan back into media theory, but I would pause to give it a bit more weight.[22] For Kittler, Lacan's famous tripartite of imaginary, symbolic and real is actually an effect of a certain moment in the development of media. It was a stage in the evolution of the cyborg of Haraway, when different technics became the mediating apparatus for different flows of sensation. For Kittler, the imaginary is the screen, the symbolic is the typewriter, and the gramophone is the real. This explains so much of the anxiety of the literate classes (nicely satirized in the Coen Brothers' *Hail Ceasar*). They struggled with their typewriters against the screen, insisting on this or that symbolic order against the self/other fluctuations of screen-generated media, while the grain of the voice echoed as a residual stand-in for the real beyond both. All of which, of course, media *convergence* erases.[23] We're differently wired cyborgs now.

It is telling that Dean wants to resist the "snares" of cognitive capitalism. Dean: "Every little tweet or comment, every forwarded image or petition, accrues a tiny affective nugget, a little surplus enjoyment, a smidgen of attention that attaches to it, making it stand out from the larger flow before it blends back in" (95). It is hard not to read it

---

21 Andrei Platonov, *Forteen Little Red Huts*, New York: Columbia University Press, 2016.

22 Friedrich Kittler, *Gramophone, Film, Typewriter*, Stanford CA: Stanford University Press, 1999.

23 Henry Jenkins, *Convergence Culture*, New York: NYU Press, 2008.

in media terms as an appeal by those invested in one media cyborg apparatus to resist the one that's replacing it. Of course the new one is part of a political economy of domination and exploitation—but so too was the old mass-media apparatus. It may just not be the same old political economy.

Of course there are things one can tease out of a conceptual frame that puts the emphasis on the subject's relation to the symbolic order. But I don't see this as a truly essential theoretical tactic. In many ways I think it more productive to think about information as a ratio of signal to noise, and beyond that as a kind of dynamics into which one might attempt to intervene with information tactics. This is what the situationists called *détournement.*

Dean: "The politics that montage suggests is a politics released from the burdens of coherence and consistency" (104). But isn't information politics always about frequency, about the probability of certain information appearing with certain other information, about affective states thereby generated? It is only intellectuals who really think political communication is anything else. Even economics may be not much more than this. In the vectoral age, as Boutang suggests, nobody knows the actual value of anything, so the problem is outsourced to a vast cyborg of plug-and-play info-filters—some human, some algorithmic.

Such an information "ecology" has its problems, of course. It knows the price of everything and the value of nothing. As Debord was already suggesting, the integrated spectacle integrated itself into the reality it was describing, and then ceased to know the difference between the two.[24] We now live in the metabolic rifts produced by the wildly improbably molecular flows this created, which in turn generate the disintegrating spectacle some call the Anthropocene.

What both Agamben and Dean miss about Debord is that the concept of spectacle was always doubled by that of détournement. This is clear in *The Society of the Spectacle*, where détournement gets the key last chapter (before the concluding coda). There Debord

24 Guy Debord, *Comments on the Society of the Spectacle*, London: Verso, 2011.

restates the case for the literary communism he and Gil Wolman first proposed in the 1950s as the avant-garde strategy for the era of spectacle. Détournement is precisely the tactic of treating all information as the commons, and refusing all private property in this domain.[25]

Contra Dean, this has nothing to do with a "participatory" politics at all. It was always about the overthrow of the spectacle as a *totality*. Nor was Debord really contributing to the undermining of "expertise." On the contrary, he dedicated his *Comments* to those few on both sides who he thought really had the knowledge to either defend the spectacle—or attack it. The same is the case with the book he helped Sanguinetti write about the Italian spectacle of the '70s—*The Last Chance to Save Capitalism in Italy*.[26] He was well aware of the dangers of recuperation back into spectacle. It was indeed one of his major themes. Dean: "The spectacle contains and captures the possibility of the common good" (112). But this is already the central point of his late work, which is about withdrawal rather than participation.

Of course, détournement itself became coopted. Free information became the basis of a new business model, one that extracts surplus information from free labor. But this means moving détournement on from free data to freeing metadata. This may require not just détournement and critique but actually building different kinds of circuit, even if it is just in the gaps of the current infrastructure.

For the time being, one tactic is just to keep putting into circulation the conjunctions of information that generate the feeling of solidarity and the commons. It's a way of taking advantage of the lateral "search" that the decline of symbolic efficiency, or at least the lack of coercive force maintaining it, affords. There is surely a place for what Dean calls "discipline, sacrifice and delay" (125). But Rome wasn't unbuilt in a day, and it may take more than one kind of subject-apparatus cyborg to make a new civilization. The party presupposes a milieu. It is an effect and not a cause. Let's build a new milieu.

---

25 Guy Debord, *Society of the Spectacle*, New York: Zone Books, 1994; Debord and Gil Wolman, "A User's Guide to Détournement," in Ken Knabb (ed.), *Situationist International Anthology*, Berkeley: Bureau of Public Secrets, 2006.

26 McKenzie Wark, *The Spectacle of Disintegration*, London: Verso Books, 2013, 105ff.

This civilization is over and everyone knows it. That is an organizational problem that calls for all sorts of different solutions to all sorts of problems. There can be no one "correct" critical theory. They are all just tools for addressing parts of a manifold problem. Dean's work seems well suited to the diagnosis of a certain subjective short-circuit and one possible solution to it.

11.

Chantal Mouffe: Democracy Versus Liberalism

Watching the American presidential primaries unfold across the spring of 2016, it seemed as if there was something else at stake besides the competition to lead the Republican and Democratic parties. It also seemed to be a contest as to whether liberal democracy is to be *liberal* or *democratic*. And if it is to be democratic, it was a contest as to what kind of *demos*—people—democracy is supposedly about. Or so it appeared to me, given that I was reading Chantal Mouffe at the time.[1] Her books provide a useful perspective on such events, although perhaps a limited one.

The two versions of the liberal in liberal democracy were represented by the campaigns of Hillary Clinton and Jeb Bush. The former was able to fend off a version of the democratic, the latter was not. It might seem tendentious to bracket both Bush and Clinton together as "liberal" and even more so to treat their challengers, Bernie Sanders and Donald Trump, as "democratic," but there's a specific meaning of both terms within which this makes sense.

Liberal here has more its classical than its American meaning. Both Clinton and Bush stood for the rule of law, private property, limited government (with some concessions to certain interest groups, of course) and a rather abstract idea of what it means to be an American citizen. Democratic also has a quite specific meaning. Both Sanders and Trump emphasize a rather stronger sense of what it means to

1 Chantal Mouffe, *Agonistics: Thinking the World Politically*, London: Verso, 2013; *The Democratic Paradox*, London: Verso, 2005.

be included as a citizen in the demos, and a corresponding sense of exclusion. For Sanders, what is excluded is Wall Street; for Trump, what is excluded is the foreigner.

These are very different versions of the demos. One comes close to being class based while the other is jingoistic, a version of what Gilroy calls *generic fascism*. Interestingly, both coupled a strong sense of who the demos are against with a strong sense of what the demos can share. At least in the initial part of his campaign, Trump was careful to support existing social-welfare and healthcare benefits for what in narrow and racist terms are perceived to be deserving members of the demos. Sanders, on the other hand, stressed making higher education free. In very different ways, these democratic challengers appealed to a stronger sense of participation in the demos. Citizenship is not just an abstract category, but a felt sense of belonging and sharing.

American politics might not be all that exceptional here. Many polities are experiencing something similar. Mainstream parties of center-right and center-left complexion find themselves challenged from the left and the right, sometimes by a left that is more clearly socialist and a right that is in direct and obvious continuity with fascist formations of the past. That version of liberalism often called *neoliberalism* finds itself under pressure from its old rivals, both of which can be seen in turn as competing versions of a democratic challenge. In some cases, such as Greece, the left-democratic force prevailed; in others, such as Poland or Hungary, the right-democratic force prevailed. In Austria, the presidential election ended up being a closely contested affair between the Green candidate and a far-right neofascist.

Two different kinds of stress might be pulling liberal democracy apart. One is *austerity*. A polity stripped to the minimum of regulatory functionality for the benefit of financial looting provokes reactions against the liberal side of liberal democracy to which both class- and nation-based versions of the democratic can appear as alternatives. In Greece, for once, this favored the demos of the left, although once Syriza was elected, it turned out there was not a whole lot they could do—or were willing to do—about austerity.

The other stress is the global refugee crisis. It seems reasonable now to say that climate change is adding to the usual raft of geopolitical shenanigans leading to destabilization on the edges of the imperial system. Aridity is spreading across North Africa, the Middle East and Central Asia.[2] Millions of people are on the move. Both in European Union states and in Australia, right-wing versions of the demos as a shared national belonging are alarmingly popular. Both center-left and center-right parties find themselves caught up in accommodating this rightist version of the demos within otherwise liberal versions of politics, more concerned with keeping the wheels of commerce turning.

How to think this further? Perhaps we could follow Mouffe, who might want to think these particular instances of politics against the background of what she takes to be a more fundamental concept: *the political.* In *Agonistics*, Mouffe thinks the political is a kind of ontological ground under any possible politics. Its most characteristic feature is what she calls *radical negativity*. There is always an ineradicable difference that cannot be annexed or subsumed or reconciled into a polity, no matter how plural. There's always a point of nonidentity. The political solution is to construct a boundary that excludes the other as a *constitutive outside*. The "moment of the political" is when a *we* confronts a *them* (A18).

Particularly in its generic fascist version, this boundary presents itself as a natural fact, but it is important for Mouffe that the distinction between an us and a them is arbitrary, contingent and constructed—no matter how much it appears as given to *common sense*. Political power is an *articulation* of particular forces linked by a *chain of equivalence* in which they can appear together as an us, forming a *hegemonic* power against a them. Thus, in the presidential primaries, for Sanders we are all in this together against "the big banks," which should be broken up. Or, for Trump we are all in this together against "Mexican rapists," to be kept out by an enormous wall for which Trump will somehow get Mexico to pay. Even the more conventionally liberal politics of Hillary Clinton is powerfully organized around

2 Eyal Weizman and Fazal Sheikh, *The Conflict Shoreline*, Göttingen: Steidl, 2015.

the struggle against "terrorism," on which she promised a rather more belligerent stance than President Obama.

All of these are versions of an American us against an un-American them with rich histories. Mouffe:

> What is at a given moment accepted as the "natural" order, jointly with the common sense that accompanies it, is the result of sedimented hegemony practices. It is never the manifestation of a deeper objectivity that is exterior to the practices that brought it into being. (A2)

Hegemony is felt rather than thought, and requires a constitutive outside. A people is called into being in the construct of a shared feeling of commitment and belonging, but which is always incomplete and unstable about the edges.

Mouffe's political theory is not governed by an ethical ideal of a perfect polity, still less a universal one. It is not driven by a desire to achieve the best state of affairs, but to avoid the worst one. But where Dean might want to heighten the antagonism of class struggle, Mouffe is more interested in how the distinction between us and them can be *agonistic* rather than *antagonistic*. Particularly where racism and misogyny are concerned, can there be institutions that can be more or less generally accepted as mediating conflict? Can institutional forms of mediation head off the danger of essentialist identities and non-negotiable demands?

Mouffe sees a role, then, for institutions that can sublimate the conflicting passions that are at the root of the political. Even if those institutions fall far short of an ethical ideal of universal justice, and are themselves the product of past hegemonic articulations. And even if those institutions fall short of being open to endless negotiation with proliferating differences, but yield to the *moment of decision* on matters of concern. There won't ever be universal peace and justice, but there need not be a war of all against all. "This agonistic encounter is a confrontation where the aim is neither the annihilation nor the assimilation of the other, and where the tensions between the different approaches contribute to enhancing the pluralism that characterizes a multipolar world" (A41).

The limited virtue of liberal democracy is that, while it won't reconcile everybody, it might manage some measure of pluralism within the constraint of the us/them boundary.

In *The Democratic Paradox*, Mouffe advances her concept of the political through a critical reading of Carl Schmitt, a particularly illiberal political theorist and Nazi jurist.[3] For Schmitt, the homogeneity of a people is the condition of possibility for democracy, where democracy means rule by the people. A people can distinguish *friend* from *enemy*. As Mouffe parses this thought, "democracy requires a conception of equality as substance" and "citizens must partake of a common substance" (D38). I'll come back to that.

The *democratic paradox* is the incompatibility of democracy with liberalism, which is not a politics of a particular people, but of an abstract humanity composed of individuals. Thus, liberals can dream of a universal polity in which the rights of individuals to own property and look after their own affairs is protected, but this isn't democracy. A democracy posits a particular people, who exist in some sort of equality with each other, but against some other people, who are unequal to us, or even as in Gilroy, less than human compared to us. "The logic of democracy does indeed imply a moment of closure which is required by the very process of constituting the 'people.' This cannot be avoided, even in a liberal-democratic model; it can only be negotiated differently" (D43).

And so: "Liberal-democratic politics consists…in the constant process of negotiation and renegotiation—through different hegemonic articulations—of this constitutive paradox" (D45). There's nothing ideal or inevitable about liberal democracy. It is just a contingent and hegemonic form of political power. As much as it likes to present itself as rational, consensual and inclusive of any reasonable objection, it is still power, and it still closes itself off against what it cannot accept. Consensus is created by eliminating pluralism from the public sphere.

Mouffe borrows some of her critique of liberal democracy from

---

3 Gopal Balakrishnan, *The Enemy: An Intellectual Portrait of Carl Schmitt*, London: Verso, 2002.

Schmitt, but then turns that critique against Schmitt as well. Schmitt wanted not only to critique but to abolish liberal democracy, and saw its paradoxical tensions as fatal. Mouffe sees them as productive. The tension between abstract individualism and the particularity of a people results in inventive compromises in political form. Schmitt could only imagine a people as a preexisting identity.

Schmitt refused any place for pluralism within a construction of a people, for in Schmitt the people is a given, not a construction of hegemonic articulation. His conception of a people is pre-political, naturalistic and essentialist. He might have understood Trump's overt appeal to nativism, but not the more plural invocation of a people made by Sanders. He may not quite grasp how the other is an internal boundary that a polity constructs, rather than an external, pre-given one.

Mouffe turns her concept of the political against two rival kinds of theory: liberal and Marxist. I find it hard to take liberal political theory seriously, as it seems mostly to be idealized versions of, and justifications for, what exists, and thus to lack any theoretical energy or stringency. Nevertheless, her points against its various flavors have a certain urgency given the inability of liberal punditry to come to terms with either the Sanders or Trump kinds of movement.

The problem with both liberal (and post-liberal) political theories is that they have to ignore antagonism. They begin and end with a (usually) rationalist faith in the possibility of a (usually) universal consensus. This is conceived as a consensus of individuals, making it hard to grasp the power of collective identity. Universal consensus based on reason has to banish not only antagonism but also the moment of decision. One might add, contra Butler, that there is more to politics than performing vulnerable bodies together. Against theories of the people as one (liberalism), and against the theory of the people as multiple (post-liberalism), Mouffe insists on the people as divided.

Looking to the international sphere, Mouffe is against the illusion of a cosmopolitan world beyond sovereignty and hegemony, whether stemming from metropolitan or postcolonial positions. (Which might include the fourth mode of exchange in Karatani.) Such approaches are trying to negotiate between cosmopolitan standards of abstract justice and specific forms of belonging. But where Mouffe finds the democratic paradox constructive, what we might call the cosmopolitan paradox is less compelling. "I do not really see the usefulness of trying to redefine the notion of cosmopolitanism to make it signify almost the opposite of its usual meaning" (A21).

Mouffe first came to attention as coauthor with the late Ernesto Laclau of *Hegemony and Socialist Strategy*, a foundational text of what would become known as the Essex School of discourse analysis.[4] That book worked its way through a series of classic Marxist positions on politics that tried to address the gap between the experience of Marxist militants, on the one hand, and a theory of politics rooted in class analysis on the other. On this reading, Rosa Luxemburg, Karl Kautsky, Eduard Bernstein and Georges Sorel are all permutations on solutions to the problem that the laws of capitalist development did not seem to result in a sharpening of class contradictions and a clarifying of political struggle down to open class antagonism.

Laclau and Mouffe rejected all three of the then-prevalent Marxist formulations of the social formation. One of these sees the commodity form as an essence and political and cultural phenomena as appearances. Another sees the economic as a base whose laws of motion are reflected in political and economic superstructures. A third grants a relative autonomy to the political and cultural superstructures but sees the economic as determinate in the last instance. This last—the formulation of Louis Althusser—was the point of departure for Laclau and Mouffe.[5] But they made the autonomy of the political from the economic absolute. They even went one further, in showing that the economic was itself political. The industrial workplace is a place of domination more than value extraction.

In Laclau and Mouffe's hands, the foundational categories of Marxist thought unravel. The development of the productive forces is not a neutral or causative historical trajectory. The economic is not

4 Chantal Mouffe and Ernesto Laclau, *Hegemony and Socialist Strategy*, London: Verso, 1985.

5 Louis Althusser, *For Marx*, London: Verso, 2006.

governed by its own regularities. Nor does it create coherent class locations and prescribe for them determinate class interests.[6] In place of the through-line of economic and historical development, they offered instead a contingent and political time.

Here Gramsci's category of *hegemony* became key: there is only a hegemonic order that produces an always incomplete construction of political power. Particularly in Mouffe's later work, the Marxist ontology of the social and historical organization of human life for the satisfaction of needs is replaced by a political ontology of a primal antagonism. Mouffe: "If our approach has been called 'post-Marxist,' it is precisely because we have challenged the type of ontology subjacent to such a conception" (A78).

From this point of view, Mouffe became a telling critic of certain attempts to revive Marxist or communist thinking. Mouffe:

> The main shortcoming of the Marxist approach lies in the inability to acknowledge the crucial role of what I call "the political"... The emancipatory project can no longer be conceived of as the elimination of power and the management of common affairs by social agents identified with the viewpoint of the social totality. There will always be antagonism, struggles, and division of the social, and the need for institutions to deal with them will never disappear. (A84)

She resists Žižek's attempt to revive communism in the guise of a kind of *via negativa*, as impossible goal. Alain Badiou's related version of communism she sees as a strange example of an ethical politics. Contra Arendt, Badiou does not think politics as a sphere of contending arguments. On the contrary, it is a singular relation to a truth event that produces a subject. The *event* is beyond matters of both fact and concern. It calls a subject into being in *fidelity* to something beyond them, an interruption of the real.[7] But where Mouffe thinks this an ethics, one might ask if it is instead not rather theological, a leap of faith into the absurd.

---

6 But see Erik Olin Wright, *Understanding Class*, London: Verso, 2015.

7 An entirely more serious account than my mere thumbnail can be found in Bruno Bosteels, *Badiou and Politics*, Durham, NC: Duke University Press, 2011.

Mouffe dismisses these kinds of (anti)politics quickly, but reserves rather more time for distancing herself from the various versions of autonomist or workerist Marxism, such as those of Hardt and Negri or Virno. These renounce the struggle for a counter-hegemony through existing institutions and propose instead an *exodus* or withdrawal from them. Theirs is an ontology in which what is given is not conflict but self-organization. In place of the self-organization of united labor, they imagine the self-organization of a differentiating multitude, which only needs to shed a parasitic capital to come into its own.

This line of thought is sometimes based on exactly the kind of analysis of changes in the forces and relations of production that Mouffe had already ruled out. Thus, the evolution of industrial organization from Fordist manufacturing to post-Fordist information industries is a mutation in the mode of production, which is now based on *immaterial*, *affective*, communicative and cooperative labor. Power is organized less through disciplinary institutions and more as control built into the social field directly. This *society of control* extends beyond the nation-state into a space of non-territorial *empire*. Political sovereignty now takes the form of *biopolitical* power over the production of life itself.[8]

Both this economy and this polity are actually reactions to the power of the self-organizing multitude, the only active agency the workerists acknowledge, in its newly emergent forms of the *mass intellectual*, *immaterial labor* or the *general intellect*. These multitudes called empire into being. Empire is the means via which the ruling class contains the unruly energies of self-organization itself. Advances in the means of production have brought the possibility of self-organization closer within the multitude's reach. The multitude's self-organizing power cannot be represented. It can't be contained within the general will. Its only political option is civil disobedience, and forms of nonrepresentative, extra-parliamentary power.

Against the strategy of withdrawal, Mouffe insists on a strategy

8 On Hardt and Negri see McKenzie Wark, "Spinoza on Speed," *Public Seminar*, November 19, 2014, at publicseminar.org.

of *engagement*. She insists on a theory of political hegemony not of the forces of production. For her what is primary is not a monism of productive and creative activity but a dualism of antagonism that cannot be reconciled. Capital has far more than a reactive role in her view. The current form of the social formation is not a product of the development of the forces of production alone but of a particular moment of hegemonic articulation. It arrived perhaps as "hegemony through neutralization" or a "passive revolution" via which the ruling class coopted forces that threatened to escape it (73). Against the seeming naturalness of the unity of the multitude, it is only through a counter-hegemonic project, creating both an us and a them, that a coherent political actor can appear. Politics is a matter of forging a chain of equivalence made by designating something as other. Against immanence and multiplicity Mouffe thinks of radical negativity and hegemony.

Here I wonder if it is possible to borrow a bit from both perspectives, but render them coherent through a somewhat different theoretical formulation. A place one might start is with Mouffe's attempt to exclude the economic domain, and indeed to make the economic turn on the stuff of politics: the workplace as a place of domination rather than value extraction. Here I want to reverse the thought, and argue that Mouffe's ontology of the political is still in part about something economic. The symptom of this is in that which forges the equality of a people as a demos: that they share in a *substance*. It turns out that what is at stake in politics is still the question of the social satisfaction of needs. Hence it might not be enough to think about the paradoxical relation between liberty and equality; one might need to think also about fraternity—which one might render now in less gendered terms as the commons. Or rather: liberalism and democracy has to confront the problem of social labor. Haraway uses the word *companion* for this, meaning those who share bread.

If against Mouffe one might resist the collapse of everything into an ontology of the political, against the workerists one might resist the collapse of everything into the self-production of the multitude. Mouffe:

> In order to challenge neoliberalism, it is necessary to engage with its key institutions. It is not enough to organize new forms of existence of the common, outside the dominant capitalist structures, as if the latter would progressively ebb away without any confrontation. (A115–16)

For the workerists, there is really only a productive class—workers, multitude—and a parasitic one. In Mouffe there are two classes—labor versus capital—and a host of social movements and other nonclass actors. But what if from the beginning one thought of more than two class actors? There is another way to read the Marxist tradition of political writings, which would make the peasant question central. Labor came to organizational consciousness at a time when there were two ruling classes—capitalists and landlords—and two subordinate classes—worker and farmer. Indeed, part of the subtlety of Gramsci's thought has to do with thinking hegemony as the articulation of more than two class positions, before he even gets to other social actors. One might ask again if there are multiple subordinate and dominant classes—including new ones.

Here one might expand the concept of hegemony using a more classically structuralist device.[9] Rather than the political as an irreducible antagonism between two nonequivalent terms, one might more modestly think a politics of four classes and four rather than two kinds of relation. To the friend and the enemy, one might add the rather more interesting categories of the *non-friend* and *non-enemy*. It was within something like the square of those four possibilities that social democracy tried to think the peasant question. Today one might think new kinds of ruling and subordinate classes beyond labor and capital.

It is one thing to use such a semiotic technique to understand social phenomena. It is another to insist that all phenomena are language based. Here one has to wonder about the usefulness of a concept of the political that seems to have excluded war, on the one hand, and labor on the other—not to mention nonlinguistic modes

9 A. J. Greimas, *On Meaning: Selected Writings in Semiotic Theory*, Minneapolis: University of Minnesota Press, 1987.

of practicing knowledge. It may be partly the case that "Nowadays, to buy something is to enter into a specific world, to become part of an imagined community" (A90). But as Lazzarato argues, modern production methods turn out subjects just as much as objects, and their organization may be coded but is barely linguistic.

The claim for an ontology of the political, whose radical negativity is an effect of the incompleteness of language, has the result of foreclosing in advance a more radical pluralism, in which nonpolitical forms of power, knowledge or institution might play a role. Thus there is something a bit unsatisfactory about Mouffe's comments on Bruno Latour. She wants to rescue some version of critique from Latour's claim that it has run out of steam, but her version of critique insists on radical negativity as a kind of essentialism in negative.

It is indeed the case, contra Latour, that not all versions of critique assert a primary distinction between nature and culture, in which nature, objectivity and reality are juxtaposed in advance against culture, subjectivity and appearances.[10] But Mouffe has cut herself off from those parts of the Marxist tradition which thought about critique outside this divide. However, her insistence that Latour's project of *composing* a common world ducks the question of antagonism is well taken, even if one remains skeptical of the ontological grandeur with which Mouffe wants to decorate it. Mouffe's *a priori* claim that there is an "antagonistic dimension which is inherent to all human societies" is not the radical break with a Marxist essentialism of labor that she imagines (A2). It is rather the same essentialism in negative.

There are some more radical encounters one could imagine for Mouffe's ontology of the political. One would be Charles Fourier, who tried to write the possibility of the *complete* absence of antagonism.[11] What is instructive in such an attempt is how, like Mouffe, his focus is on the passions rather than reason, but unlike Mouffe it is also about the passions as kinds of need. The other encounter might be to think Mouffe in relation to Johan Huizinga. This might appear a strange

10 Bruno Latour, *We Have Never Been Modern*, Cambridge, MA: Harvard University Press, 1993.

11 Charles Fourier, *Theory of the Four Movements*, Cambridge: Cambridge University Press, 1996.

choice, but Huizinga wrote *Homo Ludens* explicitly against both Carl Schmitt and the Marxists.[12] It makes no ontological claims, but it offers a much wider concept of the agonistic, in which the political is just one of the many forms that evolved for its display.

One can only agree with Mouffe that "the current crisis is civilizational," and echo her call for a "post-social-democratic ecological project" (A61). As the heightened refugee crisis makes manifest, climate change is a novel historical scenario in which "a truly Gramscian 'intellectual and moral reform' is called for" (A63). But it is one that might take rather more pluralism than Mouffe acknowledges, including a pluralism not just of political formations but of knowledge formations, none of which can claim to speak for a singular ontological ground.

While Mouffe dismisses in a sentence the famous slogan of Occupy Wall Street, "We are the 99 percent," perhaps there is some promise in the way it was taken up and expanded in the Sanders campaign. It identified an us and a them open to more than merely moral clucking about the rich. Sanders was able to forge a chain of equivalence among a number of democratic demands by identifying the ruling class as antagonist, responsible not just for austerity but also for the unchecked hell-horses of the Anthropocene. It might at least have been a better version of the democratic side of the liberal-democratic paradox than the one that prevailed—if one may be permitted a moment of understatement.

12 Johan Huizinga, *Homo Ludens*, Kettering, OH: Angelico Press, 2016.

12.

Wendy Brown: Against Neoliberalism

Different scholars get curious about different things. It turns out that I'm curious about rather different things to Wendy Brown. Her book *Undoing the Demos: Neoliberalism's Stealth Revolution* is very fine.[1] Certainly the clearest and sharpest account of *neoliberalism* I have read so far. I'll try to summarize its insights into neoliberalism, but also pose some questions regarding the things about which I am curious that get no mention in it.

Let's start with an example. Brown discusses the 2003 Bremer Orders, issued by Paul Bremer and the Coalition Provisional Authority in Iraq after the United States and its allies defeated Saddam Hussein and occupied the country. The Bremer Orders appear at first blush to be a classic instance of neoliberal *shock doctrine*.[2] The Bremer Orders decreed the sell-off of state enterprises, the opening of Iraqi companies to foreign ownership, the restriction of labor rights and a capital-friendly tax regime.

Brown concentrates on Bremer Order 81, which prohibits the reuse of crop seeds of protected varieties. The Iraq seed bank, located in Abu Ghraib, did not survive the war. The United States government handed out genetically modified seed in 2004. Iraqi farmers would now be permanently bound to agribusiness companies such

1 Wendy Brown, *Undoing the Demos: Neoliberalism's Stealth Revolution*, New York: Zone Books, 2015.

2 Naomi Klein, *Shock Doctrine: The Rise of Disaster Capitalism*, New York: Picador, 2008; Philip Mirowski, *Never Let a Serious Crisis Go to Waste*, London: Verso, 2014.

as Monsanto, Dow and DuPont. Agriculture has existed in Iraq since 8000 BC, but never like this before. Through a "legal tweak," a domain not previously incorporated into the global market economy became subject to the "best practices" of agribusiness. Brown: "Thus, *Order 81* epitomizes the neoliberal mobilization of law not to repress or punish, but to structure competition and effect 'the conduct of conduct'" (148). Order 81 subordinates farming to a market *reality principle.*

Brown's curiosity is about neoliberalism as a *political rationality.* As we shall see, it exceeds and even reverses some classic tenets of liberalism. "Neoliberalism is the rationality through which capitalism finally swallows humanity" (44). Brown constructs a compelling case for the coherence of this political rationality as a force in the world. But she does so by not being curious about some other things along the way, and one might in turn be curious about how these other curious things and neoliberal political rationality might interact.

She is not curious about the relation between politics and war. As in Mouffe and Butler, politics is a separate sphere in Brown. Quite a lot has to get bracketed off here to get down to Order 81 as a legal tweak, curious though that tweak may be. Nor is she curious about certain kinds of agency. It would appear that Order 81 was more or less drafted by agribusiness giant Monsanto, which had close ties to the Bush Administration.

Nor is she interested in the particular kind of business Monsanto represents. This would be where the story invokes the particular things I am most curious about. Is Monsanto an example of "capital" as traditionally understood, or is it some new kind of *economic* or *technical* rationality? It is interesting to me that what is at the core of this story is patents on the germ lines of cereal crops. This is a kind of business based on making *information* a commodity, and controlling the physical product in which that information is embodied through law and coercion as much as through persuasion.

Hence to me it is a story about a new kind of ruling class, which elsewhere I call the *vectoral class,* whose power lies in the control not of the means of production but of information.[3] As Peter Linebaugh

3 McKenzie Wark, *A Hacker Manifesto*, Cambridge, MA: Harvard University Press, 2004.

shows so graphically in *The London Hanged*, the imposition of capitalist relations of production in England in the eighteenth century was as much a matter of coercion and violence as anything else.[4] Not surprisingly, the imposition of vectoralist relations of production are no less coercive.

The thing I am curious about, but which Brown is not, is whether neoliberalism is a symptom of a mutation in the relations of production themselves. That might account for forms of law and politics that are "a meshing that exceeds the interlocking directorates or quid pro quo arrangements familiar from past iterations of capitalism" (149). For Brown, neoliberalism is a *political rationality*, a "normative order of reason" (9), or the "conduct of conduct" (21). Its effect is to convert the politics of democratic liberalism to an exclusively economic liberalism. Like Mouffe, Brown thinks that democracy is being hollowed out from within. Economic growth, capital accumulation and competitive positioning become the sole project of the state.

Political rationality is not an intention of a power, not an ideology, or "material conditions." It works through a "regime of truth" (115). "Political rationality is not an instrument of governmental practice, but rather the condition of possibility and legitimacy of its instruments, the field of normative reason from which governing is forged" (116). It constitutes subjects (*homo economicus*) and objects (*populations*). It is not the same as a discourse—there can be many and competing ones. Nor is it the same as governmentality, which means a shift away from the power of command and punishment. Political rationality does not originate with the state but does circulate through it. It isn't a normative form of reason so much as its implementation.

Perhaps the neoliberal renders moot a certain obsession in post-Marxist thought with the figure of The Political and of democracy as its ideal-type of procedure. It is curious to me that rare are the moments when anyone stops to question whether politics even exists, or whether like God, The Political is a myth, one about to go the way

4 Peter Linebaugh, *The London Hanged: Crime and Civil Society in the Eighteenth Century*, London: Verso, 2003.

of Zoroaster in an era when the one true faith of the market is becoming the hegemonic faith of the world.

There's no shortage of rearguard actions by believers in The Political, for whom neoliberalism is a kind of heresy, an economic god masquerading as a political one. There's attention to widening "inequality," to the vulgarity of commercialism, the endless cycle of booms and crashes in a financialized economy. Strikingly, liberals and Marxists alike all assume this is all still covered by the concept of "capitalism." There's a general consensus that capital's power has been rising, that labor suffered defeats, if rather less attention is paid to why and how. What made it possible for the ruling class to—quite literally—route around the power of labor and social movements? It is striking how rarely the *infrastructure* of twenty-first century political economy ever comes up.

In Brown, what we get is a clear articulation of a kind of fault line in political rationalities, but not much as to why it might have happened. Neoliberalism enlarges the terrain of what can be "economized." Contra classical liberalism, there is only *homo economicus*, which is then rethought as "human capital." There are only kinds of capital competing with each other, and these are imagined on the model of finance capital, as an unequal field of speculative units attempting to accumulate and augment their value. Neoliberal "liberty" is economic, not political. The old values of equality, liberty, fraternity are displaced by human capital, which is not even a humanism any more. What the young Marx called the "true realm of freedom" no longer beckons.[5]

Brown:

> Whether through social media "followers," "likes," and "retweets," through rankings and ratings for every activity and domain, or through more directly monetized practices, the pursuit of education, training, leisure, reproduction, consumption, and more are increasingly configured as strategic decisions and practices related to enhancing the self's future value. (34)

5 See Karl Marx, *Capital*, vol. 3, London: Penguin, 1993, chapter 48, "The Trinity Formula."

But notice the slippage here. This is about games and strategies, not human capital. As I proposed in *Gamer Theory*, this is a model of subjectivity in which we are all gamers, of which the speculator is just one model.[6] Perhaps it is about the arrival of a kind of tertiary infrastructure of information as value, where *sign value* controls *exchange value* controls *use value*.[7] This development would not then be well captured by the concept of neoliberalism to the extent that aspects of it are neither political nor economic.

Still, to the extent that an aspect of the present still appears political and economic, Brown shows how the neoliberal subject is no longer that of Smith, with its trucking, bartering and exchanging, nor a Benthamite maximizing of pleasure and minimizing of pain. The subject is now supposed to be a wise investor, calculator and networker, or as I would put it, a *gamer*, for as Brown acknowledges, "this does not always take monetary form" (37). Even if she is not curious as to what form it actually takes. There's not much attention here to the digital infrastructure undergirding the gamer-subject, "organizing its dating, mating, creative, and leisure practices in value-enhancing ways" (177).

Neoliberal political rationality no longer aspires to that Kantian *kingdom of ends* so dear to Karatani, where subjects are ends in themselves and a value in themselves. The human is disposable. Here I am curious whether neoliberalism is actually more a species of Gilroy's *generic fascism*, product of a petit-bourgeois culture in which the ruling class buys off the middle class through the repression of those below it. Fascism hardly appears at all in Brown's account, in which liberal democracy is taken to be the normal model of modern politics.

But what if we took generic fascism as the norm rather than an historically quarantined exception? This would at least make sense of the casual acceptance not just of inequality but the possibility of the extinction of those units of "human capital" that fail to successfully compete. It would also bring us closer to the exercise of state violence

6 McKenzie Wark, *Gamer Theory*, Cambridge, MA: Harvard University Press, 2007.

7 Jean Baudrillard, *For a Critique of the Political Economy of the Sign*, St. Louis: Telos Press, 1980.

in our time and to social movements like Black Lives Matter, for whom the state remains a repressive apparatus of violence above all else.

To see everything as capital is a petit-bourgeois worldview. Labor disappears as a category. It is Marx inverted: for Marx, capital was dead labor. For neoliberalism, labor is extinct and there is only capital. Supposedly there are many capitals, all competing with each other. There's no foundation for citizenship, for human capital can go bankrupt and cease to exist. (Unless of course it is "too big to fail"—a telling exception.) There is no public good and no commons. Perhaps, in an era when Donald Trump is a successful candidate for a presidential election, there is no politics, either.

For Brown, the mission of the neoliberal state is to help economic growth, competitiveness and credit rating. Actually, I wonder if that is really the case. Perhaps *austerity* is not about growth at all, but maintaining the transfer of wealth upwards in the absence of growth. Following in the steps of Foucault, Brown is interested in how neoliberal rationality is a regime of truth, but it might help to be a bit more curious as to how much of neoliberalism is not a rationality at all.[8] Certainly in its own terms it is a (semi-)coherent set of norms for economic management. However, I would not want to forego the tools with which to show its incoherence, irrationality and magical special pleading for an emergent ruling class, based on truth claims made with methods outside its orbit, and derived from the struggles against it.

Undoing the Demos is among other things a reconstructive reading of Foucault's lectures on *biopolitics* as an account of how liberalism became neoliberalism in the postwar years.[9] This is not Foucault at his best. Here he is doing something close to old-fashioned intellectual history. Brown: "neoliberalism for Foucault was intellectually conceived and politically implemented" (50). And yet both he and Brown want to make claims for this as more than a superstructural development.

As Brown candidly acknowledges, parts of the lectures read as an

---

8 See Philip Mirowski, *The Road From Mont Pelerin: The Making of Neoliberalism,* Cambridge, MA: Harvard University Press, 2009.

9 Michel Foucault, *The Birth of Biopolitics*, New York: Picador, 2010.

"anti-Marxist rant," even as other parts might lend themselves to a less than cautious reader to a sort of "neo-Marxist critique" (55). But it can never be such. Nowhere does Foucault ask what transformations in the forces of production, putting pressure on the relations of production, might generate such a break in political and ideological forms. In that sense the lectures remain what Nicos Poulantzas would have called a regional study.[10]

Foucault begins with the question of limits to state power, with rights as a constraint on sovereignty, but alongside this there is a second principle of limit: the market as not just an alternate form of organization but also of a certain truth: *market veridiction*. The neoliberal turn pushes rights aside and makes the market not just a limit to the state but its very principle of operation.

Unlike Marxists, Foucault is not interested in property rights, the occlusion of class by nation, or the state as ruling class in committee. Instead, the focus is on the market as *truth* and *limit* to government. For Foucault, neoliberalism emerges out of a crisis of liberalism—and in this he accepts its own narrative about itself. Neoliberalism does not want to be perceived as a response to the crisis of capitalism; it wants to present itself as a response to the failure of the state.

Here Foucault's old-style intellectual history links the Freiburg school and the Chicago school with Hayek as the go-between. The former contributes the idea of the state's role in fostering competition, the latter the idea of human capital. Interestingly, Hayek is also the person who, whatever his ideological commitments, really thought about the problem of *information* in economic theory. But explaining that would be to connect these intellectual developments to what was happening with the forces of production at the time, whereas Foucault wants to think The Political as autonomous and primary.

Brown:

> Neoliberalism is not about the state leaving the economy alone. Rather, neoliberalism activates the state on behalf of the economy not to undertake economic functions or to intervene in economic effects, but rather

10 Nicos Poulantzas, *Fascism and Dictatorship*, London: Verso, 1974.

> to facilitate economic competition and growth and to economize the social, or, as Foucault puts it, to "regulate society by the market." (62)

The missing concept there for me is *information*. It is no accident that neoliberalism has its moment in the postwar period, when the infrastructure of command and control through information that had developed during the war for managing complex systems was extended out of the military industrial complex into civilian industry.

Hayek had said that only the price signal could function as a rational management of information in a complex economy, and yet as Ronald Coase showed, market transactions are not free.[11] In cases where the cost of market transactions outweighed their efficiency, the nonmarket organizational form of the firm would prevail. The corporation emerged as a truly enormous *nonmarket* form of resource allocation. The state is called upon to perform all sorts of functions to enable these behemoths to coexist and survive. Meanwhile, the ideological fixation on "competition" covered up the lack of it.

For neoliberalism, "the economy is at once model, object and project" (62). Precisely because it can only be an *artificial* construct at this point. Civil society seems to have worked its charms on Foucault. He could not see the other side of the picture. Looked at from the point of view of neoliberalism, the state has to become more like the market. (And one can celebrate or decry that proposition.) But one can also see it the other way around: the market has to be propped up and kept going by the state.

The developed world became the overdeveloped world. Commodification ran up against the limits of what it could claim to organize efficiently or effectively. Whole chunks of social life had to be hacked off and fed into the flames to keep the steam up. Commodification moved on from land to things to information. A whole infrastructure grew, of information vectors, backed up by the growth of "intellectual property" into a comprehensive set of full private property rights. This for me would be a sketch that makes sense of neoliberalism as effect rather than cause.

---

11 R. H. Coase, *The Firm, the Market and the Law*, Chicago: University of Chicago Press, 1990.

If "economy" is not a static, unmoving thing in the postwar period, neither is the "state." Both are transformed by the same *techne*. As Sandra Braman shows, the functions of the state start to work differently when what the state runs on is information.[12] If there's a connection between state and private organizational units in the postwar period, it is that they both run on the same computational infrastructure, from the mainframe era to the PC to today's so-called cloud computing. One might wonder, with Chun, if these were the vector more of military rationalities than of market ones. This would help make sense of an aporia in Foucault and Brown: that the neoliberal subject is not only autonomous and self-managing, but also obeys commands. Autonomy is constrained. Initiative is welcome but only in fulfilling a task commanded from without. This is the principle of military organization.

One might also wonder if it is not at least in part from the generalization of military models that inequality becomes naturalized and normalized. It is certainly the case that another component of this, as Brown astutely observes, is a move away from the category of exchange to one of competition. In bourgeois economics, all exchanges are equal, including that of labor and capital. Barring a few outlier situations, the price at which an exchange takes place will tend to equilibrium. Or so it was once believed. Competition implies not equality but inequality. Some are just better than others and deserve more. It is as ideological and self-proving a nostrum as exchange, of course.

Success at this game becomes the only measure of success: "those who act according to other principles are not simply irrational, but refuse 'reality'" (67). It is a wild and unpredictable reality. The market is now frankly acknowledged to be convulsive. The state has to prop up the economy, and becomes responsible for it even though the state cannot predict or control it. The politics that goes with this is a *centrist extremism*. You can be for gay marriage or for prayer in schools, but the market is not to be questioned. The market is not there to enable the good life; all of life is to be sacrificed to keeping the market going.

12 Sandra Braman, *Change of State: Information, Policy and Power*, Cambridge, MA: MIT Press, 2009.

Brown: "Where others saw only economic policy, Foucault discerned a revolutionary and comprehensive political rationality, one that drew on classical liberal language and concerns while inverting many of liberalism's purposes and channels of accountability" (67). Brown points to rather different limitations to Foucault's thinking than I would. For Brown, his view is state centric. There's only the state and its subjects. For Brown, it is the citizen who is excluded here (rather than labor, praxis). Foucault sees things from the point of view of power. He is a little too fascinated with neoliberal "freedom." There's no subtending world of exploitation. Brown questions "his acceptance of the neoliberal claim that the economy constitutes the limit of government for liberalism and neoliberalism, that it must not be touched because it cannot be known" (77).

For Foucault, *homo economicus* as a man of interest is a constant, but for Brown, self-interest does not quite capture the latest iteration. "*Homo economicus* is made, not born, and operates in a context replete with risk, contingency, and potentially violent changes, from burst bubbles and capital or currency meltdowns to wholesale industry dissolution" (84). To me this is the subjectivity of the gamer, or the "Army of One."[13]

For Brown, *homo politicus* is the main casualty of neoliberalism. She explains this via the just-so story of political theory, for which *homo politicus* is something of an ironic founding myth. "In the beginning, there was *homo politicus*" (87). Humans live together as political animals, where politics means the capacity for association, language, law and ethical judgment (but not, as Stiegler notes, *techne*[14]).

Aristotle is quite candid about the prerequisites for political life: slavery and private property. The household is at the same time the model of rule and site of relations of production. But Aristotle is a bit troubled by production beyond household needs, which might ground not *homo politicus*, but another kind of figure. There're two kinds of production, one natural, one unnatural. Unnatural wealth is

13 McKenzie Wark, *Gamer Theory*, Cambridge, MA: Harvard University Press, 2007, 8ff.

14 Bernard Stiegler, *Technics and Time*, vol. 1, Stanford, CA: Stanford University Press, 1998.

accumulated for its own sake. Proper acquisition concerns the household; the improper, the marketplace and money. The former has limits and grants leisure, the latter becomes an end in itself.

No mention is made here of war, which might ground the right to citizenship in the first place, and determine the extent of those rights. Nor is any mention made of *techne*. How is political communication actually and materially conducted? Are not the agora and rhetoric technologies of the polis? There is also a bit of an elision between the classical concept of man as political and the modern one, skipping the intervening millennia in which the leisure of the man of means was not for politics but for God. One might also ask, with Karatani, if this is just a provincial Western myth.

Even modern liberal political thought respects the foundational fiction of *homo politicus*. In Smith we are not exactly political animals, but creatures of truck and barter—of exchange. But we're not creatures of pure self-interest. We might be *homo economicus* already in Smith, but we are also creatures of deliberation, restraint and self-direction—in a word, we have *sovereignty*. The rise of *homo economicus* is not incompatible with a presumed power of the political over the economic. The state could choose mercantilism or free trade, for example. Smith was intent on proving why the latter was better state policy.

In Locke there is more strain between *homo politicus* and *homo economicus*. The danger of the latter is made clearer in Rousseau, who is perhaps the main source of the investment in The Political that persists in critical theory today. Rousseau is the prophet of the return of *homo politicus* in the form of popular sovereignty rising up against self-interest. In Hegel this becomes the universality of the state versus the mere particularity of civil society. The young Marx begins with the unrealized nature of sovereign political man. Mill offers a world of little sovereigns, choosing their own means and ends. Here the boundary between state and liberty is a political question. The state is beginning to recede as guarantor of liberty, equality, fraternity. It becomes rather the manager of what Foucault calls the biopolitical. But *homo politicus* still lingers in a subject's relation to itself, even in Freud, for whom the superego is the politician of the self.

This thumbnail account of the mythic history of *homo politicus* is for Brown a story which shows the novelty of neoliberalism: "the vanquishing of *homo politicus* by contemporary neoliberal rationality, the insistence that there are only rational market actors in every sphere of human existence, is novel, indeed revolutionary, in the history of the West" (99).

Brown shows that there's a slippage in neoliberal thought about the subject, between the individual and the family. *Homo economicus* is still imaged as a male head of a household, or at least one with the benefits of such a household. He may no longer have slaves, but someone tends the kids and does the dishes. The family remains a nonmarket sphere that cannot be economized. It's a space of needs, interdependence, love, loyalty, community and care—where it is women who take care of all that "stuff." I might venture that for all its patriarchal faults, the family is the minimal unit of communism, not as a utopia of course, but strictly understood as a domain of shared or pooled resources outside of both exchange and even gift, as Karatani might see it.

Neoliberalism puts pressure on the family, and in particular on "women's work."

> Either women align their own conduct with this truth, becoming *homo economicus*, in which case the world becomes uninhabitable, or women's activities and bearing as *femina domestica* remain the unabowed glue for a world whose governing principle cannot hold it together. (104)

Neoliberalism intensifies gender subordination, not least because its demolition of social services leaves women propping up more than half the sky. Women's domestic labor is incidentally the only time labor really appears as a category in Brown's text.

If the point of liberalism was liberty, the point of neoliberalism is, perversely enough, *sacrifice*.

> This is the central paradox, perhaps even the central ruse, of neoliberal governance: the neoliberal revolution takes place in the name of

> freedom—free markets, free countries, free men—but tears up freedom's grounding in sovereignty for states and subjects alike. (108)

One is "free" only to submit to market "discipline." Brown:

> But when citizenship loses its distinctly political morphology and with it the mantle of sovereignty, it loses not only its orientation toward the public and towards values enshrined by, say, constitutions, it also ceases to carry the Kantian autonomy underpinning individual sovereignty. (109)

"Enshrined" is a curious word choice there. For believers in the political, neoliberalism really does appear either as an attack on the sacred or a heretical form of it.

It is, as Foucault predicted in a rather different context, the end of Man as sacred stand-in for the hidden God.[15] No longer are people able to pursue the good life in their own way, as nothing adheres to "man" other than as human capital, as servant of the market. It is, for Brown, "an existential disappearance of freedom from the world" (110). When Weber attacked the iron cage of rationality and Marx the commodity as reification, both presumed a subjectivity outside of both rationality and commodity, although I am not sure that in the case of Marx that subject was necessarily a political one. I think for Marx that subject was labor, in its capacity to know and imagine and transform the world. And I am not sure that this other agency of Marx is erased by neoliberalism. It is more contained by a vectoral technology, in which all of labor's agency is siphoned off as "creativity" and captured as intellectual property for a new iteration of a ruling class that may not be strictly capitalist any more.

Brown thinks that Foucault's sources for thinking the political rationality of neoliberalism are Max Weber and Herbert Marcuse. From Weber he takes the distinction between the rationality of means and ends, which was developed into a whole critique of modernity in Adorno and Horkheimer. In Marcuse, the object is more specifically

---

15 Foucault, *The Order of Things*, New York: Vintage, 1973, 387.

a *technological* rationality, extending out of capitalist relations of production and colonizing other parts of life.

Here Foucault's project is an explicitly anti-Marxist one. He restores the autonomy of the political that is questioned in Marcuse, but in the form of a rationality thought to extend beyond mere ideology. "For Foucault, political rationalities are world-changing, hegemonic orders of normative reason, generative of subjects, markets, states, law, jurisprudence, and their relations" (121). Brown gives a bit more weight to agency in her version, where the agent is "capital," but not much is said about its historical form, other than that it is now "financial." We're not told at any point how or why it became so.

One hint at what's missing here is Brown's account of *governance*, which she thinks converged with neoliberalism but is not of it. Governance is the move from hierarchy to network, from institution to process, from command to self-organization. As I suggested earlier, this is actually not that far removed from modern military organizational forms. And it shares with it an infrastructure of communication technology that makes information the key to both control and autonomy. This is contemporary *logistics*.[16] The political is made technical—as indeed Marcuse had already suggested. There is a devolution of responsibility to smaller and weaker units. "Thus, responsibilized individuals are required to provide for themselves in the context of powers and contingencies radically limiting their ability to do so" (134).

A particularly interesting part of *Undoing the Demos* is Brown's discussion of law. For her, "neoliberal law is the opposite of planning. It facilitates the economic game, but does not direct or contain it" (67). Her example is the 2010 decision in *Citizens United v. Federal Election Commission*. This famously gives corporations the standing of people with unqualified free-speech rights, and mobilizes even the constitution for the project of a neoliberal makeover of governance.

In Brown's reading, Justice Kennedy's decision in that case, writing for the majority, essentially argues that speech is *like* capital, and thus

16 Sylvère Lotringer and Paul Virilio, *Pure War*, Los Angeles: Semiotext(e), 2008.

should be another domain of unfettered competition. Curiously, while for Brown, Kennedy's proposition makes speech *like* capital, what speech *is* for Kennedy is *information*. This once again appears as the elided concept. It is curious that it shows up in nearly all of Brown's quotations from the decision. Kennedy writes of the right of citizens to "use information to reach consensus" (157). He is concerned with "where a person may get his or her information" (160). He worries about situations where one is "deprived of information" (165).

For Kennedy, speech is innovative and productive, which is a bit like capital, but it also has attributes of information in a commodity economy in which it too has become a commodity. Hence while Brown stresses that in Kennedy's decision "There is only capital, and whether it is human, corporate, financial or derivative," this is a metaphorical leap which steps over the key word: information (161). And it is information that composes the means of control and accumulation of all the leading forms of corporate power now.

Information is what Monsanto and Wall Street have in common, and have in common too with the tech companies, the drug companies, even Walmart, which is essentially a logistics company rather than a retailer. Corporations compete with their brand or their supply-chain management, rather than by trucking and bartering things, let alone making them. Of course there are still things for sale in the market, but never without their wrappings of information, not to mention the end-user agreements protecting their proprietary code. It is from the point of view of information that it makes perfect sense for corporations to have untrammeled rights to speech, for corporations "compete" with, as and for information. This is the point of view from which it even makes perverse sense to Kennedy that corporations are a disadvantaged minority group in that the state curtails their speech rights in elections.

That the postwar commodity economy, having run out of things to sell, has to sell information is also a good way of making sense of the "neoliberal" turn in education. Business now thinks it has the tools to take on, and make money from, things that could not even be quantified with the old Fordist forces of production. In the neoliberal "truth" regime, no amount of evidence will convince anyone that the charter schools and for-profit colleges are doing a mediocre to terrible job of this.

Brown's focus is on the decline of liberal arts in higher education. College is now about "return on investment" and "removing quaint concerns with developing the person or the citizen" (23). Here Brown strikes something of a nostalgic note. "Once about developing intelligent, thoughtful elites and reproducing culture...higher education now produces human capital" (24). Anyone attentive to the aggressive purging from higher education of suspected reds during the Cold War could question that rosy assessment of its recent past.[17]

A liberal arts education was once appropriate to free men, not slaves. It lifted a student's sights from the immediate and local to wider horizons—to become citizens. For Brown, the extension of such an education beyond a narrow elite was a significant achievement of postwar America. But one might wonder here, as in the ancient context, how citizenship is connected to war. The GI Bill could be seen as a way of recognizing and also defusing the demands the citizen-soldier makes on the polity it has risked itself defending. One might question how much this concern for educating citizens was a Cold War project, sustained by the Soviet "menace." And one might also ask if it already had an economic rationale, in turning out labor with the broader "skill set" for a more complex and increasingly information-driven economy.

Perhaps it is also worth recalling that the postwar university was a complex beast. In part it delivered a broadened liberal arts education. But it was also the heart of the military-industrial complex, from which today's *military-entertainment complex* was born.[18] (Not to mention a parallel medical-industrial one, as Haraway and Préciado remind us.) From wartime through to the '70s, the state funded basic research, much of it on the Pentagon's dime, contributing to a common stock of "innovation." The crucial change was

17 Noam Chomsky et al., *The Cold War and the University*, New Press, New York, 1978.

18 McKenzie Wark, *Gamer Theory*, Cambridge, MA: Harvard University Press, 2007, 8ff.

to allow universities to own the intellectual property they created, which put places like Stanford and MIT into the information business in an unprecedented way. Perhaps it is because I am not a product of it that I am not so enamored of the myth of the great American university. It is, after all, where one of the two branches of neoliberalism in Foucault's account actually came from. It was not just a safe haven for humanisms, of the *homo politicus* variety and otherwise.

The disinvestment in higher education may be more explicable in terms of labor-market requirements. Today's *vectoral class* has no need of the mass worker. Labor is bifurcated between a small core of a highly skilled *hacker class* using or designing information technology and a vast *precarious* population whose jobs have been deskilled by the same information technology.[19]

In sum, Brown's account holds capital constant and locates a break in the regime of political rationality. The latter has a certain primacy, as in Foucault, but is also to some extent emerging *for* capital. Capital is understood somewhat metaphorically, as a category that includes both actual corporations and forms of subjectivity. This capital is understood to be somewhat modified, to be financial capital, even if the only example—Monsanto—does not fit that category.

What we're missing is the possibility that the mutation in political rationality has an external driver—a transformation in the commodity form itself. The key ingredient in this transformation—information—actually appears in the margins of the analysis, but can't rise to the level of a concept where there are only two regimes of subject-formation theorized: *homo economicus* and *homo politicus*. That not only politics and economics but also war, strategy and education are now all made of information, both as concept and real infrastructure, remains unthought.

Brown offers an excellent diagnosis of the *what* of neoliberalism, but not the *why*. Perhaps Foucault is of less help here than one might hope, and for quite specific historical reasons. He was among other things a late artifact of the Cold War struggle around Marxism in

19 McKenzie Wark, *Telesthesia*, Cambridge: Polity Press, 163ff.

the university. There was a time when his heroic dissent from communist orthodoxies had relevance. Now that the latter has ceased to exist, it might be time to rethink the how the archive even of critical theory is no neutral resource but is itself a product of a historical struggle.

13.

Judith Butler: Bodies on the Line

Judith Butler's *Notes Towards a Performative Theory of Assembly* is a series of occasional pieces which, taken together, show both the extraordinary range of her thought, and perhaps also some of its limitations.[1] Here her thinking extends from questions of *gender performativity*, seen as an instance of *precarity* more generally, to a view of the political grounded in *interdependency*.

Along the way, Butler touches on questions of *antagonism*, media, infrastructure, the living and nonliving, and labor, but each of these are perhaps limit points beyond which she could not go without modification of her essential theses. Butler: "there is a war on the idea of interdependency, on … the social network of hands that seeks to minimize the unlivability of lives" (67). Indeed, but one might need to press on into some of these other questions to understand why.

A *performative theory of assembly* is where these texts are headed. Butler reprises her famous theory of gender performativity as a place to start.[2] "One does not begin as one's gender and then later decide how and when to enact it" (57). A performative utterance brings what it names into being (*illocutionary act*) or makes an event happen (*perlocutionary act*), but Butler is more interested in what bodies do than what they say. One could think of Butler's performativity as

1 Judith Butler, *Notes Towards a Performative Theory of Assembly*, Cambridge, MA: Harvard University Press, 2015.

2 Judith Butler, *Gender Trouble*, New York: Routledge, 2007; *Bodies That Matter*, New York: Routledge, 2011.

starting from Althusser's famous theory of ideology as interpellation.[3] Ideology works by calling to us, addressing us. We misrecognize ourselves in the address, adopting the point of view provided for us.

To this Butler adds a soupçon of Derrida, where the act of repeating something brings with it an unavoidable variation.[4] Hence while gender performativity does not mean being free to choose one's gender, there is still always some slippage in the performance of gender norms. That gender comes into being through its performance implies that there is always something a bit *off* about it. Butler: "something queer can happen, where the norm is refused or revised" (64). Gender norms not only hail us but call us to repeat them, and even if we don't intend to, our performances will be a bit different.

The reproductions of the norm reveal its weaknesses. The very repetition of the norm risks undoing it. The norm is enacted bodily, but with little turnings, deviations, inadvertent agency. One cannot separate genders and sexualities from the right to assert them publicly. Their power—and also their vulnerability—is in the act. Gender is always a bit precarious. But those who are furthest from the norm are likely to be particularly precarious. We need an ethics of protecting those who break from such norms.

But first, a word on this word *precarious*. Its roots are Latin, and it means something obtained by asking or praying. It used to mean dependent on the whim or favor of another, but over time its core meaning has shifted to dependency on circumstances, being at risk. One might wonder, however, if the discourse around a more general concept of *precarity* has tended to privilege the first meaning over the second. I'll come back to this. Butler: "Precarity names both the necessity and difficulty of ethics" (109). Perhaps, but maybe it also hints at what exceeds not only ethics, but also the politics in which Butler will ground an ethics.

Certainly, *precarity* can be felt as a kind of expendability.[5] As Brown

3 Louis Althusser, *On Ideology*, London: Verso, 2008.

4 Gilles Deleuze, *Difference and Repetition*, New York: Columbia University Press, 1995.

5 Lauren Berlant, *Cruel Optimism*, Durham, NC: Duke University Press, 2011.

explains it, one is supposed to be a self-reliant unit of human capital. But as Berardi shows, one becomes isolated, which in turn makes one feel more precarious, escalating anxiety. However, gender norms are not just about individual identity, they are about how and who and where one can appear publicly. Butler: "the term queer does not designate identity, but alliance" (70).

So who can be recognized in a field of appearances, and as what? Gender politics should make alliances among precarious populations. Precarity brings together all such claims to act in public, whether as a particular sexuality, as disabled, as stateless or homeless. Politics is about looking beyond one's own subjectivity. Butler: "identity politics fails to furnish a broader conception of what it means, politically, to live together, across differences, sometimes in modes of unchosen proximity" (27).

Precarity is about a differential exposure to suffering. Why are only some human subjects recognizable? "Which humans count as the human?" (36). One answer is in the very slogan "Black Lives Matter."[6] "The struggle becomes an embodied one for recognizability, a public insistence on existing and mattering" (37). Precarity is the performance of unspeakable peoples, whose appearance is disruptive. What they claim is what they need. They have to act politically to secure the means of existing.

What precarity performs is not so much its power as its weakness. What it claims is the right to be recognized as something other than the self-sufficient body. In Butler, all bodies are dependent and interdependent. They are dependent on *infrastructures* that support them. They are also *interdependent*, dependent on each other. The latter is reciprocal but not symmetrical; the former is not reciprocal at all, as we shall see. Dependency is a transhistorical quality of the body. This body that has needs is what political theory tends to exclude. "The republican ideal is yet to give way to a broader understanding of sensate democracy" (207).

Butler makes this a problem for critical theory. Who are these

---

6 Keenga-Yamahtha Taylor, *From #BlackLivesMatter to Black Liberation* Chicago: Haymarket, 2016.

needy bodies that don't appear as subjects? What do the excluded call themselves? Can the illegible form a group? Can they be recognized? Full recognition may well be a fantasy for anybody. As Althusser and Mulvey would insist, when ideology hails us, we misrecognize ourselves in its calling.[7] But what would it feel like to not be called at all? To be a subject, to become a political being, means performing some version of the norms that call us.

What the gender-nonconforming and the undocumented share then is a demand to be recognized which puts a lot of pressure on existing norms of the good subject. Hence Butler's call for alliances of the unrecognizable that seek to expand what we mean when we say *we*. "I am already an assembly, even a general assembly" (68). This might not in the end be a demand for some kind of universality, so much as a practice of showing, through what it excludes, its impossibility.

Such a politics happens in the context of a war against interdependency. A politics of precarity demands access to an equally livable life for all by linking groups from diverse class, racial, religious or other backgrounds. But here we strike one of the things Butler still has to exclude: what Mouffe would call *antagonism*. Who or what is conducting this war on interdependency? Agency is all on the side of resisting it. The ruling class never appears, is hardly mentioned.

Not only are gender and precarity performative, so too is the public space in which such performances happen. "Plural and public action is the exercise of the right to place and belonging, and this exercise is the means by which the space of appearance is presupposed and brought into being" (59). Occupying such space together calls into question accepted distinctions between the public and the private. Public space is *refunctioned*, as Brecht would say, or perhaps what the situationists called *détournement* was and is always performative.[8]

Butler: "What does it mean to act together when the conditions for acting together are devastated or falling away?" (23). It means calling

7 Laura Mulvey, *Visual and Other Pleasures*, London: Palgrave, 2009.

8 On détournement, see Guy Debord, *The Society of the Spectacle*, New York: Zone Books, 1994, chapter 8.

into question forms of the political that exclude too many people and too much of the conditions of a liveable life. Butler acknowledges Mouffe's insistence that a polity always excludes someone, and constitutes its ability to name an *us* by an exclusion of a *them*. But perhaps extending who can be included extends at the same time the unrecognizable to its constitutive limit. "The body politic is posited as a unity that can never be" (4). Democratic politics is more about changing the relation between what can be recognized and what can't than aspiring to some Kantian universality (as in Karatani). Butler: "acting in concert can be an embodied form of calling into question the inchoate and powerful dimensions of reigning notions of the political" (9).

At issue here are forms of action that might take the form of assemblies, strikes or vigils, although the paradigmatic examples are movements of the squares, the first of which to my mind is Tiananmen Square.[9] Butler privileges bodies together. These are not versions of Virno's multitude, however. Butler is more interested in what a body can't do that what it can. She does not celebrate the active body so much as the fragile one. In appearing in its fragility, the precarious, dependent body performs the right to appear and reveals that part of the population deemed disposable. It challenges what Achille Mbembe calls the *necropolitics* which decides without consultation which bodies can live and which not. Not to mention Ruth Gilmore's definition of racism as exposure to premature death.[10] Against that, the public assembly shows a shared situation of people enduring, "obdurately living" (18).

Interdependency is not a matter of making an ethical choice about the other. Following Levinas, Butler thinks that the other impinges on me before I can even make any ethical choice.[11] Those who act on us are other to us. It is not sameness that makes the ethical relation. This relation is reciprocal but asymmetrical. The other has priority

9 McKenzie Wark, *Virtual Geography*, Bloomington IL: Indiana University Press, 1995, 95ff.

10 Achille Mbembe, *On the Postcolony*, Berkeley: University of California Press, 2001; Ruth Wilson Gilmore, *Golden Gulag*, Berkeley: University of California Press, 2007.

11 Sean Hand (ed.), *The Levinas Reader*, London: Blackwell, 1989.

over me. Ethics is not a matter of either self-interest or altruism. The face of the other demands my ethical attention regardless of my will.

Butler wants to join Levinas to Hannah Arendt as thinkers who refuse bourgeois liberal individualism.[12] Much of what Butler has to say about politics here takes shape against a running commentary on Arendt. In Arendt the body does not enter politics, which is a realm of the speech act. Her model of the polis is the one handed down through the ancient texts, where men occupy a public space and discuss matters of state in a world of freedom separated from everyday necessity. Arendt did not think the poor in the streets, demanding bread, was quite politics. Necessity is not politics to her, only freedom is politics. Butler wants to ask if one can be hungry and rational, but this still insists on a certain distinction between necessity and politics as the sphere of reason. But what if to be hungry is already rational? Or what if politics is not rational at all?

And yet there is something useful in Arendt in the idea of the right to have rights, the claim of the stateless, a claim made outside the claim itself. To which Butler adds: those ineligible for rights need to form alliances, to bring about a tension in the realm of appearances, in which gender-nonconformers and undocumented immigrants might, in their different ways, be making analogous claims. "To be a political actor is a function, a feature of acting on terms of equality with other humans" (52). The freedom to appear is central to democratic struggles of all kinds, whether Occupy, Black Lives Matter or movements for trans visibility or the undocumented.

Butler's is a politics of bodies assembling, but as more than a mass of individual bodies. Politics emerges *between* bodies. "Those who find themselves in positions of radical exposure to violence, without basic political protections by forms of law, are not for that reason outside the political or deprived of all forms of agency" (79). To say so is already to accept that they are nonpersons—Gilroy's *infrahuman*. Unlike Giorgio Agamben, Butler refuses to reduce the excluded body to *bare life*, which might be how biopolitics might view a body from

12 Hannah Arendt, *The Human Condition*, Chicago: University of Chicago Press, 1998.

above but is not necessarily how the body of the excluded appears to itself or its neighbors.[13] "If we claim that the destitute are outside of the sphere of politics—reduced to depoliticized forms of being—then we implicitly accept as right the dominant ways of establishing and limiting the political" (78).

From Arendt, Butler extracts the principle that nobody has the right to choose who to live with on earth. We are obliged to cohabit with others. There is an unchosen condition of freedom in Arendt just as there is an unchosen condition of ethics in Levinas. Community has to be subordinated to this non-communitarian refusal of genocide. But could this be extended even further? Or are we stuck with a politics (Arendt) and an ethics (Levinas) that begins with other people (Arendt) even if it then skips off toward a more theological other (Levinas)? Is there a way to let in the copresence of nonhumans, even the nonliving? That might be the sort of ethics and politics Haraway wants, but it seems beyond the limits of where Butler wants to go.

There is no one part of the species-being that can claim the whole of the earth. "Thus, from unchosen co-habitation, Arendt derives notions of universality and equality that commit us to institutions that seek to sustain human lives" (115). Arendt thought the lesson of Nazi genocide, internment and dispossession was opposition to illegitimate use of state violence. Equality has to extend beyond language, ethnicity, religion, to those nobody ever chose to be around. Politics is about obligations to unchosen people. Butler: "everyone is precarious, and this follows from our social existence as bodily beings who depend upon one another for shelter and sustenance, and who, therefore, are at risk of statelessness, homelessness, and destitution under unjust and unequal political conditions" (118).

Butler mentions the problem of the unchosen cohabitation forced upon the colonized, but that case clearly puts more pressure on this Arendtian and Levinasian framework than they would have wanted to acknowledge. Butler: "our precarity is to a large extent dependent upon the organization of economic and social relationships…

13 Giorgio Agamben, *Homo Sacer*, Stanford, CA: Stanford University Press, 1998.

So as soon as the existential claim is articulated in its specificity, it ceases to be existential" (119). Even if in Butler it never quite becomes historical.

Against forms of politics that increasingly restrict the possibility of livable lives to fewer and fewer, Butler counterposes those gatherings that embody demands for justice and equality as those that are worthy. But is there ever an unmixed example? That the people constitute themselves performatively through a détournement of norms that they take over and inhabit queerly is going to mean that the people are never quite a consistently ethical collective subject. A hostile media played up the existence of anti-Semites among Occupy Wall Street and misogynistic Bernie-bros who supported Senator Sanders against Hillary Clinton in the 2016 Democratic primary. Media reproduce familiar stories, extracting elements from situations that can only be known retrospectively as fragments of such simulations.

The media remain only marginally present in Butler's body-centric political theory. Yet media is necessary to the performance of gender.[14] "Recognizing a gender depends fundamentally on whether there is a mode of presentation for that gender, a condition for its appearance; we can call this its media or its mode of presentation" (38–9). And media is necessary for assembly: "there is an indexical force of the body that arrives with other bodies in a zone visible to media coverage" (9). But we never arrive at much of a concept of media, which can't really be grasped from the point of view of that which it produces.

For Butler, "the media have entered into the very definition of the people" (20). There is a sort of humanism at work here, where the bodies gathered in and as a body come first, and their technical, mediated double comes second. But surely it is the other way around in any modern polity. The media are the primary space; public squares and so forth are sets for media performances. One cannot simply add media onto some fantasy of the Greek polis and call it modern politics. The thing to occupy is media time; the way to do it is to take

14 McKenzie Wark, *Telesthesia: Communication, Culture and Class*, Cambridge: Polity Press, 2012, chapter 17.

space. It is not the case that "the media extends the scene" (91). The scene is a retroactive production of media. If an assembly gathered and nobody noticed, did it make a sound?

While mediation is characteristic of all modern polities, it is not all that new. It is not the case that "this conjuncture of street and media constitutes a very contemporary version of the public sphere" (94). Unless by contemporary one means a century and a half of "Twitter revolutions." Already by the 1840s, telegraphy starts to shape a *virtual geography* of the event.[15] At first it may appear as something added to contiguous, physical and embodied space, but really it constitutes a new geography of the event, dominated by *telesthesia*, or perception at a distance. "There is a specter haunting Europe," as Marx and Engels famously said, precisely because of the changing materiality of space and time, where information starts to move faster than the merchant, the soldier or even the revolutionary.

Butler: "Does the media not select what can appear, and who can appear?" (55). Indeed, but there's been a long debate on what might constitute its criteria of selection. Do the media replicate the forces of production (as in Benjamin), or the relations of production (as in Adorno)? Or do they *reproduce* the relations of production (as in Althusser)? Do they express a hegemonic compromise (as in Gramsci) or a hybrid of dominant, residual and emergent cultures (as in Williams)? And is there not something performative in the manner in which people make meaning out of media, as an active audience (as in Ang) or through negotiated or resistant readings (as in Hall) or even by injecting subcultural noise (as in Hebdige)?[16]

There is at least the beginning of an inkling of media theory in Butler, which I suppose is to be welcomed, given how much political theory still thinks it is in the Greek polis, and indeed thinks the Greek polis is more than a myth. Butler:

---

15 James Carey, *Communication as Culture*, 2nd edition, New York: Routledge, New York, 2008; McKenzie Wark, *Virtual Geography*, Bloomington IN: Indiana University Press, 1995.

16 These classic texts can all be found in Meenakshi Gigi Durham and Douglas Kellner (eds.), *Media and Cultural Studies: Keyworks*, 2nd edition, Hoboken, NJ: Wiley-Blackwell, 2012.

> Of course, we have to study those occasions in which the official frame is dismantled by rival images, or where a single set of images sets off an implacable division in society, or where the numbers of people gathering in resistance overwhelms the frame. (20)

But which are those occasions? Perhaps what is crucial here is the capacity to interrupt the temporality and narrative coherence of virtual geography.

Mediated narratives precede events. The function of the news is to fit events into the template of a handful of simple stories, as Benjamin already knew.[17] The event that frustrates the narrative framing held open for it in advance is the one most likely to receive inconsistent presence in the media and be most open, at least for a time, to queer acts of performativity. This of course need not always be a good thing. The first twenty-four hours after the planes flew into the World Trade Center are a signal instance of a dismantled frame. After that, the frame was put back in place and insisted upon relentlessly.

That was an example of what I call a *weird global media event*. Being global, the range of interpretive performances can be even wider. Butler: "its locality is not denied by the fact that the scene is communicated beyond itself and so constituted in global media" (92). Indeed, but again, this is backwards. Its locality is determined by the variable range of significance of that locus in a particular instance of a global media imaginary. Global media imaginaries are transnational but partial and plural. A particular locus can mean something quite different there to what it means to those local to it. To New Yorkers, the World Trade Center was a bunch of second-tier office real estate; in a global media imaginary, it meant rather more than that. To give a very different example, Zuccotti Park is not even all that close to Wall Street, and in any case, Wall Street is an abstraction. How do you occupy an abstraction?[18] It is a nicely performative example, but it depends on making meaning in a virtual geography rather than an actual one.

---

17 Walter Benjamin "The Storyteller," in *Selected Writings*, vol. 3, Cambridge, MA: Harvard University Press, 2002, 143ff.

18 Wark, *Telesthesia*, 207.

Butler's approach to media is stuck in a representational way of thinking, viz:

> The term "media" names any mode of presentation that relays to us some version of reality from the outside; it operates by means of a series of foreclosures that make possible what we might call its message, which impinges on us, by which I mean both the foreclosure—what is edited out, what is outside the margins—and what is presented. (102)

Or as Debord put it rather more pithily: "That which appears is good; that which is good appears."[19] Note that this way of thinking about media is contrary to the performativity Butler insists on elsewhere. Here, there's reality; then there's its selected representation. There's no sense here of how the mediated performance calls the real into being and designates in that act both what is included and what is ignored.

This might complicate Butler's effort to apply Levinas's ethics to mediated images, where we are "solicited by images of distant suffering" (100). For Butler, these unchosen images of suffering bring the fate of the other near. I am here but also more than just here. "It is not just that one discrete population views another through certain media moments but that such a response makes evident a form of global connectedness" (105). Consent and community don't mark the range of obligation. But one has to ask: Which images do we see of the other suffering? Is it not most often images of children? The other is mediated within the narrative of the humanitarian obligation, which might be ethical but is never political. As both Jackie Wang and I have argued in different contexts, only the "innocent" are the subject of an ethical responsibility.[20] Hence the adult refugee, or the Black American teenager who may have had some minor run-in with the law, are excluded from the field of livable lives, for which we might care or grieve.

In Butler, media is not, or is not consistently, performative. The same is the case with infrastructure. Bodies are *supported* "by

19 Guy Debord, *Society of the Spectacle*, Zone Books, New York, 1994, 15.

20 Jackie Wang, "Against Innocence," *LIES* 1, 2012; Wark, *Telesthesia*, 16ff.

environments, by nutrition, by work, by modes of sociality and belonging" (84). Bodies are *dependent*: "Assembled creatures such as these depend upon a set of living and institutional processes, infrastructural conditions, to persist and to assert together a right to the conditions of its persistence" (18–19). Occasionally infrastructure is a "collaborative actor" (127). But mostly it is like this: "bodily movement is supported and facilitated by nonhuman objects and their particular capacity for agency" (72).

This is because Butler has not really strayed all that far from Arendt. In Arendt, politics is a meeting of minds; in Butler, it is also a meeting of bodies. But what is not really part of this politics of bodies is the *laboring* body. Hence infrastructure appears as that which supports a political body; it is not that which a laboring body also builds and maintains. Like media, infrastructure is not really performative. In Butler, political bodies perform with public spaces, making them part of their assembly, but the reciprocal kind of performance is lacking, in which infrastructure makes labor part of itself. "So the pavement and the street are already to be understood as requirements of the body" (128). But the (laboring) body is not a requirement of the pavement.

To be fair, Butler does acknowledge a world beyond the assembling of bodies. "We cannot presume the enclosed and well-fed space of the polis, where all material needs are somehow being taken care of elsewhere by beings whose gender, race or status render them ineligible for public recognition" (96). Not to mention their class. Butler: "the organization of infrastructure is intimately tied with an enduring sense of individual life"—with an emphasis on *individual* (21). Or as Sartre might have put it, the practico-inert of a world built out of dead labor arranges us into relations of seriality rather than interdependency.[21] There are other registers in which one could think this. For Pasolini, infrastructure is not only the mass production of objects but also of subjects, a line of thought picked up by Lazzarato.[22] It is

21 Jean-Paul Sartre, *Critique of Dialectical Reason*, vol. 1, London: Verso, 2004.

22 Pier Paolo Pasolini, *Heretical Empiricism*, Washington, DC: New Academia Publishing, 2005; McKenzie Wark, "Pasolini: Sexting the World," *Public Seminar*, July 15, 2015, at publicseminar.org.

curious that the one form of assembly that does attack dependency on infrastructure does not appear in Butler—that of the riot.[23]

It is a strategy throughout this text that Butler includes the name of what her concepts exclude: antagonism, media, infrastructure, the inhuman, but not the name of labor, which hardly appears at all. Butler:

> I'm using one word after another, searching for a set of related terms as a way of approaching a problem that resists a technical nomenclature; no single word can adequately describe the character and the aim of this human striving, this striving in concert or this striving together that seems to form one meaning of political movement or mobilization. (133)

Perhaps, but the term that might cover a lot of it is labor. The labor of many genders, the labor of many species, the labor of the dead and the living, not to mention Haraway's cyborg hybrids.

And so I can agree in part with Butler that "forms of political resistance that champion forms of autonomy freed of all dependency perhaps make this mistake of understanding dependency as exploitation" (147). Eliminating exploitation would not leave a world of autonomous bodies. But the concept of dependency does not really go far enough. Precarious bodies are interdependent in Butler, but then dependent on infrastructure as support. Interdependence is a kind of reciprocal but not symmetrical ethical relation, where the other impinges upon me independently of my will. And it only seems to apply to the other that has a face, behind which lurks an infinite and essentially theological demand. But this line of thought tends from the human toward the gods. It doesn't tend much in the other direction. The unchosen ethical obligation starts with the human and then might be extended to other forms of life. And the ethical call of other forms of life is modeled on that of human life.

Despite some gestures towards Haraway and Stengers, I don't think Butler has really heard them, or through them; the unbidden demand

23 Joshua Clover, *Riot. Strike. Riot*, London: Verso Books, 2016.

impinging on us, beyond ethics and even politics, of that which has no face. An ethical obligation to *nonlife* doesn't really seem thinkable within Butler at all. Infrastructure supports the body, but the body owes it nothing. Faceless things don't call for any care. They simply are. Having remaindered labor as a category of what bodies are and do, infrastructure can't appear as part of the body itself, as what the laboring body has made, as dead labor.

What we're left with then is not a logocentrism but a *corporeocentrism*. It isn't reason or speech or the individual human body that is the alpha and omega, but it is still the human body. It is an inclusive liberalism, of differences but not antagonism. It wants to eschew any claim to universality, but still takes the Greek polis as the model for political thought, and political thought to be a generalizable category. It stresses the vulnerability of the body rather than its capacity for labor. As such, it can only think the inhuman as the support of the body. As such, this is an exemplary set of essays on how far one can extend political theory, but the book remains limited by the partial category of the polis itself.

14.

Hiroki Azuma: Otaku Philosophy

I started going to Tokyo sometime in the '80s. I had access to an apartment in a good location, thanks to someone who would later become rather powerful in the media world, whose name I hesitate to mention. Since my host was a workaholic, I was left to my own devices.

Tokyo was a real metropolis centuries before any European city got much beyond the small-town stage. By the '80s it had a heavy overlay of pervasive media culture, of a kind that would not happen anywhere else for decades. The contemporary media-urban landscape was born here. Not speaking the language, I learned what I could by walking the city, in the company of foreigners who made a living by teaching English to bored housewives, or by wrestling naked in milk.

What prompted me to go there was the video art of Peter Callas, who worked in Tokyo for a time.[1] That and Chris Marker's essay-film *Sunless*. But it was hard to find much to read about this postmodern, mediated Tokyo. You could see classic modern Japanese art cinema and read some high points of its literature, but the transformation of everyday life was not much documented for foreign readers.

Akira Asada had published a surprise bestseller in 1983 called *Structure and Power*, which introduced French theory to a Japanese readership, and which offered the tools for analyzing what was happening. Fragments of his work appeared in translation in various European languages in all sorts of avant-garde magazines. In Japan

1 Peter Grilli (ed.), *Peter Callas 1973–2003*, New York: Earth Enterprise, 2003.

itself it seemed as if theory had been absorbed the same way Japanese media culture absorbed everything else—by turning it into a spectacular subcultural style. But unfortunately there was very little interest in Japan's "New Academicism" in the West. Which was a shame. If we had paid attention to Japan in the '80s we might not have been so surprised by things that happened in the West twenty years later.

All this is by way of explaining my amateur interest in Japanese media culture and Japanese theory. I think it should be a bigger part of the global conversation. Fortunately, there is now a small band of scholars and translators generating new material to help facilitate that.[2] Unfortunately, Japan may also be ahead of the United States in the plan to abolish the study of the humanities in the university, so time may be running out.

This brings me to the work of Hiroki Azuma, two of whose books are available in English. Born in 1971, he is of a younger generation to Asada (b. 1957) and Kojin Karatani (b. 1941), whose major works are now being translated.[3] Azuma's work first received attention in 1993 in a journal those two more senior theorists edited, back when New Academicism was still in full swing.

As Asada said when he introduced Azuma in 1998: "Azuma's future will prove that his 'otaku philosophy' is not at all the same thing as an 'otaku *of* philosophy.'" This bears at least a couple of comments. An *otaku* is usually a young man with an obsessive interest, sometimes in anime or manga, but sometimes in other things. It was a phenomenon about which there was a moral panic in Japan in the early '80s, but it is by no means restricted to Japanese culture. Indeed, there seems to no shortage of theory-otaku around these days, who know everything about it as consumers and curate their collections of it on blogs.

Asada put his finger on something profound, even if in a throwaway line, in proposing a possible path from the obsessive cultivating of theory as media to coming up with a theory native to this culture and this mode of its communication. Although Asada had shown up

2 See the *Mechamedia* journal from University of Minnesota Press, Minneapolis.

3 Such as Kojin Karatani, *History and Repetition*, New York: Columbia University Press, 2011.

on our radar, those of us trying to do netkritik in the '90s on listservs like nettime.org (or people like Jodi Dean with her blog theory a bit later) did not know much about this parallel development in Japan.[4]

Azuma's *Otaku: Japan's Database Animals* is different from the New Academicism of Asada in fully inhabiting a pop-media universe without ironic detachment.[5] It translates theory into the media rather than vice versa. Like Francis Fukuyama's *End of History* (1992), and Asada's essay on "Infantile Capitalism," its point of departure is Alexandre Kojève's Marxist-Hegelian philosophy of history.[6] Where Fukuyama celebrated the end of history as the victory of liberal capitalism, Azuma was rather more interested in the "last humans" obliged to inhabit such a moment.

Kojève had noted in a throwaway footnote that postwar America had actually realized a certain terminus that both Marxist and Soviet thought had long anticipated. All basic needs could immediately be sated, and there was thus nothing to desire and struggle for. At the end of history desire is foreclosed and man reduced to an animal state, for man no longer desires to negate nature and make history.

The exception was postwar Japan. There the ruling class had laid down its arms and devoted itself to cultivating a purely ceremonial and ritual culture, which kept desire alive in form but not in substance. Kojève thought postwar Japan had overcome its militarist interlude by reverting to this "snobbish" practice. The snob keeps desire going, and with it the possibility of being human, through the negation of the world. But the world that was negated was no longer nature and the result was no longer historical action.

Azuma manages to twist this story—well known in Japan since Fukuyama's famous book—into something else. He notes that Japanese culture had become thoroughly "American," in being a consumer culture of the immediate gratification of needs. The otaku

4 Josephine Bosma et al. (eds.), *Readme!*, New York: Autonomedia, 1999.

5 Hiroki Azuma, *Otaku: Japan's Database Animals*, Minneapolis: University of Minnesota Press, 2009.

6 Akira Asada, "Infantile Capitalism", in Masao Miyoshi and Harry Harootunian (eds.), Postmodernism and Japan, Durham NC: Duke University Press, 1989. A text clearly riffing on Kojève and Fukuyama.

cultures of the '80s and '90s were actually the furthest shores of it. Rather than pathologize otaku, Azuma treats them as a contemporary aesthetic practice, rather like Dick Hebdige's treatment of British subcultures.[7]

The otaku subculture passes through three stages. The first wave of otaku were born in the early '60s. The emblematic media work for them to obsess over was the TV anime *Mobile Suit Gundam* (1979), along with B-grade monster and sci-fi movies. The second was, like Azuma, born around 1970 and watched *Megazone 23* (1985). The third were born around 1980 and for them the emblematic work is the TV anime *Neon Genesis Evangelion* (1995), along with mysteries and computer games.

Some, such as the famous *superflat* visual artist Takashi Murakami, think of otaku as connected to Edo-era Japanese woodblock print art, with its supposedly unique approach to derivative works, where artists recycle motifs from each other. But for Azuma, otaku is a product of a transnational postmodernism. Its origins are in cultural forms imported from the United States after the war.

> The history of otaku culture is one of adaptation—of how to "domesticate" American culture...Otaku may very well be heirs to Edo culture, but the two are by no means connected by a continuous line. Between the otaku and Japan lies the United States. (O11)

A key example is animation, borrowed as a technology from the United States after the war. One strand of it developed Disney and Looney Tunes character animation, which would result in the masterpieces of Hayao Miyazaki. The other developed limited animation, a cheaper method more suited to the small budgets of television. A classic early instance is Osamu Tezuka's *Astro Boy*, although as a little kid I preferred *Prince Planet*.

Whereas in the United States only character animation was really developed to a high level, in Japan limited animation became something of an art form, particularly in *Mobile Suit Gundam*, a TV

7 Dick Hebdige, *Subculture: The Meaning of Style*, London: Routledge, 1979.

show with no parallels in American models. But for Azuma this is an instance of a hybrid rather than a purely Japanese cultural form. Postwar Japanese culture was obsessed with Japanese-ness because of a *lack* of continuity. "Lurking at the foundations of otaku culture is the complex yearning to produce a pseudo-Japan" (O13). This took a strange turn in the '80s, and accounts for the globally unique popularity of postmodern theory in Japan under the banner of New Academicism. The idea was that since Japan had never quite managed to be a proper modern society, it could get a jump-start on being a postmodern one. "Whereas modernity equals the West, postmodernity equals Japan" (O17).

As I remember well, there was a certain charm about Japanese cultural confidence in the '80s, but a certain willful blindness as well. As Azuma notes, celebrating an obscure footnote from Kojève fit into this quite nicely. "Nothing better expresses the reality of Japanese postmodernists' desires than this choice" (O18). It was a way of forgetting the recent past and celebrating the present and future. In the anime *Megazone 23* by Noboru Ishiguro, '80s Tokyo turns out to be a computer simulated world created on a futuristic spaceship. Azuma: "Japan in the eighties was entirely a fiction. Yet this fiction, while it lasted, was comfortable to dwell in" (O19). Until the economic bubble burst, at least. But for otaku the simulated, CGI Japan kept on going.

The preferred worlds to simulate were either sci-fi or Edo-period Japan, as if the two breaks of the Meiji restoration (1868) and the occupation (1945) had not happened. Azuma links simulation to the practice of détournement or the fan-based making of derivative works, which "official" products then borrow from in turn: "the products of otaku culture are born into a chain of infinite imitations and piracy" (O26). Simulacra thus float free from both the notion of an historical time and from the authoring of original works.

Azuma sees otaku cultural practice as a response to what Jean-François Lyotard called the decline in *grand narratives*.[8] This is

8 Jean-François Lyotard, *The Postmodern Condition*, Minneapolis: University of Minnesota Press, 1984.

perhaps not unrelated to what Jodi Dean and other Lacanians call the decline in symbolic efficiency. In the Lyotard version, there's a loss of faith in an underlying story of historical time, particularly its Marxist form, but perhaps also liberal-capitalist grand narratives of progress tied to reason, technology, peaceful trade and consumer comfort.

For Azuma this decline in grand narratives is connected to loss of prestige of paternal and national authority. There is neither a big-picture story or authorized storyteller. Kinji Fukasaku's film *Battle Royale* (2000), in which the state compels the seniors of the most troublesome school to kill each other might stand as an emblem of that loss.

Otaku refer to themselves as otaku, a word related to home and family—perhaps meaning something like "homeboy." With their libraries of magazines and anime and figurines, they create a carapace in which to live. Azuma: "we can view otaku's neurotic construction of 'shells of themselves' out of materials from junk subcultures as a behavior pattern that arose to fill the void from the loss of grand narrative" (O28).

Azuma proceeds by asking: what kind of culture can be made out of simulacra, and for what kinds of human, or maybe post-human, life? What is curious about his account is that the decline of grand narratives does not give way to a precession of simulacra, to decoded flows, to open-ended language games, or to blank parody—to give the code words for some versions of the postmodern. Rather, what replaces the grand narrative "behind" the text or the screen of the individual work is not an invisible grand narrative, but a *database*.

Otaku extinguish the grand narrative in stages. The first wave replaced the official grand narratives of postwar progress with fictional ones. The second wave cared more about the detailed exposition of an alternative universe that all particular works abide by. By the third stage the database itself emerges as the organizing principle behind particular cultural artifacts.

Key to this is the emergence of *chara-moé*, where moé means the emotional appeal of some point of detail of a character. The word probably comes from one meaning budding or blooming. Where the otaku fans of *Mobile Suit Gundam* insisted on the stability of the worldview underlying the various anime series and peripheral products, Azuma thinks things are different once we get to *Neon Genesis Evangelion*, whose fans would rather draw erotic pictures of its heroine Rei Ayanami.

Evangelion is not so much an original as itself already a copy of popular anime elements, "an aggregate of information without a narrative" or a "grand non-narrative" (O38). This results in part from industrial changes. By the '90s, any product can spawn all the others: a series of stickers or a company logo could bloom into a series of manga, TV or film anime, games and more. By now "the narrative is only a surplus item" (O41).

One level of fan attention attends to moé-points out of which characters are assembled, such as pointy hair, cat's ears, glasses, maid costumes or the flat affect popularized by the Rei Ayanami character in *Evangelion*. There is even a website—tinami.com—where you can search for characters by specifying which moé-points you like. Characters start to appear with excessive moé-points—bells, cat's ears, antennae hair all on the same character. Attention shifts from the production of narratives or worlds to the production of characters who can appear in various product lines independently of either unifying narrative or world.

One could push back a bit on Azuma's insistence on a break with the past. In *Evangelion*, the Rei Ayanami character and others are named after World War II Japanese naval ships. The allegorical may still be with us. But surely one of the struggles in critical thought is to detect the appearance of the new as something other than a binary reversal of the old; or worse, to simply erase novelty as a mere appearance of an underling sameness. Hence I think it is worth speculatively pursuing Azuma's line of thought to see where it goes.

Azuma thinks there's a new kind of double articulation, of database and simulacra. The latter do not float free but are constrained by the database, and here he differs from much postmodern writing in not seeing the loss of an old cultural architecture as leading to something wild and anarchic. The tension of simulacra versus database replaces that of grand narrative versus allegorical fragment, and hence the world cannot be cognitively mapped.

Here we are closer to Galloway's concept of interface as simulation. "A copy is judged not by its distance from an original but by its distance from the database" (O61). In that sense Walter Benjamin's contrast of copy and original no longer gives much purchase either.[9] "The surface outer layer of otaku culture is covered with simulacra, or derivative works. But in the deep inner layer lies the database of settings and characters, and further down, the database of moé-elements" (O58).

Gone is the narrative and cinematic passage through the world. Rather, it's a matter of the mediation of database and simulacra by search engines and interfaces, which make actual and material the intuition of an earlier phase of otaku culture about the database behind the particular work.

That this is an organized culture is key: "the simulations that are filling up this society have never propagated in a chaotic fashion… their effective functioning is warranted first and foremost by the level of the database" (O60). The author is no longer even a producer of copies. Rather, in place of the creative agency of the author is the permutation of moé-elements.

What becomes, not just of the author, but of the human, after this erasure of the invisible depth behind the work once provided by the grand narrative, whether in the form of the Marxist totality or the completion of Enlightenment rationality or postindustrial progress? Here Azuma returns to Kojève. The human is not human in itself, as the human is merely another animal. What makes us human is the struggle to negate nature and make ourselves something other. History is the struggle to negate both nature and human animal nature.

Azuma does not note the class dimension to this in Kojève, for whom the master is the one who faces the threat of death and forces the other to bow before him. Only the master appears fully human, in forcing the servant back toward nature and animality. The slave fulfills the master's needs, but also the master's desire, which is for the

9 McKenzie Wark, "Benjamedia," *Public Seminar*, August 27, 2015, at publicseminar.org.

other's desire, for command over the desire of the slave. We'll come back to this missing part of Kojève in Azuma later.

The problem with postwar modernity for Kojève is that "Fordist" industrial production fulfills immediate animal needs so completely that it erases the struggle against nature, and even against the human nature of the other that might ground a desire and an act of making history. Kojève made of a tourist's glimpse of Japan the thought that Japanese snob culture found another way out. The snob creates a purely formal game of desire. Seppuku, or ritual suicide, is then Kojève's emblem of the snob making a formal distinction between human honor and animal instinct, by overcoming the latter with the former.

Cultural clichés aside, perhaps the otaku reverses the snob's formal construction of the human with a kind of formal and artificial construction of the animal. The otaku know they are dealing only with simulacra, but the moé-points extracted from the database enable real emotions. These simulacra immediately sate emotional needs, foreclosing the formation of the desire to overcome and negate nature. The post-historical human, or post-human animal, detaches form from content and no longer aims to transform the content, only the form, the simulacra.

Azuma dates postwar culture in three stages: the idealistic age (1945–70), the fictional age (1970–95) and the animal age (1995 onwards). Azuma sees the cynical relation to grand narratives thematized by Žižek and Sloterdijk, or the snob as it appears in Kojève's Japanese admirers, as only the second of these stages. The third stage of the otaku no longer needs to maintain a negative relation to grand narratives. They dispense with them in favor of the database. Hence with the otaku the collapse of modernity is complete. If it is an acceleration it is not an acceleration of modernity, but of and as something else.

It is curious that while there are erotic works that appeal to otaku, in Azuma's account the erotic is subordinated to the emotional. For example, "games produced by Key are designed not to give erotic satisfaction to consumers but to provide an ideal vehicle for otaku to efficiently cry and feel moé, by a thorough combination of the moé-elements popular among otaku" (O78).

Nevertheless, there is a tension in otaku needs between small fragments of narrative that deliver emotional payoffs and the interest in understanding the underlying database. Some would even take something of a hacker approach and extract the content files from the software to make derivative works directly with the game or other content materials.

While needs can thus be sated, desire cannot, as desire is always for Kojève desire for the other's desire. For Azuma this also explains the difference between the sometimes rather conservative sexuality of otaku and their tastes for what might otherwise be considered highly fetishistic material. The latter efficiently satiates a genital need disconnected from residual notions of love and sex and desire.

Azuma deflects the idea that otaku behavior is fetishistic, although it is a topic that could do with some elaboration. In the now classic Freudian screen theory popularized by Laura Mulvey, the male gaze partakes in a scopophilic desire to look, but is threatened by the castrating power of the image of the woman.[10] One strategy for containing that threat is fetishism, where the body of the woman is reduced to a fetishistic part. Perhaps Azuma is talking about a second-order development. Having reduced the threatening image of the female body to parts, it can then be reconstructed out of the database at will as ensembles of moé-points. The movie *Ex Machina* (2015) might be the furthest end point of this theme so far.

The old model of grand narrative and allegorical fragment lent itself to a hermeneutic procedure in which the fragment of a particular work could be read as a lost or ruined bit of a larger historical time. But perhaps the new model is no longer a depth model. Azuma calls this *hyper-flatness*. He anticipates Lev Manovich's insistence on the software layer as a generalized meta-medium.[11] For Azuma, there's only view control. You can look at the data different ways, but there's no way to read through the fragment to the underlying truth of the totality to which it belongs, other than as database.

---

10 Laura Mulvey, *Visual and Other Pleasures*, London: Palgrave, 2009.

11 Lev Manovich, *Software Takes Command*, London: Bloomsbury, 2013; McKenzie Wark, "On Manovich," *Public Seminar*, September 15, 2015, at public seminar.org.

Otaku reading practices can only go sideways, as it were, from one view of the database to another.

> All such information is consumed in parallel, as equivalents, as if to open different "windows." So today's Graphical User Interface, much more than simply a useful invention, is a marvelous apparatus in which the world image of our time is encapsulated. (O104)

There's no path from what is visible on the screen to the actual database, only other ways of representing fragments of its content.

In a later work, Azuma explores the political implications of the database. *General Will 2.0: Rousseau, Freud, Google* is about a moment after a loss of confidence in political institutions.[12] This book too is a kind of derivative work, détournement or simulacrum, reusing not Kojève in this case but Rousseau's *The Social Contract*.

From Rousseau, Azuma cuts the concept of the *general will*, or popular sovereignty. For Rousseau it is a fictional construct. "He probably never dreamed that it would become possible to see and feel the texture of the 'general will'" (GW7). In political theory, the general will is a symptom of a repressed desire for a non-deliberative form of government. Now it is a latent content beginning to use information as the tech of its material actualization.

In Rousseau's version the social contract creates the social, and the sovereignty of this sociality is the general will. There is first the social, and then secondly a government. There is a difference between sovereignty and government. The latter is merely the instrument of general will. The social contract thought in this manner does not legitimate any existing government, but rather the possibility of revolution when governments fail the general will.

The general will is an ideal construct, perhaps part of a grand narrative, which can generate critical purchase on the corruption of actual governments. But the general will in Rousseau is not public opinion. Public opinion can be false; the general will is never false. The general will is a shared interest, whereas public opinion is merely a motley of

---

12 Hiroki Azuma, *General Will 2.0*, New York: Vertical Books, 2014.

particular interests. Public opinion is the sum of wills; general will is the sum of the *difference* of wills.

Azuma offers a useful analogy: public opinion is scalar; the general will is vectoral. Public opinion is an averaging of the "masses"; the general will is the sum of differences between velocities. Rousseau sometimes writes as if the general will is computable, a mathematical entity. He posits a matheme of collective intelligence centuries before it could exist.

Rousseau is a problem for theorists of democratic governance because of his aversion to not only public opinion but also representative democracy and parties. The general will does not come from citizens communicating with each other at all.

> Rousseau thought that the general will is generated not through a process of members of a group affirming a single will cancelling out the differences but instead all at once, through allowing diverse wills to appear in the public sphere will retaining their respective differences. (GW33)

The general will is a sum of all differences.

The hidden ideal model underlying actual polities and according to which they are to be judged is a politics without communication. The general will belongs to the order of things, not to the social world. It is not a politics made by the social, but a politics conforming to nature. (And in this sense pointing away from Kojève.) Like the otaku, Rousseau preferred solitude to public life. For Rousseau (and subsequently for Fourier) civilization with its cultural artifice is the origin of all evil.

Azuma is skeptical of the value of normative models of deliberative democracy, such as one might find in Hannah Arendt or Jürgen Habermas.[13] For this school of thought, the public sphere detached from labor is where one might find the conditions of rational communication necessary for deliberation. This would be not a mere gathering of needs or desires but their transformation through rational deliberation.

---

13 Jürgen Habermas, *The Theory of Communicative Action*, Boston: Beacon Press, 1985.

Azuma distances his approach both from deliberative democracy and from one other very different idea of the political, one central to Mouffe: Carl Schmitt's concept of politics as the making of friend-versus-enemy distinctions and the ontological extermination of the enemy. Just as the general will does not deliberate, nor does it distinguish between friend and enemy. Perhaps it is the domain of that rather more interesting part of politics, which is always about the non-friend and the non-enemy.

So if the general will is neither a deliberative democracy nor the fight to the death, what is it? For Rousseau it is a regulative ideal, but for Azuma it is rapidly becoming a kind of reality: it's the database. Ubiquitous computing extracts patterns of unconscious need directly from environments—in the form of big data—quite without the conscious participation of citizens—or should I say users. The general has been made concrete, but also privatized—it's Google. "No-one being conscious of Google, but everyone rendering a service to Google—this contradiction is the crucial point here" (GW58).

Some might immediately thematize this as *control society* or *biopower* or *neoliberalism*, and not without justice. But Azuma's approach is at least novel in relation to such received ideas. It seems the otaku were onto something: that underlying the moé-points of attraction there's a database unconscious. People's wants become a thing. "Rousseau…remarked that the general will is etched into the hearts of citizens. Therefore, it cannot be perceived. On the other hand, the general will 2.0 is etched into the information environment" (GW63).

But where general will 1.0 was a mythic grand narrative, general will 2.0 is an actual database. "So far, access to general will 2.0 is exclusively in the hands of private corporations" (GW64). This is a point Azuma chooses not to linger over, however. To put it in my own conceptual language, which here neatly fits with Azuma's: the governmental power that can be extracted from the database is in the hands of a ruling class—what I call the *vectoral class*.[14]

Azuma distances his approach, however, from that of Tim O'Reilly

14 McKenzie Wark, *A Hacker Manifesto*, Cambridge, MA: Harvard University Press, 2004.

and other Silicon Valley boosters of the tech-industry fraction of the vectoral class. To some extent his database general will is still something of a regulative ideal, indeed even a grand narrative. It is potentially, rather than actually, a means to supplement a deliberative democracy that can no longer function as such. Politics has in his view become too complex for deliberation by all citizens. But perhaps the database of needs can come to their assistance, and enable a combining of rational deliberation with "a government guided by the unconscious" (GW72).

One might expect a great deal of push-back at this point from intellectuals for whom The Political is still something sacred and transcendent. But it has to be acknowledged that actual politics is in rather poor shape in much of the overdeveloped world. It turns out we human animals are not very good at using reason to overcome our particular sympathies and strive instead for the universal. Reason does not trump empathy, nor universality particularity, nor communication private interest.

Communication leads to networks, not universality. It creates island worlds and echo chambers—as anyone who uses the internet these days would know. What people want from their media tools now is the reduction of information complexity, not endless deliberation. How can there be deliberative democracy when nobody writes comments except trolls and nobody reads them—except other trolls? Perhaps we need a whole new architecture for politics. One that can visualize unconscious needs and desires.

If psychoanalysis is a way of uncovering an individual unconscious unknown to the subject, then the database is a way of uncovering the collective unconscious unknown to the people. And just as in dream analysis, there is no negation. Take Google's PageRank, for example: it measures links to a given page, but it does not judge that page. Hence if you google a "sensitive" term such as "Judaism" it is likely that among the top hits is some anti-Semitic bile. It is possible that anti-anti-Semitic sites that link to it to attack it are part of what generates its high rank.

But perhaps there is a bit missing here. Who owns and controls the database? If the old grand narratives were products of the superstructure, then as Pasolini had already noticed, the new forms of cultural power are actually directly infrastructural. What I would call the vectoral class ends up in charge of the means of detecting the general will as the social unconscious. They use it mostly to make a buck off rewarding our animal needs with simulacra. As Lazzarato has noted, the affective life of the species is now one of machinic enslavement.

Still, there's a certain pleasure in reading Azuma's writing, in selecting it from the database. He seems to have grasped sooner than many that the material conditions of theory writing and reading had themselves changed, and become also part of the database. His own writing works like otaku practice, moving sideways through simulacra, whether of anime or philosophy.

15.

Paul B. Préciado: The Pharmo-Porno Body Politic

"Read, this!" he said, thrusting a soiled photocopy of a typescript into my hands. "It will change your life!" Then he disappeared back into the public toilet he was cruising. This was my introduction to the works of Foucault. It was a "pirate" translation, made by a self-described "nasty street queen." And it did change my life, after a fashion. The most interesting books for me are always works of *low theory*. They may be written by people schooled in the high theory of the seminar room, but they take those sorts of intellectual resources and apply them directly to life. *Testo Junkie* by Paul B. Préciado is such a book.[1]

Préciado grew up in the dying days of Franco's Spain, and was educated by Jesuits. Préciado has traveled through at least four cities, three languages and two genders. He met Derrida while studying philosophy at the New School, when Derrida was writing about St. Augustine, whose *Confessions* about changing faith reminded Préciado of contemporary writings about changing genders. Préciado lived in Paris for a while, then got a PhD in architecture from Princeton.[2]

In *Testo Junkie*, Préciado documents a short period of life dedicated to taking testosterone. The book builds out an astonishing conceptual frame for thinking what that experience might mean. It is not a memoir. It may be a study of emotions, but only those ones that are not private. It is a "single point in a cartography of extinction" (12).

1 Paul B. Préciado, *Testo Junkie*, New York: Feminist Press at CUNY, 2013.

2 Béatriz Préciado, *Pornotopia*, New York: Zone Books, 2014.

Préciado is not sure if they are "a feminist hooked on testosterone, or a transgender body hooked on feminism" (22). As for testosterone:

> I take it to foil what society wanted to make of me, so that I can write, fuck, feel a form of pleasure that is post-pornographic, add a molecular prosthesis to my low-tech transgender identity composed of dildos, texts, and moving images; I do it to avenge your death. (16)

The death is that of French autofiction writer Guillaume Dustan. The book hovers between a memorial for him, and a celebration of her relations with writer and filmmaker Virginie Despentes: "fucking her is harder than factory work," but she comes to be "covered with my feminism as if with a diaphanous ejaculation, a sea of political sparkles" (97–8).[3]

The bulk of the book is not about such things. It is rather about what one can think by extension from such experience. It is about mapping the commodity economy centered on the management of bodies, sexes, identities, or what Preciado calls the "somatico-political," of how it finds itself both making and made over by "the sex-gender industrial complex" (28). It is an exercise in what Bogdanov calls substitution, building a metaphoric account of how the whole world is made out of one's own experience of labor. The most interesting kind of labor is now that of the "production of the species as species."

"I look for keys to survival in books," Préciado writes (135). Scattered in *Testo Junkie* are useful lists of writers and artists for anyone who feels they need similar keys to survival: Jean Genet, Walter Benjamin, Monique Wittig, Susan Stryker, Edmund White, Faith Ringgold, Faith Wilding, Jill Johnson, Valerie Solanas, Silvia Federici, Ellen Willis, Kathy Acker, Sandy Stone, Shu Lea Chang, Diane Torr, Del LaGrace Volcano, Pedro Lemebel, Michelle Tea. As in any low-theory book, the reading list is determined by a need to live rather than disciplinary boundary keeping. What is of interest is how Préciado pulls it off.

---

3 Guillaume Dustan, *In My Room*, New York: High Risk Books, 1998; Virginie Despentes, *King Kong Theory*, New York: Feminist Press at CUNY, 2010.

Testo Junkie goes far beyond a narrative account of the *affect* of a queer, bohemian experience. It starts producing its *concept*:

> There is nothing to discover in sex or in sexual identity; there is no *inside*. The truth about sex is not a disclosure; it is *sexdesign*. Pharmaco-pornographic biocapitalism does not produce *things*. It produces mobile ideas, living organs, symbols, desires, chemical reactions. (35)

It is not about the personal affects so much as the systematic effects that produce them.

The key objects to the sex-gender industrial complex are synthetic steroids, porn and the internet. What results is a pharma-porno-punk hypermodernity. It was hidden under the Fordist economy and is now revealed by the latter's displacement onto the so-called underdeveloped parts of the world. In what Gilroy calls the overdeveloped world of Europe, America and Japan, this hypermodernity now emerges as the engine of commodification.

If there's an agency within the system, it is not identifiable with a natural body. But there is nevertheless an agency that could have a politics, in and against the mesh.

> What if, in reality, the insatiable bodies of the multitude—their cocks, clitorises, anuses, hormones, and neuro-sexual synapses—what if desire, excitement, sexuality, seduction, and the pleasure of the multitude were all the mainsprings of the creation of value added to the contemporary economy? And what if cooperation were a masturbatory cooperation and not the simple cooperation of brains? (37)

There's a challenge here to rethink what labor is in the twenty-first century. "The raw materials of today's production process are excitation, erection, ejaculation, and pleasure and feelings of self-satisfaction, omnipotent control, and total destruction." The production of sex-affect is now the model for all other kinds of production. "Sex is the corollary of capitalism and war, the mirror of production" (40).

But rather than labor power or the general intellect, Préciadio identifies that which is both producer and produced, the agency of the system, as *potentia gaudendi*, or orgasmic force, a capacity for being excited, exciting and being-excited-with. Not so much the invisible hand as the invisible hand-job. Capital is about "the transformation of our sexual resources into work" (131). Capital tries to privatize *potentia guadendi* but it exists really as an event, a practice, or perhaps an evolutionary process.

I'll come back to this *potentia gaudendi* later. For now, it is crucial to grasp that for Préciado, it does not exist outside of techno-science. It isn't a natural core. In this regard its different to the *sex-pol* of Wilhelm Reich and all that descends from it.[4] The market isn't an outside power repressing or even making work some natural given sexuality. Nor is the body even a coherent unit within this economy. "Sexual bodies are the product of a sort of division of flesh whereby each organ is reduced to a function. Here Préciado comes close to the media archaeology practiced by Chun and others, but of all of the sex organs rather than just the sense organs.

Others have written about how the internet changes certain things about the commodity form, including me.[5] Préciado connects it to two other regimes: pharmacology and pornography. The pharma part includes the production of the Pill, Prozac, Viagra, while the porno part is a corresponding shot list of blow jobs, penetrations, spit roastings and so forth. What the internet plus pharma and porno produce is a distinctive kind of control of women's bodies, while being attentive to the ejaculatory function of bodies coded as male.

To the extent that pharma-porno capitalism produces objects, they are just props for producing subjects. Those subjects are less coherent than they appear. It is more a system of plugging pills or dicks into mouths, dildos into vaginas, inserting silicone into breasts or transferring skin and fat from arms to make penises, spritzing images at eyeballs—and introducing hormones into bodies of all kinds.

It's a squishy version the *control society* thesis, originated by Deleuze and extended by Galloway.[6] Préciado: "A politically programmed

4 Wilhelm Reich, *Sex-Pol: Essays, 1929–1934*, London: Verso, 2013.

5 McKenzie Wark, *Gamer Theory*, Cambridge, MA: Harvard University Press, 2007.

6 "Postscript on Control Societies" in Gilles Deleuze, *Negotiations 1972–1990*, New York: Columbia University Press, 1997.

ejaculation is the currency of this new molecular-informatic control" (77). This is the age of the soft machine. There's a new regime of power more sophisticated than what Foucault called the *disciplinary*. "The body no longer inhabits disciplinary spaces but is inhabited by them (79)."[7]

There are certain tensions in this system. On the one hand, these are technologies which have the potential to disassemble gender binaries, but on the other, there's a massive effort to produce and reproduce exactly those binaries. Pharma-porno capitalism fabricates the idea of a naturalism of sex and gender all the better to make tech that approximates that idea. All the better to sell image and chemical props to make bodies appear as if they follow the codes.

The sex-gender distinction, Preciado usefully reminds us, did not originate in feminism or the trans community, but in the biotech industries. By producing a conceptual distinction between bodily sex and subjective gender, a whole industry could then emerge in which the one could be technically realigned with the other. But to be clear, Préciado does not think that the lack of naturalism of the trans body in any way disqualifies it. All bodies lack this naturalism, and that's no bad thing. Préciado is not against the techno-body, which may have as yet unexplored affordances. Rather, he is against the commodification and disciplinary control of the techno-body.

The existing sex-gender industrial complex produces and reproduces bodies according to a Platonic ideal of male/female forms.[8] These are produced, varied, but also policed by the production of normative codes of gender aesthetics, of recognition, etc., which allow subjects to default towards identities as male or female, hetero or homo, cis or trans. Sex-assignment procedures are based not just on external morphology but also on reproductive capacity and social role—a shifting and unstable terrain anchored by a relentless production of images that reduce the messy nodes of both sex and gender to a binary form.

7 On disciplinary society, see Michel Foucault, *Discipline and Punish*, New York: Vintage Books, 1995.

8 Wark, *Telesthesia*, 176ff.

All kinds of codes are invented and reinvented for every sexualizable zone of the Platonic ideal of the body, but the anus has a problematic status in this schema:

> it creates a short circuit in the division of the sexes. As a center of primordial passivity and a perfect locale for the abject, positioned close to waste and shit, it serves as the universal black hole into which rush genders, sexes, identities, and capital. (71)

No wonder ass-fucking is one of the defining genres of internet-era porn, the site at one and the same time of all kinds of fantasies of male power and domination and of the ever present possibility of their destabilization.

Platonic sexual ideals of male and female are in ever increasing need of tech and image props. Far from being "natural," heterosexual reproduction is part of a vast technical apparatus. There is no *bare life*, there is only a bare techno-life.[9] Heterosexuality is a politically assisted reproductive technology. While it is not part of Préciado's beat, any cis woman (or trans man) who has negotiated a "birth plan" with a hospital will have a lot of thoughts about this! Already by the end of the '50s, the supposedly natural reproductive system was becoming something else. Formula replaced or supplemented breast milk. Oral contraceptive pills were poised to become one of the most commonly ingested prescriptions of them all.

Préciado's thinking builds here on Teresa de Laurentis, and her critique of second-wave feminism's naturalizing of femininity.[10] As we now know, under the universality of the category of woman a host of other things are hiding, from race and class to technologies for producing and sustaining genders. De Laurentis introduced the provocative concept that there are technologies of gender. Gender becomes real when a representation of it becomes a self-representation, and those representations are industrially produced.

9 Giorgio Agamben, *Homo Sacer*, Stanford, CA: Stanford University Press, 1998.

10 Teresa de Laurentis, *Technologies of Gender*, Bloomington IL: Indiana University Press, 1987.

There's a tension between the pharma and porno wings of the sex-gender industrial complex. Image production has at its core a relentlessly Platonic ideal of two genders, and spends quite a bit of time exposing and categorizing ambiguous images in between. But from the point of view of medical, rather than media, production, the category of gender reveals the arbitrary and constructive character of biomedical interventions.

For example, hormone therapy is used to treat "hirsutism" in women. There are standard tests for how hairy is too hairy, and these allow women access to hormone treatments to reduce things like facial hair. But the scale of hairiness is not an objective constant. The white female has a different standard of hairiness than, say, a Jewish or Hispanic one. Medical-technical regimes are complicated applications of boundaries to bodies.

Another kind of example: the different legal-medical regimes that apply to getting a nose job versus a dick job. Your nose is your private property. If you think it is too big or too broad or something, that's your concern, as are any complicated racialized assumptions about the Platonic form of perfection of the nose. But if you want a dick job, that's something else. Removing one, or having one constructed on your body, is not a matter of the body as your private property. It's a matter of your body as a thing whose normative sex and gender is assigned by the state.

Bodies are not such coherent things, then. They are fabricated in meshes of images, tech, laws and so on. "We are not a body without organs, but rather an array of heterogeneous organs unable to be gathered under the same skin" (116). Pharma-porno gender is not just an ideology or an image or a performance. It gets under the skin. It's a political technology, "and the state draws its pleasure from the production and control of our porngore subjectivity."

But it is capital and tech rather than the state that most interests Préciado.

> These artifacts (us) can't exist in a pure state, but only within our enclosed sexual techno-systems. In our role as sexual subjects, we're inhabiting bio-capitalist amusement parks. We are men and

> women of the laboratory, effects of a kind of politico-scientific bio-Platonism. (119)

Préciado usefully extends what is basically a Foucauldian way of thinking onto new terrain, where commodification and power meet.

In some ways this is a book about what Lyotard called *libidinal economies*, which now work on digital and molecular tech that produce sex, gender, sexuality and subjectivity.[11] The pharma and the porno parts of this economy work in opposition as much as together. Porn is mostly propaganda for Platonic sex division. Gender codes are continually mutating, distributing and redistributing, if mostly curling around the same bifurcated distribution.

But when it comes to pharma, there are only techno-genders, of increasingly ambiguous kinds. The cyclist Lance Armstrong and F2M trans men are the product of the same kinds of hormones from the same kinds of labs. Préciado wrote this book while taking testosterone. Préciado thinks of themself at the time as neither testogirl nor technoboy, but a port for inserting the hormone. He is aware that testosterone isn't masculinity. This self-directed endocrinal reprogramming only makes sense together with a certain political agenda. Préciado did it outside of any medical regime, because to partake in that is to give one's body over to the state's decisions about what your sex and gender are or should be, and what technologies will "properly" align these divergent parts of the state's own property.

However, to do so is to risk getting caught in another disciplinary net—the one strung to catch "addicts." If Préciado's testosterone-taking is not sanctioned by one kind of medicalized discourse, it risks another. If Préciado wants to convince a doctor that there is a misfit in this case between sex and gender, there's a regime to deal with that. But what if someone wants to remain ambiguously between genders? If someone wants to take hormones for aesthetic reasons? And what is at stake in taking a drug which transforms the physical body as

11 Jean-François Lyotard, *Libidinal Economy*, Bloomington IL: Indiana University Press, 1993.

its direct goal and changes subjective feeling only secondarily, rather than the other way around? What, in other words, is at stake in the industrialization of the hormone?

The unconscious and the hormone were discovered around the same time. The former is about linguistic signs, but the latter about chemical signals in the body. The study of hormones—endocrinology—is a part of the founding or refounding of a wide range of knowledge on an episteme of communication and information.[12] There were some bumps along the way, as with any new science. (Even Bogdanov fell for some total pseudoscience about monkey glands as a way of promoting longevity and vitality.[13]) In retrospect the surrealist monkey-gland moment in endocrinology actually did foreshadow what the field's ambitions were, if not its methods. "Hormonal theory represents another form of mass communication." Hormones act at a distance—they are a kind of *telesthesia*. As such they can act to "discipline" a body without having to restrain it.

"Hormones are bio-artifacts made of carbon chains, language, images, capital, and collective desires" (160). They are part of a genealogy of the techno-molecular control first of women (the Pill), now of men too: testosterone, Viagra, etc. All sorts of bodies can be produced via artificial hormones, but they are still organized around the Platonic binary. Interestingly, the FDA at first rejected the Pill. The early versions suppressed menstruation altogether, which was too radical a technical reprogramming of gender. It was approved once the period cycle—or something mimicking it—was restored by lower-dose formulations.

If Préciado wants to go beyond Foucault's thinking on the disciplinary apparatus, he also wants to go beyond Butler's thinking about *gender performativity*. Gender isn't just performative at the level of gesture and language, but also via a kind of biomimicry or biodrag. There's a molecular dimension, the pharma dimension. Perhaps we all do biodrag, a mimesis, more or less parodic, of the Platonic gender

12 How could one forget Jean Baudrillard, *Forget Foucault*, Los Angeles: Semiotext(e), 2007?

13 Nikolai Krementsov, *A Martian Stranded on Earth*, Chicago: University of Chicago Press, 2011.

ideals, propping up our bodies with chemical assistance as much as dress codes.

These relatively new kinds of molecular power modify bodies themselves as living platforms:

> We are certainly still confronting a form of social control, but this time it's a matter of control lite, a bubbly type of control, full of colors and wearing Mickey Mouse ears and the Brigitte Bardot low-cut look, as opposed to the cold, disciplinary architecture of the panoptic illustrated by Foucault. (211)

Weaponized adorables for grown-ups.[14] The movie *Sucker Punch* could well be a kind of weird Hollywood allegory for all that.

In a nightmare image, Préciado writes of

> a new type of high-tech heterosexuality ... : the techno-Barbie, remaining eternally young and super-sexualized, almost entirely infertile and non-menstruating but always ready for artificial insemination and accompanied by a sterile super-macho whose erections are technically produced by a combination of Viagra and audio-visual pornographic codes. (220)

Which suggests to me that there are no cis-gender bodies, as the term implies that one could be "on the side" of a pregiven standard, when all such standards are now products of a sex-gender industrial complex. The innovation of Préciado's work is to insist so thoroughly that all of sex, gender and identity are on the same level, all produced industrially, and by the same systems.

Préciado does not mention hormone-replacement therapy for menopausal women, but one could add that to this picture. The next frontier for the sex-gender industrial complex is probably marketing hormones to men without undermining their sense of masculinity. The masculine body has its own honor codes of supposed naturalism.

---

14 Rachel Law and McKenzie Wark, *W.A.N.T.: Weaponized Adorables Negotiation Tactics*, Iceland: Oddi, 2013.

Taking steroids to improve athletic performance is somehow always "wrong," even if Viagra can now be an accepted chemical modification of the male body for "erectile dysfunction."

For Préciado, liberal feminism made a pact with the state and the pharmacology industry. It is not that defending Planned Parenthood is a bad thing, but that the unexamined component of state intervention in reproduction is the hormonal transformation of the body. Préciado is also wary of feminisms that are complicit with the state, including on issues of pornography. It hardly bears repeating that when states increase the policing of pornography it is usually images of nonnormative sexualities that are criminalized or excluded.[15]

"Pornography is sexuality transformed into spectacle" (266). It is now the paradigm of the culture industry. "The culture industry is *porn envy*" (271). Porn is the management of the excitation-frustration circuit. The culture industry now wants to produce the same physiological effect. Porn may have more to do with freak shows and the circus than cinema. "Paris Hilton represents the zenith of the sexopolitical production of the luxury white heterosexual techno-bitch" (280). Or more recently—the Kardashians. But it only appears that they are living a reality-TV life of languid uselessness: their whole lives are under surveillance. Pornography is doubled by scrutiny and control of the affects and discharges of bodies.

Porn is regulated by a kind of "Spermatic Platonism" in which only the cum shot is real. Porn produces the illusion of *potentia gaudendi*, when excitation is actually a more or less involuntary response. However, "pornography tells the *performative* truth about sexuality" (270). One can claim that the sex in porn is merely performed and is thus unreal, or that the bodies are unreal, but this very unreality is precisely the Platonic normative forms around which the whole sex-gender industrial complex is made to circulate.

Not only sex but labor is becoming pornified. In the overdeveloped world, we are all coming to work in a porn factory fueled by bodily fluids, synthetic hormones, silicon, stimulants, mood regulators and digital signs. Sexual labor transforms *potentia gaudendi* into

15 Carol Vance (ed.), *Pleasure and Danger*, New York: Routledge, 1984.

commodities. If one were to look for what Gramsci would call the *organic intellectuals* of labor now, it would be among pornographers and sex workers.[16] Sex workers are still the "other" to many "respectable" people, but perhaps a wider definition of sex work would help. On a spa day with Virginie Despentes, Préciado discovers the erotics of the personal care industry. Perhaps some people would just rather have the actual massage than the happy ending, but in a way it is all sex work. Or perhaps, to riff off Préciado's line of thought further, we should think about both sex workers and "gender workers" as on a continuum in the industrial production of bodies and their identities.

At variance here from McRobbie, Préciado wants to look at a *pornification of labor* rather than a feminization of labor. The concept of a feminization of labor assumes certain things about femininity. For one thing, it "omits the cum shot" (49). And it still buys into Platonic gender absolutes. Affective labor is a girl thing; effective labor is a boy thing. Flexibility is a girl thing; stability is a boy thing.

Préciado is also hostile to the *cognitive* or *immaterial labor* thesis that bedevils the thought of the inheritors of Italian workerist theory such as Boutang, Virno, Lazzarato and Berardi. "None of them mention the effects on their philosopher's cocks of a dose of Viagra accompanied by the right image" (293). Perhaps this is a time of über-material, not immaterial, labor.

And it is not a "sexual division of labor" but a pornographic one. The term "sexual" in sexual division of labor silently sanctions a hetero view of reproduction, as if it goes without saying that only hetero reproduction is normal. It also takes the asymmetries of the hetero sex act as the norm. The list of body types that can be willingly penetrated includes at least the bodies of cis females, trans females and gay men. The sexual division of labor concept also leaves out the technical apparatus within which it is produced.

There is no immaterial labor, nor is there a *general intellect*. There is general sex. This might be another name for the *potentia guardini*, "the impulse for communal joy that travels through the multitude,

16 Antonio Gramsci, *Selections from the Prison Notebooks*, New York: International Publishers, 1971.

convulsing the totality of excitable producer-bodies of capital" (309). Modernity is the sexualization of the domestic and the domestication of the sexual. The sexual-domestic coupling has mostly taken place under the sign of private property. (Infidelity is theft.) But there's another side: *potentia guardini*, that which is both produced by, and enfettered by, the sex-gender industrial complex.

Can we just admit that immaterial labor was a terrible, useless concept? What is refreshing about low theory is that when it works it starts from actual experiences, then it appropriates and adapts concepts to fit the articulation of the experience. It is always a kind of détournement or highjacking of high theory for other purposes.[17] As such it tends to shun what might otherwise be endlessly productive research programs just for lack of evidence that their conceptual objects actually correspond to anything. Hence Préciado pretty ruthlessly cuts through some decades of social theory.

Préciado doesn't see psychoanalysis, as traditionally understood, as all that much help either:

> The father and mother are already dead. We are the children of Hollywood, porn, the Pill, the TV trashcan, the internet, and cyber-capitalism. The cis-girl wants to transform her body into a consumable image for the greatest number of gazes … She wants her pornification … to transform her body into abstract capital. (408)

Unlike Butler, Préciado finds *queer* becoming too commodified. Critical thought and practice has to move on. But critical theory has to steer away from both the neutered objects of speculative realism (Morton) and the messianic leap of spiritualized subjects (Žižek). It has to talk about labor, but not just the kind involved in pretty things like fashion (McRobbie) or other supposedly immaterial practices (Berardi). "Let us be worthy of our own fall and imagine for the time left the components of a new porno-punk philosophy."

Préciado's program is to transform minority knowledge into collective experimentation, to work for the common ownership of the

17 Debord, *Society of the Spectacle*, 129ff

biocodes. Like Suely Rolnik, he sees psychiatry as a foreclosing of aesthetic responses to creating subjectivity.[18] Préciado puts gender dissent in an aesthetic context, rather than one of dysphoria, pathology, etc. Préciado compares their taking of testosterone to Walter Benjamin taking hash, or Freud taking cocaine, or Bogdanov's blood exchange: a protocol for experiment not sanctioned by the state or the professions, and to be understood more as the construction of situations in everyday life.

Political subjectivity does not emerge when a subject recognizes itself in its representation, but when it doesn't. That break creates the space not just for another kind of representation, but another life. It's time to become gender pirates or gender hackers: "We're copyleft users who consider sex hormones free and open biocodes" (55). Préciado calls for a "molecular revolution of the genders" (235). There's no natural or private acts to which to return.

Praxis, then, is "a matter of inventing other common, shared, collective, and copyleft forms of the dominant pornographic representations and standardized sexual consumption." Those who are its objects can become its subjects. The organic intellectuals of such a movement are pornographers and sex workers as theorists. And as for practice, "since the '70s, the only major revolution has been carried out by gays listening to music while getting high and fucking" (417).

I love the following line in particular, as it could have come from (and yet critique) my *A Hacker Manifesto*: "Power experienced slippage; it shifted, throughout the previous century, from the earth to manufacturing, then toward information and life" (277). But Préciado opens up a space for thinking that last bit—life—in a fresh way. Desire and sexuality, like information, or even *as* information, defy ownership: one's possession of a bit of information (or desire, or sex, or gender) doesn't take it away from another. Sharing multiplies desire, sex and gender.

But the idea of sexual liberation is obsolete. There's no preexisting natural state of sex that is repressed, as we all learned from Foucault,

18 Félix Guattari and Suely Rolnik, *Molecular Revolution in Brazil*, Los Angeles: Semiotext(e), 2008.

whether from a "street" photocopy or in grad school. Now we have to think about how to hack pharma-porno domination from within. Préciado has some slogans for it, each of which could equally well name a punk band or a conference: FreeFuckware! OpenGender! BodyPunk! PenetratedState! PostPorn! There is monstrous fun to be had. There are new bodies and their relations to sexdesign. But it all involves the prior step of letting go of a theoretical ideal of species-being, and working experimentally with actual cyborg assemblies instead. Préciado: "Humanity does not exist under the sign of the divine … but of the monstrous" (239).

16.

Wendy Chun: Programming Politics

Is the relation *between* the analog and the digital itself analog or digital? That might be one way of thinking the contrast between the work of Alex Galloway and Wendy Hui Kyong Chun. I write in the following chapter about Galloway's notion of software as a *simulation* of ideology. Here I take up Chun's concept of software as an *analogy* for ideology, through a reading of her book *Programmed Visions: Software and Memory.*[1]

Software as analogy is a strange thing. It illustrates an unknown through an unknowable. It participates in, and embodies, some strange properties of information. Chun: "digital information has divorced tangibility from permanence" (5). Or as I put it in *A Hacker Manifesto*, the relation between matter as support for information becomes arbitrary.[2] The history of the reification of information passes through the history of the production of software as a separate object of a distinct labor process and form of property. Chun puts this in more Foucauldian terms:

> the remarkable process by which software was transformed from a service in time to a product, the hardening of relations into a thing, the externalization of information from the self, coincides with and

---

1 Wendy Hui Kyong Chun, *Programmed Visions: Software and Memory*, Cambridge, MA: MIT Press, 2011.

2 McKenzie Wark, *A Hacker Manifesto*, Cambridge, MA: Harvard University Press, 2004. See the "Information" chapter.

> embodies larger changes within what Michel Foucault has called *governmentality*. (6)

Software coincides with what Chun follows Foucault and Brown in calling the *neoliberal*. I'm not entirely sure "neoliberal" holds much water as a general concept, but the general distinction would be that in liberalism, the state has to be kept out of the market, whereas in neoliberalism, the market becomes the model for the state. In both, there's no sovereign power governing from above so much as a *governmentality* that produces self-activating subjects whose "free" actions can't be known in advance. Producing such free agents requires a management of populations, a practice of *biopower*.

Such might be a simplified explanation of the standard model. What Chun adds is the role of computing in the management of populations and the cultivation of individuals as "human capital." The neoliberal subject feels mastery and "empowerment" via interfaces to computing which inform the user about past events and possible futures, becoming, in effect, the future itself. The "source" of this mode of governmentality is source code itself. Code becomes *logos*: in the beginning was the code. On some level the user knows code does not work magically on its own but rather controls a machine, but the user acts as if code had such a power. Neither the work of the machine nor the labor of humans figures much at all.

Code as logos organizes the past as stored data and presents it via an interface as the means for units of human capital to place their bets. "Software as thing is inseparable from the externalization of memory, from the dream and nightmare of an all-encompassing archive that constantly regenerates and degenerates, that beckons us forward and disappears before our very eyes" (11). As Berardi and others have noted, this is not the tragedy of alienation so much as what Baudrillard called the *ecstasy of communication*.[3]

Software is a crucial component in producing the appearance of transparency, where the user can manage their own data and imagine

3 Jean Baudrillard, *The Ecstasy of Communication*, Los Angeles: Semiotext(e), 2012.

they see all the variables relevant to their investment decisions about their own human capital. Oddly, this visibility is produced by something invisible, that hides its workings. Hence computing becomes a substitutable metaphor for everything we believe is invisible yet generates visible effects. The economy, nature, the cosmos, love are all figured as black boxes that can be known by the data visible on their interfaces.

The interface appears as a device of some kind of *cognitive mapping*, although not the kind Fredric Jameson had in mind, which would be an aesthetic intuition of the totality of capitalist social relations.[4] What we get is a map of a map, of exchange relations among quantifiable units. On the screen of the device, whose workings we don't know, we see clearly the data about the workings of other things we don't know. Just as the device seems reducible to the code that makes the data appear, so too must the other systems it models be reducible to the code that makes their data appear.

But this is not so much an attribute of computing in general as a certain historical version of it, where software emerged as a second- (and third-, and fourth- . . .) order way of presenting the kinds of things the computer could do. Chun: "Software emerged as a thing—as an iterable textual program—through a process of commercialization and commodification that has made code logos: code as source, code as true representation of action, indeed code as conflated with, and substituting for, action" (18).

One side effect of the rise of software was the fantasy of the all-powerful programmer. I don't think it is entirely the case that the coder is an ideal neoliberal subject. Rather, this figure was absorbed into, and subtly transformed, a range of existing archetypal figures. The programmer could be either a figure of control or rebellion and much else. Sometimes it was a figure of order; sometimes a romantic one, an outlaw looking for *exploits*.[5]

4 Alberto Toscano and Jeff Kinkle, *Cartographies of the Absolute*, Winchester, UK: Zero Books, 2015.

5 Alexander R. Galloway and Eugene Thacker, *The Exploit: A Theory of Networks*, Minneapolis: University of Minnesota Press, 2007.

I think it is more helpful to focus less on the supposedly unique attributes of the programmer and to ask rather what kind of labor she or he does, and what other kinds of labor it might be like. The very peculiar qualities of information, in part a product of this very technical-scientific trajectory, makes the coder a primary form of an equally peculiar kind of labor. But labor is curiously absent from parts of Chun's thinking. The figure of the coder as romantic outlaw hacker may indeed be largely myth, but it is one that poses questions of agency that don't typically appear when one thinks through Foucault.[6]

Contra Galloway, Chun does not want to take as given the technical identity of software as means of control with the machine it controls. She wants to keep the materiality of the machine in view at all times. Code isn't everything, even if that is how code itself gets us to think. "This amplification of the power of source code also dominates critical analyses of code, and the valorization of software as a 'driving layer' conceptually constructs software as neatly layered" (21).

Code becomes fetish, as Haraway has also argued.[7] However, this is a strange kind of fetish, not entirely analogous to the religious, commodity or sexual fetish. Where those fetishes supposedly offer imaginary means of control, code *really does* control things. One could even reverse the claim here. What if *not* accepting that code has control was the mark of a fetishism? One where particular objects have to be interposed as talismans of a power relationship that is abstract and invisible, yet real?

I think one could sustain this view and still accept much of the nuance of Chun's very interesting and persuasive readings of key moments and texts in the history of computing. She argues, for instance, that code ought not to be conflated with its execution. One cannot run "source" code itself. It has to be compiled. The relation between source code and machine code is not a mere technical identity. "Source code only becomes a source after the fact" (24).

---

6 Gabriella Coleman, *Coding Freedom*, Princeton, NJ: Princeton University Press, 2012.

7 McKenzie Wark, *Molecular Red*, London: Verso, 2015, 132ff.

Mind you, one could push this even further than Chun does. She grounds source code in machine code and machine code in machine architectures. But these in turn only run if there is an energy "source," and can only exist if manufactured out of often quite rare materials.[8] All of which, in this day and age, are subject to forms of computerized command to bring such materials and their labors together. To reduce computers to command, and indeed not just computers but whole political economies, might not be so much an anthropomorphizing of the computer as a recognition that information has become a rather *nonhuman* thing.

I would argue that perhaps the desire to see the act of commanding an unknown, invisible device through interface, through software, in which code appears as source and logos is at once a way to make sense of neoliberal political-economic opacity and indeed irrationality. But perhaps command itself is not quite so commanding, and is a gesture that only appears to restore the subject to itself. Maybe command is not "empowering" of anything but itself. Information has control over *both* objects and subjects.

To develop this idea, Chun usefully recalls a moment from the history of computing—the "ENIAC girls." Early computing had a gendered division of labor, where men worked out the mathematical problem and women had to embody the problem in a series of steps performed by the machine. "One could say that programming became programming and software became software when the command structure shifted from commanding a 'girl' to commanding a machine" (29).

Although Chun does not quite frame it as such, one could see the postwar career of software as the result of struggles over labor. Software removes the need to program every task directly in machine language. Software offers the coder an environment in which to write instructions for the machine, or the user to write problems for the machine to solve. Software appears via an interface that makes the machine invisible but offers instead ways to think about the

8 Jussi Parikka, *A Geology of Media*, Minneapolis: University of Minnesota Press, 2015.

instructions or the problem in a way more intelligible to the human and more efficient in terms of human abilities and time constraints.

Software obviates the need to write in machine language. This made programming a higher-order task, based on mathematical and logical operations rather than machine operations. But it also made programming available as a kind of industrialized labor. Certain tasks could be automated. The routine running of the machine could be separated from the machine's solution of particular tasks. One could even see it as in part a kind of *deskilling*.[9]

The separation of software from hardware also enables the separation of certain programming tasks in software from each other. Hence the rise of *structured programming* as a way of managing quality and labor discipline when programming becomes an industry. Structured programming enables a division of labor and secures the running of the machine from routine programming tasks. The result might be less efficient from the point of view of organizing the "work" of the machine but more efficient from the point of view of organizing human labor. Structured programming recruits the machine into the task of managing itself. It is a step towards *object-oriented programming*, which further hides the machine, and also the interior of other "objects," from the ones with which the programmer is tasked within the division of labor.

Like Wendling, Chun notes that Charles Babbage rather than Marx foresaw the industrialization of cognitive tasks and the application of the division of labor to them.[10] Neither foresaw software as a distinct commodity; or (I would add) one that might be the product of a quite distinct kind of labor. More could be said here about the evolution of the private property relation that will enable software to become a thing made by labor rather than a service that merely applies naturally occurring mathematical relations to the running of machines.

Crucial to Chun's analysis is the way source code becomes a thing that erases execution from view. It hides the labor of the machine,

9 Harry Braverman, *Labor and Monopoly Capital*, New York: Monthly Review Press, 1998.

10 See also Nick Dyer-Witheford, *Cyber-Marx*, Urbana: Illinois University Press, 1999, 2–5.

which becomes something like one of Derrida's *specters.*[11] It makes the actions of the human at the machine appear as a powerful relation. "Embedded within the notion of instruction as source and the drive to automate computing—relentlessly haunting them—is a constantly repeated narrative of liberation and empowerment, wizards and (ex)slaves" (41).

I wonder if this might be a general quality of labor processes. A car mechanic does not need to know the complexities of the metallurgy involved in making a modern engine block. She or he just needs to know how to replace the blown gasket. What might be more distinctive is the way that these particular "objects," made of information stored on some random material surface or other, can also be forms of private property, and can be designed in such a way as to render the information in which they traffic also private property. There might be more distinctive features in how the code-form interacts with the property-form than in the code-form alone.

If one viewed the evolution of those forms together as the product of a series of struggles, one might then have a way of explaining the particular contours of today's devices. Chun: "The history of computing is littered with moments of 'computer liberation' that are also moments of greater obfuscation" (45). This all turns on the question of who is freed from what. But in Chun such things are more the effects of a structure than the result of a struggle or negotiation.

Step by step, the user is "freed" from not only having to know about her or his machine, but then also from ownership of what runs on the machine, and then from ownership of the data she or he produces on the machine. There's a question of whether the first kind of "liberation" —from having to know the machine—necessarily leads to the other all on its own—to "liberation" from owning the information we produce. Rather, it may act in combination with the class conflicts that drove the emergence of a software-driven mode of production with intellectual property as the form of the relations of production.

In short: programmers appeared to become more powerful but more remote from their machines; users appeared to become more

11 Jacques Derrida, *Specters of Marx*, New York: Routledge, 2006.

powerful but more remote from their machines. The programmer and then the user work not with the materiality of the machine but with information. Information becomes a thing, perhaps in the sense of a fetish, but perhaps also in the senses of a form of property and an actual power over and against those who work it.

But let's not lose sight of the gendered thread to the argument. Programming is an odd profession, in that at a time when women were making inroads into once male-dominated professions, programing went the other way, becoming more a male domain. Perhaps it is because it started out as a kind of feminine clerical labor but became—through the intermediary of software—a priestly caste, an engineering and academic profession. Perhaps its male bias is in part an artifact of timing: programming becomes a profession rather late. I would compare it then to the well-known story of how obstetrics pushed midwives out of the birth business, masculinizing and professionalizing it, now over a hundred years ago; but more recently it has been challenged as a male-dominated profession by the reentry of women as professionals.[12]

My argument would be that while the timing is different, programming might not be all the different from other professions in its claims to exclusive mastery based on knowledge of protocols shorn of certain material and practical dimensions. In this regard, is it all that different from architecture? What might need explaining is rather how software intervened in, and transforms, *all* the professions. Most of them have been redefined as kinds of information-work. In many cases this can lead to deskilling and casualization, on the one hand; and to the circling of the wagons around certain higher-order, but information-based, functions on the other. It is not that programming is an example of "neoliberalism," so much as that neoliberalism has become a catch-all term for a collection of symptoms of the role of computing in its current form in the production of information as a control layer.

Hence my problem with the ambiguity in formulations such as this: "Software becomes axiomatic. As a first principle, it fastens in place a certain neoliberal logic of cause and effect, based on the erasure of

12 Silvia Federici, *Caliban and the Witch,* New York: Autonomedia, 2004.

execution and the privileging of programming" (49). What if it is not that software enables neoliberalism, but rather that neoliberalism is just a rather inaccurate way of describing a software-centric mode of production? The invisible machine joins the list of other invisible operators: slaves, women, workers. They don't need to be all that visible so long as they do what they're told. They need only to be seen to do what they are supposed to do. Invisibility is the other side of power.[13] To the extent that software has power or is power, it isn't an imaginary fetish.

Rather than fetish and ideology, perhaps we could use some different concepts, what Bogdanov calls *substitution* and the *basic metaphor*.[14] In this way of thinking, *actual* organizational forms through which labor are controlled get projected onto other, unknown phenomena. We *substitute* the form of organization we know and experience for forms we don't know—life, the universe, etc. The *basic metaphors* in operation are thus likely to be those of the dominant form of labor organization, and its causal model will become a whole worldview.

That seems to me a good basic sketch for how code, software and information became terms that could be substituted into any and every problem, from understanding the brain, or love, or nature or evolution. For example, *object-oriented programming* gets picked up, shorn of this technical and economic history, and used as a metaphor by Morton and others—as *object-oriented ontology*. Computation creates a way of thinking about relations of power, even of mapping them, in a world in which both objects and subjects can be controlled by information.

As Chun acknowledges, computers have become metaphor machines. From being universal machines in Turing's mathematical sense, they become universal machines also in a poetic sense.[15] The computer is in Chun's terms a sort of *analogy*, or in Galloway's a *simulation*. This is the sense in which for Chun the relation between analog and digital is analog, while for Galloway it is digital. Seen from

13 Nicholas Mirzoeff, *The Right to Look*, Durham, NC: Duke University Press, 2011.

14 Wark, *Molecular Red*, 13ff.

15 Andrew Hodges, *Alan Turing: The Enigma*, Princeton, NJ: Princeton University Press, 2014.

the machine side, one sees code as an analogy for the world it controls; seen from the software side, one sees a digital simulation of the world to be controlled. Woven together with Marx's circuit of money -> commodity -> money, there is now another: digital -> analog -> digital. The question of the times might be how the former got subsumed into the latter.

For Chun, the promise of what the "intelligence community" calls "topsight" through computation proves illusory. The production of cognitive maps via computation obscures the means via which they are made. But is there not a kind of modernist aesthetic at work here, where the truth of appearances is in revealing the materials via which appearances are made? I want to read her readings in the literature of computing a bit differently. I don't think it's a matter of the truth of code lying in its execution by and in and as the machine. If so, why stop there? Why not further relate the machine to its manufacture? I am also not entirely sure one can say, after the fact, that software encodes a neoliberal logic. Rather, one might read for signs of struggles over what kind of power information could become.

This brings us to the history of interfaces. Chun starts with the legendary SAGE air defense network, the largest computer system ever built. It used 60,000 vacuum tubes and took three megawatts to run. It was finished in 1963 and already obsolete, although it led to the SABRE airline reservation system. Bits of old SAGE hardware were used in film sets where blinky computers were called for—as in *Logan's Run*.

SAGE is an origin story for ideas of real-time computing and interface design, allowing "direct" manipulation that simulates engagement by the user. It is also an example of what Brenda Laurel would later think in terms of *computers as theater*. Like a theater, computers offer what Paul Edwards calls a *closed world* of interaction, where one has to suspend disbelief and enter into the pleasures of a predictable world.[16]

The choices offered by an interface make change routine and shape a notion of what is possible. We know that our "folders" and

16 Paul Edwards, *The Closed World*, Cambridge MA: MIT Press, 1997; Brenda Laurel, *Computers as Theater*, Upper Saddle River NJ: Addison Wesley, 2013.

"desktops" are not real but we use them as if they were anyway. Mind you, a paper file is already a metaphor. The world is not better or more poorly represented by my paper folders than it is by my digital "folders," even if they are not quite the same kind of representation.

Chun: "Software and ideology fit each other perfectly because both try to map the tangible effects of the intangible and to posit the intangible causes through visible cues" (71). Perhaps this is one response to the disorientation of the postmodern moment. Galloway would say rather that software simulates ideology. I think in my mind it's a matter of software emerging as a basic metaphor, a handy model from the leading labor processes of the time substituted for processes unknown. Cognitive mapping is now something we all have to do all the time, and in a somewhat restricted form—mapping data about costs and benefits, risks and rewards—rather than grasping the totality of commodified social relations.

In perhaps the boldest intuition in the book, Chun thinks that computation is part of a general disposition, an *episteme*, at work in modern thought, where the inscrutable body of a present phenomenon could be understood as the visible product of an invisible process that was in some sense encoded. Such a process requires an archive, a past upon which to work, and a process via which future progress emerges out of past information.

JCR Licklider, Douglas Engelbart and other figures in postwar computing wanted machines that were networked, ran in real time and had interfaces that allowed the user to "navigate" complex problems while "driving" an interface that could be learned step by step. Chun: "Engelbart's system underscores the key neoliberal quality of personal empowerment—the individual's ability to see, steer, and creatively destroy—as vital social development" (83). To me it makes more sense to say that the symptoms shorthanded by the commonplace "neoliberal" are better thought of as "Engelbartian." His famous "demo" of interactive computing for "intellectual workers" ought now to be thought of as the really significant cultural artifact of 1968.[17]

Chun:

17 Easily found online as Douglas Engelbart, 'The Mother of All Demos', 1968.

> Software has become a common-sense shorthand for culture, and hardware shorthand for nature…In our so-called post-ideological society, software sustains and depoliticizes notions of ideology and ideology critique. People may deny ideology, but they don't deny software—and they attribute to software, metaphorically, greater powers that have been attributed to ideology. Our interactions with software have disciplined us, created certain expectations about cause and effect, offered us pleasure and power—a way to navigate our neoliberal world—that we believe should be transferrable elsewhere. It has also fostered our belief in the world as neoliberal; as an economic game that follows certain rules. (92)

But does software really "depoliticize," or does it change what politics is or could be?

Digital media both program the future and the past. The archive is first and last a public record of private property, which was why the situationists practiced détournement, to treat it not as property but as the *commons*. Political power requires control of the archive, or better, of memory—as Google surely has figured out.[18] Chun:

> This always there-ness of new media links it to the future as future simple. By saving the past, it is supposed to make knowing the future easier. The future is technology because technology enables us to see trends and hence to make projections—it allows us to intervene on the future based on stored programs and data that compress time and space. (97)

Here is what Bogdanov would recognize as a *basic metaphor* for our times: "To repeat, software is axiomatic. As a first principle, it fastens in place a certain logic of cause and effect, a causal pleasure that erases execution and reduces programming to an act of writing" (101). Mind, genes, culture, economy, even metaphor itself can be understood as software. Software produces order from order, but as such it is part of a larger episteme:

---

18 Siva Vaidhyanathan, *The Googlization of Everything*, Berkeley: University of California Press, 2011.

> The drive for software—for an independent program that conflates legislation and execution—did not arise solely from within the field of computation. Rather, code as logos existed elsewhere and emanated from elsewhere—it was part of a larger epistemic field of biopolitical programmability. (103)

As indeed Foucault's own thought may be too.

In a particularly interesting development, Chun argues that both computing and modern biology derive from this same episteme. It is not that biology developed a fascination with genes as code under the influence of computing. Rather, both computing and genetics develop out of the same space of concepts. Actually, early cybernetic theory had no concept of software. It isn't in Norbert Wiener or Claude Shannon.[19] Their work treated information as *signal*. In the former, the signal is *feedback*, and in the latter, the signal has to defeat *noise*. How then did information thought of as code and control develop both in cybernetics and also in biology? Both were part of the same governmental drive to understand the visible as controlled by an invisible program that derives present from past and mediates between populations and individuals.

A key text for Chun here is Erwin Schrödinger's *What is Life?* (1944), which posits the gene as a kind of "crystal."[20] He saw living cells as run by a kind of military or industrial governance, each cell following the same internalized order(s). This resonates with Shannon's conception of information as negative entropy (a measure of randomness) and Wiener's of information as positive entropy (a measure of order). Schrödinger's text made possible a view of life that was not *vitalist*—no special spirit is invoked—but which could explain organization above the level of a protein, which was about the level of complexity that Needham and other biochemists could explain at the time. But it comes at the price of substituting "crystal," or "form," for the organism itself.

19 Norbert Wiener, *Cybernetics*, Cambridge MA: MIT Press, 1965; Claude Shannon and Warren Weaver, *The Mathematical Theory of Communication*, Bloomington IL, University of Illinois Press, 1971.

20 Erwin Schrödinger, *What Is Life?*, Cambridge: Cambridge University Press, 2012.

Drawing on early Foucault, Chun thinks some key elements of a certain episteme of knowledge are embodied in Schrödinger's text. Foucault's interest was in discontinuities. Hence his metaphor of "archeology," which gives us the image of discontinuous strata. It was never terribly clear in Foucault what accounts for "mutations" that form the boundaries of these discontinuities. The basic metaphor of "archaeology" presents the work of the philosopher of knowledge as a sort of detached "fieldwork" in the geological strata of the archive.

Chun: "The archeological project attempts to map what is visible and what is articulable" (113). One has to ask whether Foucault's work was perhaps more an exemplar than a critique of a certain mode of knowledge. Foucault said that Marx was a thinker who swam in the nineteenth century as a fish swims in water.[21] Perhaps now we can say that Foucault is a thinker who swam in the twentieth century as a torpedo swims in water. Computing, genetics and Foucault's archaeology are about discontinuous and discrete knowledge.

Still, he has his uses. Chun puts Foucault to work to show how there is a precursor to the conceptual architecture of computing in genetics and eugenics. The latter was a political program, supposedly based on genetics, whose mission was improving the "breeding stock" of the human animal. But humans proved very hard to program, so perhaps that drive ended up in computing instead.

The "source" for modern genetics is usually acknowledged to be the rediscovered experiments of Gregor Mendel.[22] Mendelian genetics is in a sense "digital." The traits he studied are binary pairs. The appearance of the pea (phenotype) is controlled by a code (genotype). The recessive-gene concept made eugenic selective breeding rather difficult in practice. But it is a theory of a "hard" inheritance, where nature is all and nurture does not matter. As such, it could still be used in debates about forms of biopower on the side of eugenic rather than welfare policies.

Interestingly, Chun makes the (mis)use of Mendelian genetics as

21 Foucault, *Order of Things*, New York: Vintage, 1973, 261–2.

22 A rich topic. Here I'll just mention JBS Haldane, *The Causes of Evolution*, Princeton NJ: Princeton University Press, 1990. One of the founding texts of population genetics, it is rather prescient about what the field might imply.

a eugenic theory a precursor to cybernetics. "Eugenics is based on a fundamental belief in the knowability of the human body, an ability to 'read' its genes and to program humanity accordingly…Like cybernetics, eugenics is a means of 'governing' or navigating nature" (122). The notion of information as a source code was already at work in genetics long before either computing or modern biology. Control of, and by, code as a means of fostering life, agency, communication and the qualities of freely acting human capital is then an idea with a long history. One might ask whether it might not correspond to certain tendencies in the organization of labor at the time. What links machinic and biological information systems is the idea of some kind of archive of information out of which a source code articulates future states of a system. But memory came to be conflated with storage. The active process of both forgetting and remembering turns into a vast and endless storage of data.

Where I would want to diverge from Chun is on two points. One has to do with the ontological status of *information*, and the second has to do with its political-economic status. In Chun I find that information is already reduced to the machines that execute its functions, and then those machines are inserted into a historical frame that sees only governmentality and not a political economy. Chun: "The information travelling through computers is not 1s and 0s; beneath binary digits and logic lies a messy, noisy world of signals and interference. Information—if it exists—is always embodied, whether in a machine or an animal" (139). Yes, information has no autonomous and prior existence. In that sense neither Chun nor Galloway nor I are Platonists. But I don't think information is reducible to the material substrate that carries it.

Information is a slippery term, meaning both order, neg-entropy, form, on the one hand, and something like signal or communication on the other. These are related, but not the same. The way I would reconstruct technical-intellectual history would put the stress on the dual production of information both as a concept and as a fact in the design of machines that could be controlled by it, but where information is meant as signal, and as signal becomes the means of producing order and form.

One could then think about how information was historically produced as a reality, in much the same way that energy was produced as a reality in an earlier moment in the history of technics. In both cases certain features of natural history are discovered and repeated within technical history. Or rather, features of what will *retrospectively* become natural history. For us there was always information, just as for the Victorians there was always energy (but no such thing as information). The *nonhuman* enters human history through the *inhuman* mediation of a technics where labor deploys it.

So I take the point of refusing to let information float free and become a kind of new theological essence or given, wafting about in the "cloud."[23] But there is a certain historical truth to the production of a world where information can have arbitrary and reversible relations to materiality. Particularly when that rather unprecedented relation between information and its substrate is a control relation. Information controls other aspects of materiality, and also controls energy. Of the three aspects of materiality—matter, energy and information—the latter now appears as a form of controlling the other two.

Here I think it worth pausing to consider information not just as governmentality but also as commodity. Chun:

> If a commodity is, as Marx famously argued, a "sensible supersensible thing," information would seem to be its complement: a supersensible sensible thing...That is, if information is a commodity, it is not simply due to historical circumstances or to structural changes, it is also because commodities, like information, depend on a ghostly abstract. (135)

As retrospective readers of how natural history enters social history, perhaps we need to reread Marx from the point of view of information. He had a fairly good grasp of thermodynamics, as Wendling observes, but information as we know it today did not yet exist.

23 Tung-Hui Hu, *A Prehistory of the Cloud*, Cambridge, MA: MIT Press, 2006.

To what extent is information the missing "complement" to the commodity? There is only one kind of (proto-)information in Marx, and that is the *general equivalent*—money. The materiality of a thing—let's say "coats"—its use value, is doubled by its informational quantity, its exchange value, and it is exchanged against the general equivalent, or information as quantity. But notice the missing step. Before one can exchange the thing "coats" for money, one needs the information "coats." What the general equivalent meets in the market is not the thing but another kind of information—let's call it the *general nonequivalent*—a general, shared, agreed-upon kind of information about the *qualities* of things.[24]

Putting these sketches together, one might then ask what role computing plays in the rise of a political economy (or a post-political one) in which not only is exchange value dominant over use value, but where use value further recedes behind the general nonequivalent, or information about use value. In such a world, fetishism would be mistaking the body for the information, not the other way around, for it is the information that controls the body.

Thus we want to think bodies matter, lives matter, things matter—when actually they are just props for the accumulation of information and information as accumulation. "Neo"liberal is perhaps too retro a term for a world which does not just set bodies "free" to accumulate property, but sets information "free" from bodies, and makes information property in itself. Perhaps bodies are shaped now by more than one kind of code. Perhaps it is no longer a time in which to use Foucault and Derrida to explain computing, but rather to see them as side effects of the era of computing itself.[25]

---

24 McKenzie Wark, 'Capture All', *Avery Review*, 2015, at averyreview.com.

25 Lydia Liu, *The Freudian Robot*, Chicago: University of Chicago Press, 2011.

17.

Alexander Galloway: The Intraface

The thing about an interface is that when it is working smoothly you hardly notice it is there at all. Rather like ideology, really. Perhaps in some peculiar way it is ideology. That might be one of the starting points of Alexander Galloway's book *The Interface Effect.* Galloway revives, and revises, Fredric Jameson's idea of *cognitive mapping*, which might in shorthand be described as a way of tracing how the *totality* of social relations in our commodifed world show up, in spite of themselves, in a particular works of literature, art or media.[1]

Take the TV show *24.* In what sense could one say that the show is "political"? It certainly appears so in a "red state" sort of way. The Jack Bauer character commits all sorts of crimes, including torture, in the name of "national security." But perhaps there's more to it. Galloway draws attention to how certain formal properties of narrative and editing might help us see "politics" at work in *24* in other ways.

24 is curiously a show about the totality, but in a rather reactionary way. Characters are connected to something much greater than their petty interests, but that thing is national security, whose overriding ethical imperative justifies any action. This is of course much the same "moral relativism" of which both the conservative right and the liberal center accused communists and then postmodernists.

1 Alexander R. Galloway, *The Interface Effect*, Polity, Cambridge: 2012; Alberto Toscano and Jeff Kinkle, *Cartographies of the Absolute*, Winchester, UK: Zero Books, 2015.

The hero, Jack Bauer is a kind of hacker, circumventing the protocols of both technologies and institutions. Everything is about informatics as weapon. Interrogation is about extracting information. "The body is a database, torture a query algorithm" (112). Time is always pressing, and so shortcuts and hacks are always justified. The editing often favors "windowing," where the screen breaks into separate panels showing different simultaneous events, cutting across the older logic of montage as succession.

The show's narrative runs on a sort of networked instantaneity. Characters in different places are all connected and work against the same ever ticking clock. Characters have no interiority, no communal life. They are on the job (almost) 24/7, like perfect post-Fordist workers, and like them their work is under constant surveillance. There is no domestic space. They have nothing but their jobs, and as Berardi and McRobbie also show, a heightened ownership of their labor is their only source of spiritual achievement. "Being alive and being on the clock are now essentially synonymous" (109).

But Galloway takes a step back and looks at a broader question of form and its relation to the content of the show. The twenty-four episodes of a season of *24*, each an hour long, are supposed to be twenty-four consecutive hours in the story—but there's actually only 16.8 hours of television. The show makes no reference to the roughly 30 percent of the viewer's time spent watching the ads. Watching television is "work," and we might now add, a precursor form of the vast amount of more detailed nonlabor we all perform on all kinds of screens.[2]

Galloway: "*24* is political because the show embodies in its formal technique the essential grammar of the control society, dominated as it is by specific and information logics" (119). One might add that it is probably watched now in a specific way as well, by viewers checking their text messages or with Facebook open on their laptops while it plays on the big screen. It has to compete with all our other interfaces.

---

2 Dallas Smythe, *Counterclockwise: Perspectives on Communication*, Boulder, CO: Westview, 1994; Sut Jhally, *The Codes of Advertising*, New York: Routledge, 1990.

"Today the 'culture industry' takes on a whole new meaning, for inside software the 'cultural' and the 'industrial' are coterminous" (59).

How then can the interface be a site where the larger historical and political forces can be detected playing themselves out as they articulate individual experiences and sensibilities into that larger world? How is the one transformed into the other, as a kind of parallel world, both attuned and blind to what is beyond it? What is the dialectic between culture and history? What lies between might be called *allegory*?[3] For Galloway, allegory today takes the specific form of an interface, and even more specifically of the workings of an *intraface*, which might be described as the relation between the center and the edge within the interface itself.

Culture is history in representational form, as social life as a whole cannot be expressed directly (to say nothing of social-natural metabolic life). Culture is not a representation of social life per se, but of the *impossibility* of its representation. Hence one might pay as much attention to the blind spots of an instance of cultural work—like the missing 30 percent of *24*, where the ads run.

Further, might there be a certain homology between the mode of production at work at large in history and the specific way in which the form of a cultural work does its work? This was perhaps what Jameson was proposing in his famous essay on the "postmodern."[4] But these times are not "post-" anything: they just are what they are. If this is, in a term Galloway borrows from Deleuze, a society of control, then perhaps the interface is a kind of *control allegory*.[5]

I can remember a time when we still called all this *new media*.[6] It is an absurd term now, especially for students whose whole conscious life has existed pretty much within the era of the internet and

---

3 Fredric Jameson, *The Political Unconscious*, Ithaca, NY: Cornell University Press, 1982, 17–29.

4 Fredric Jameson, *Postmodernism, or, The Cultural Logic of Late Capitalism*, London: Verso, 1991.

5 Gilles Deleuze, "Postscript on Control Societies," in *Negotiations, 1972–1990*, New York: Columbia University Press, 1997.

6 Wendy Hui Kyong Chun et al. (eds.), *New Media, Old Media: A History and Theory Reader*, 2nd Edition, New York: Routledge, 2015.

increasingly also of the web and the cell phone. I can also remember a time when the potentials of "new media" appeared to be, and in some ways really were, quite open. That past is now often read as a kind of teleology where it was inevitable that it would end up monopolized by giant corporations profiting off nonlabor in a society of control and surveillance. But this is selective memory. There were once avant-gardes who tried, and failed, to make it otherwise. That they—or we—failed is no reason to accept the official Silicon Valley ideologies of history.

I mention this because Galloway starts *The Interface Effect* by recalling in passing the avant-garde in listserv form that was nettime.org and rhizome.org—but without flagging his own role in any of this. His work with the Radical Software Group and rhizome.org is not part of the story. That world appears here as just the place of the first reception for that pioneering attempt to describe it, Lev Manovich's *The Language of New Media*.[7]

Manovich came at this topic from a very different place from either the techno-boosters of Silicon Valley's Californian Ideology or the politico-media avant-gardes of Western Europe. His own statement about this, which Galloway quotes, turned out to be prescient: "As a post-communist subject, I cannot but see Internet as a communal apartment of Stalin era: no privacy, everybody spies on everybody else, always present line for common areas such as the toilet or the kitchen."[8] How ironic, now that Edward Snowden, who showed that this is where we had ended up, had to seek asylum of sorts in Putin's post-Soviet Russia.

As Galloway reads him, Manovich is a modernist, whose attention in drawn to the formal principles of "new media." He found five: numeric representation, modularity, automation, variability and transcoding. Emphasis shifts from the linear sequence to the database from which it draws, or from syntagm to paradigm. Since that pioneering work, the formal properties of media are often seen as a mask

---

7 Lev Manovich, *The Language of New Media*, Cambridge, MA: MIT Press, 2000.

8 Lev Manovich, "On Totalitarian Interactivity," *Telepolis*, April 3, 1996.

for underlying political-economic essence—neoliberalism. But the form of new media doesn't change the understanding of that essence, nor is there attention to the relation between appearance and essence, which remain a metaphysical given.

Galloway's distinctive, and subtle, argument is that digital media are not so much a new ontology as a simulation of one. The word "ontology" is a slippery one here, and perhaps best taken in a naïve sense of "what is." A medium such as cinema has a certain material relation to what is, or rather what was. The pro-filmic event ends up as a sort of trace in the film, or, put the other way around, the film is an index of a past event. Here it is not the resemblance but the sequence of events that make film a kind of sign of the real, in much the same way that smoke is an indexical sign for fire.

Galloway: "Today all media are a question of synecdoche (scaling a part for the whole), not indexicality (pointing from here to there)" (9). Galloway doesn't draw on Benjamin here, but one could think Benjamin's view of cinema as a kind of organizing of indexical signs from perceptual scales and tempos that can exceed the human—signs pointing to a bigger world. It takes a certain masochistic posture to even endure it, and not quite in the way Laura Mulvey might have thought one of cinema-viewing's modes as masochistic. For any viewer it is a sort of giving over of perceptual power to a great machine.[9]

To the extent that it helps perceive often subtle, continuous changes by sharpening the edges through a binary of language, let's say that by contrast digital media is sadistic rather than masochistic. "The world no longer indicates to us what it is. We indicate ourselves to it, and in so doing the world materializes in our image" (13). This media is not about indexes of a world, but about the profiles of its users.

Galloway does not want to go too far down this path, however. His is a theory not of media but of *mediation*, which is to say not a theory of a new class of objects but of a new class of relations: mediation, allegory, interface. Instead of beginning and ending from technical media, we are dealing instead with their actions: storing, transmitting, processing. Having learned his anti-essentialism—from

9 Laura Mulvey, *Visual and Other Pleasures*, London: Palgrave, 2009.

Haraway among others—he is careful not to seek essences for either objects or subjects.

A computer is not an ontology, then, but neither is it a metaphysics, in that larger sense of not just what is, but why and how what is, is. Most curiously, Galloway proposes that a computer is actually a *simulation* of a metaphysical arrangement, not a metaphysical arrangement: "the computer does not remediate other physical media, it remediates metaphysics itself" (20).

Here Galloway gives a rather abbreviated example, which I will flesh out a bit more than he does, as best I can. That example is *object-oriented programming.*

> The metaphysico-Platonic logic of object-oriented systems is awe inspiring, particularly the way in which classes (forms) define objects (instantiated things): classes are programmer-defined templates, they are (usually) static and state in abstract terms how objects define data types and process data; objects are instances of classes, they are created in the image of a class, they persist for finite amounts of time and are eventually destroyed. On the one hand an idea, on the other a body. On the one hand an essence; on the other, an instance. On the one hand the ontological, on the other the ontical. (21)

One could say a bit more about this, and about how the "ontology" (in the information-science sense) of object-oriented programming, or of any other school of it, is indeed an ontology in a philosophical sense, or something like it. Object-oriented programming (OOP) is a programming paradigm based on objects that contain data and procedures. Most flavors of OOP are class-based, where objects are instances of classes. A class defines data formats and procedures for its objects. Classes can be arranged hierarchically, where subordinate classes inherit attributes from the "parent" class. Objects then interact with each other as more or less black boxes.

In some versions of OOP, those boxes cannot only hide their code, they can lock it away. Among other things, this makes code more modular, and enables a division of labor among coders. Less charitably, it means that half-assed coders working on big projects can't fuck too much of it up beyond the particular part they work on. Moreover, OOP offers the ability to mask this division of labor and its history. The structure of the software enables a social reality where code can be written in California or Bangalore.

A commercially popular programming language that is substantially OOP based is Java, although there are many others. They encourage the reuse of functional bits of code but add a heavy burden of unnecessary complexity and often lack transparency. It is an "ontology" that sees the world as collections of things interacting with things but where the things share inputs and outputs only. How they do so is controlled at a higher level. Such is its "metaphysico-Platonic logic," as Galloway calls it, although to me it is sounding rather more like Leibnitz.

The structure of software—its "ontology" in the information-science sense—makes possible a larger social reality. But perhaps not in the same way as the media of old. Cinema was the defining medium of the twentieth century; the game-like interfaces of our own time are something else.[10] The interface itself still looks like a screen, so it is possible to imagine it still works the same way. Galloway: "It does not facilitate or make reference to an arrangement of being, it remediates the very conditions of being itself" (21). The computer simulates an ontological plane with logical relations. "The computer instantiates a practice not a presence, an effect not an object" (22).

Perhaps the computer is more of an ethic (what *ought*) than an ontology (what *is*).

> The machine is an ethic because it is premised on the notion that objects are subject to definition and manipulation according to a set of principles for action. The matter at hand is not that of coming to know a world, but rather that of how specific, abstract definitions are executed to form a world. (23)

(I would rather think this as a different kind of index, of the way formal logics can organize electrical conductivity, for example.)

---

10 McKenzie Wark, *Gamer Theory*, Cambridge, MA: Harvard University Press, 2007.

"The computer is not an object, or a creator of objects, it is a process or active threshold mediating between two states" (23). Or more than two—there can be many layers. "The catoptrics of the society of the spectacle is now the dioptrics of the society of control" (25). Or: we no longer have mirrors, we have lenses. Despite such a fundamental reorganization of the world, Galloway insists on the enduring usefulness of Marx (and Freud) and of their respective *depth models* of interpretation, which attempt to ferret out how something can appear as its opposite.[11]

Galloway tips the depth model sideways, and considers the interface in terms of centers and edges, as "the edges of art always make reference to the medium itself" (33). This center-edge relation Galloway calls the *intraface*. It is a zone of indecision between center and edge, not unlike what Roland Barthes called the *studium* and the *punctum*.[12] Making an intraface internally consistent requires a sort of neurotic repression of the problem of its edge. On the other hand, signaling the real presence of an edge to the intraface ends up making the work itself incoherent and schizophrenic—what Maurice Blanchot called the unworkable.[13]

In cinema the great artists of the neurotically coherent and schizophrenically incoherent intrafaces respectively might be Hitchcock and Godard. The choice appears to be one of a coherent aesthetic of believing in the interface, but not enacting it (Hitchcock); and an incoherent aesthetic of enacting the interface, but not believing in it (Godard). But Galloway is wary of assuming that only the second kind of intraface is a "political" one. The multiplayer computer game *World of Warcraft* is as much an example of a schizophrenic intraface as any Godard movie. "At root, the game is not simply a fantasy landscape

11 Although in Alexander R. Galloway, Eugene Thacker and McKenzie Wark, *Excommunication: Three Inquiries in Media and Mediation*, Chicago: University of Chicago Press, 2013, Galloway is rather more skeptical of depth models of interpretation.

12 Roland Barthes, *Camera Lucida: Reflections on Photography*, New York: Hill & Wang, 2010.

13 Maurice Blanchot, *The Space of Literature*, Lincoln NE: University of Nebraska Press, 1989, 13.

of dragons and epic weapons but a factory floor, an information-age sweat-shop, custom tailored in every detail for cooperative ludic labor" (44).

Galloway doubles the binary of coherent vs. incoherent *aesthetics* with a second: coherent vs. incoherent *politics*, to make a four-fold scheme.[14] The coherent aesthetics + coherent politics quadrant is probably a rare one now. Galloway doesn't mention architecture here, but Corbusier would be a great example, where a new and clarified aesthetic geometry was supposed to be the representative form for the modern ruling class.[15]

The quadrant of incoherent aesthetics + coherent politics is a lively one, giving Berthold Brecht, Alain Badiou, Jean-Luc Godard or the punk band Fugazi. All in very different ways combine a self-revealing or self-annihilating aesthetic with a fixed political aspiration, be it communist or "straight edged." The *World of Warcraft* interface might fit here too, with its schizo graphics interfacing with an order whose politics we shall come to later.[16]

Then there's the coherent aesthetic + incoherent politics quadrant, which for Galloway means art for art's sake, or a prioritizing of the aesthetic over the political, giving us the otherwise rather different cinema of Billy Wilder and Alfred Hitchcock, but also the aesthetics of Gilles Deleuze, and I would add Oscar Wilde, and all those with nothing to declare but their "genius."

The most interesting quadrant combines incoherent aesthetics with incoherent politics. This is the "dirty" regime, of the inhuman, of nihilism, of "the negation of the negation." Galloway will also say the interface of truth. Here lurks Nietzsche, Georges Bataille and I would add the situationists or the Jean-François Lyotard of *Libidinal Economy*. Galloway will by the end of the book place his own approach here, but to trouble that a bit, let me also point out that here lies the

---

14 See A. J. Greimas, *On Meaning: Selected Writings in Semiotic Theory*, Minneapolis: University of Minnesota Press, 1987.

15 On Corbusier, see McKenzie Wark, *The Beach Beneath the Street*, London: Verso, 2015, 19–31.

16 On *World of Warcraft*, see Mikko Vesa, *There Be Dragons!*, Helsinki: Edita Prima, 2013.

strategies of Nick Land and his epigones.[17] Or, more interestingly, Préciado's *Testo Junkie*.

So in short there are four modes of aesthetic-political interface. The first is *ideological*, where art and justice are coterminous (the dominant mode). The second is *ethical*, which must destroy art in the service of justice (a privileged mode). The third is *poetic*, where one must banish justice in the service of art (a tolerated mode). The last is *nihilist*, and wants the destruction of all existing modes of art and justice. Which for Galloway is a banished mode—unless one sees it, in the spirit of Nick Land, as rather the mode of capitalist deterritorialization itself, in which case it is actually dominant and the new ideological mode. Its avatar would perhaps be Joseph Schumpeter.[18]

Galloway thinks one can map the times as a shift from the ideological to the ethical mode, and (as in Dean) a generalized "decline in ideological efficiency" (51). I suspect it may rather be a shift from the ideological to the nihilist, but which cannot declare itself, leading to a redoubling of efforts to produce viable ideological modes despite their waning effect. (The sub rosa popularity of Nick Land among blogosphere philosophers finds its explanation here as delicious and desirable wound and symptom.)

Either way, the mechanism—in a quite literal sense—that produces this effect might be the transformation of the interface itself by computing, producing as it does a simulated relation to ideological conditions, where ideology itself is modeled as software. The computer interface is an incoherent aesthetic that is either in the service of a coherent politics (Galloway's reading), or wants to *appear* as such but is actually in the service of an incoherent politics that it cannot quite avow (my reading).

Galloway usefully focuses attention on the intraface as the surface between the problems of aesthetic form and the political-historical totality of which it is a part. Where he sees the present aesthetico-politics of the interface as oscillating between regimes two and three,

17 Nick Land, *Fanged Noumena: Collected Writings 1987–2007*, Falmouth: Urbanomic, 2011.

18 Joseph Schumpeter, *Capitalism, Socialism and Democracy*, New York: Harper Perennial, 2008.

I think it is more about regimes one and four, and entails a devaluing of the old aesthetic-political compromises of the Godards and Hitchcocks, or Badious and Deleuzes of this world. I think we now have a short-circuit between ideology and nihilism that *accepts no compromise formations.*

The interface is an allegorical device for Galloway, a concept that is related to, but not quite the same as, Chun's idea that "software is a functional analog to ideology." Certainly both writers have zeroed in on a crucial point. Where Galloway and Chun differ is that he does not follow her and Kittler in reducing software to hardware. Kittler's view is part of a whole conceptual field that may be produced by the interface effect itself. There is a kind of segregation where data are supposedly immaterial ideas and the computer is a machine from a real world called "technology." The former appears as a sort of idealist residue reducible to the latter in a sort of material-trumps-immaterial move.

This might correct for certain idealist deviations, such as in Lazzarato, where the "immaterial" or the "algorithm" acquire mysterious powers of their own without reference to the physical logic gates, memory cores, not to mention energy sources that actually make computers compute. However, it then runs the risk of treating data and information as somehow less real and less "material" than matter and energy. Hence, as usual, a merely philosophical "materialism" reproduces the idealism it seeks to oppose.

I think Galloway wants to accord a little more "materiality" to information than that, although it is not a topic the book tackles directly. But this is a theory not of media but of *mediation*, or of action, process, and event.[19] Galloway also has little to say about labor, but that might be a useful term here too, if one can separate it from assumptions about it being something only humans do. A theory of mediation might also be a theory of information labor. An interface would then be a site of labor, where a particular, concrete act meets social, abstract labor in its totality.[20]

---

19 Galloway et al., *Excommunication.*

20 McKenzie Wark, *A Hacker Manifesto*, Cambridge, MA: Harvard University Press, 2004.

Software is not quite reducible to hardware. I think we can use a formula here from Raymond Williams: hardware sets *limits* on what software can do, but does not determine what it does in any stronger sense.[21] Software is not then "ideological," but something a bit more complicated. For Galloway, software is not just a vehicle for ideology, "instead, the ideological contradictions of technical transcoding and fetishistic abstraction are enacted and 'resolved' within the very form of software itself" (61).

Of course not all interfaces are for humans. Actually most are probably now interfaces between machines and other machines. Software is a machinic turn for ideology, an interface which is mostly about the machinic. Here Galloway also takes his distance from those who, like Katherine Hayles, see code as something like an *illocutory speech act.*[22] Just as natural languages require a social setting, code requires a technical setting. But to broaden the context and see code as a subset of enunciation (a key term for Lazzarato) is still to anthropomorphize it too much. I am still rather fond of a term Galloway has used elsewhere—*allegorithm*—an allegory that takes an algorithmic form.[23]

What does it mean to *visualize* data? What is data? In simple terms, maybe data are "the givens," whereas information might mean to give (in turn) some form to what is given. Data is empirical; information is aesthetic. But data visualization mostly pictures its own rules of representation. Galloway's example here is the visualization of the internet itself, of which there are many examples, all of which look pretty much the same. "Data have no necessary information" (83). But the information that is applied to it seems over and over to be the same, a sort of hub-and-spoke cloud aesthetic, which draws connections but leaves out protocols, labor or power.

Maybe one form of what Dean calls the *decline in symbolic efficiency* is a parallel increase in *aesthetic information* that goes hand in hand with a decline in *information aesthetics*. There's no necessary

21 Raymond Williams, *Culture and Materialism*, London: Verso, 2006.

22 N. Katherine Hayles, *How We Became Posthuman*, Chicago: University of Chicago Press, 1999.

23 Alexander R. Galloway, *Gaming: Essays on Algorithmic Culture*, Minneapolis: University of Minnesota Press, 2006.

visual form for data, but the forms it gets seem to come from a small number of presets. Galloway thinks this through Jacques Rancière's *distribution of the sensible*.[24] Once upon a time there were given forms for representing particular things in particular situations. But after that comes a sort of sublime regime, which tries to record the trace of the unrepresentable. It succeeds the old distribution, as a result of breakdown between subjects of art and forms of representation.

The nihilism of modernity actually stems from realism, which levels the representational system, for in realism everything is equally representable. Realism can even represent the Shoah, and its *representability* is actually the problem, for there is nothing specific about the language in which it is represented, which could just as easily represent a tea party. The problem might be not so much about the representability of the Shoah as that its representation seems to have negligible consequences. Representation has lost ethical power.

But perhaps Rancière was speaking only of the former society of the spectacle, not the current society of control. Galloway: "One of the key consequences of the control society is that we have moved from a condition in which singular machines produce proliferations of images, into a condition in which multitudes of machines produce singular images" (91). We have no adequate pictures of the control society. Its unrepresentability is connected to what the mode of production itself makes visible and invisible.

Galloway: "the point of unrepresentability is the point of power. And the point of power today is not in the image. The point of power today resides in networks, computers, algorithms, information and data" (92). Mark Lombardi's work, and that of the Bureau d'études might be interesting attempts at the *allegorithm*.[25] One that might actually restore questions of power and protocol to images of "networks." But these are still limited to certain affordances of the map-form as interface.

---

24 Jacques Rancière, *The Politics of Aesthetics: The Distribution of the Sensible*, London: Bloomsbury, 2006.

25 Patricia Goldstone, *Interlock: Art, Conspiracy and the Shadow Worlds of Mark Lombardi*, Berkeley: Counterpoint, 2015; Bureau d'Etudes, *An Atlas of Agendas*, Onomatopee, 2014.

So we have no visual language (yet) for the control society. Although we have them for some of its effects. Galloway does not mention climate modeling, but to me that is surely the key form of the *data-> information -> visualization* problem to which to attend in the Anthropocene. As I tried to show in *Molecular Red*, the data -> information interface is actually quite complicated.[26] In climate science each coproduces the other. Data are not empirical in a philosophical sense, but they are wedded to specific material circumstances of which they are unwitting indexes.

One could also think about the problems of visualizing the results, particularly for lay viewers. I see a lot of maps of the existing continents with data on rising temperatures, and a lot of maps of rising seas making new continents which omit the climate projections. Imagine being at a given GPS coordinate sixty years from now where *neither* the land form nor the climate were familiar. How could one visualize such a *terra incognita*? Most visualizations hold one variable constant to help understand the other. In *Gamer Theory* I showed how the *SimEarth* game actually made some progress on this—but then that game was a commercial failure.[27]

There are lots of visualizations of networks and of climate change—curious how there are few visualizations which show both at the same time. And what they tend to leave out is agency. Both social labor and the relations of production are not pictured. Images of today's social labor often land on images of elsewhere. Galloway mentions the Chinese gold farmers, those semi-real, semi-mythical creatures (under)paid to dig up items worth money in games like *World of Warcraft*.[28] Another might be the call-center worker, who we might more often hear but never see.[29] These might be the allegorical figures of labor today.

For Galloway, we are all Chinese gold farmers, in the sense that all

26 McKenzie Wark, *Molecular Red*, London: Verso, 2015. See the chapter "Climate Science as Tektology."

27 Wark, *Gamer Theory*, 145ff.

28 Julian Dibbell, *Play Money*, New York: Basic Books, 2007.

29 On call center workers, see the Kolinko Group, "Hotlines: Call Center Inquiry," 2010, available at libcom.org.

computerized and networked activity is connected to value extraction. One might add that we are all call-center workers, in that we are all responding to demands placed on us by a network, to which we are obliged to respond. There is of course a massive inequity in how such labor (and nonlabor) is rewarded, but all of it may increasingly take similar forms.

All labor and even nonlabor becomes abstract and valorized, but race is a much more stubborn category, and a good example of how software simulates ideology.[30] In a game like *World of Warcraft*, class is figured as something temporary. By grinding away at hard work you can improve your "position." But race is basic and ineradicable. The "races" are all fantasy types, rather than "real" ones, but perhaps it is only in fantasy form that race can be accepted and become matter-of-fact. Control society may be one that even encourages a certain relentless tagging and identifying through race and other markers of difference—all the better to connect you at a fine-grained level of labor and consumption, as Gilroy suggests.

The answer to Gayatri Spivak's question—can the subaltern speak? —is that the subaltern not only speaks but *has* to speak, even if restricted to certain stereotypical scripts.[31] "The subaltern speaks and somewhere an algorithm listens" (137). In an era when difference is the very thing that what Galloway calls *ludic capitalism* feasts on, it is tempting to turn, as Badiou and Žižek do, back to the universal. But questions of what the universal erases or suppresses are not addressed in this turn, just ignored.

Galloway advocates instead a politics of subtraction and disappearance: to be neither the universal nor differentiated subject, but rather the *generic* one of *whatever being*. I'm not entirely convinced by this metaphysical-political turn, at least not yet. It is striking to me that most of *The Interface Effect* is written under the sign of Fredric Jameson, for whom politics is not a separate domain, but is itself an

30 Lisa Nakamura, *Cybertypes: Race, Ethnicity and Identity on the Internet*, New York: Routledge, 2002.

31 Gayatri Spivak, "Can the Subaltern Speak?," in Lawrence Grossberg and Cary Nelson (eds.), *Marxism and the Interpretation of Culture*, Champaign, IL: University of Illinois Press, 1988.

allegory for the history of capitalism itself. And yet the concluding remarks are built much more on the Jacobin approach to the political of the post-Althusserians such as Dean or Mouffe, for whom the political is an autonomous realm *against* the merely economic.

From that Jacobin-political-philosophical point of view, the economic itself starts to become a bit reified. Hence Galloway associates the logic of the game *World of Warcraft* with the economics of capital itself, because the game simulates a world in which resources are scarce and quantifiable. But surely *any* mode of production has to quantify. Certainly precapitalist ones did.[32] I don't think it is entirely helpful to associate use value only with the qualitative and uncountable, and to equate exchange value with quantification *tout court*. One of the lessons of climate science, and the earth science of which it is a subset, is that one of the necessary ways in which one critiques exchange value is by showing that it attempts to quantify imaginary values. It is actually the "qualities" of exchange value that are the problem, not its math.[33]

So while Galloway and I agree on a lot of things, there are also points of interesting divergence. Galloway: "The virtual (or the new, the next) is no longer the site of emancipation…No politics can be derived today from a theory of the new" (138). I would agree that the virtual became a way in which the theological entered critical theory, once again, through a back door. I tried to correct for that, between *A Hacker Manifesto* and *Spectacle of Disintegration*, through a reading of Debord's concept of *strategy*, which I think tried to mediate between pure, calculative models and purely romantic, qualitative ones.[34] It was also a way of thinking with a keen sense of the *actual* affordances of situations rather than a hankering for mystical "events."

But I think there's a problem with Galloway's attempt to have done with an historicist (Jamesonian) mode of thought in favor of

32 V. Gordon Childe, *What Happened in History*, Harmondsworth: Penguin, 1985.

33 Paul Burkett, *Marx and Nature*, Chicago: Haymarket Books, 2014.

34 McKenzie Wark, *The Spectacle of Disintegration*, London: Verso, 2013, chapters 18 and 19; see also Alexander R. Galloway, "The Game of War: An Overview," *Cabinet*, Spring 2008, at cabinetmagazine.org.

a spatialized and Jacobin or "political" one. To try to supersede the modifier of the "post-" with that of the "non-" is still in spite of itself a temporal succession. I think rather that we need to propose other past-present configurations. It's a question of going back into the database of the archive (of the *Marx-field*, for example) and understanding it not as a montage of successive theories but as a field of possible paths and forks—and selecting other (but not "new") ones.

Galloway is quite right to insist that "Another world is not possible"[35] (139). But I read this more through what the natural sciences insist are the parameters of action than through what philosophy thinks are the parameters of thought. I do agree that we need to take our leave from consumerist models of difference and the demand to always tag and produce ourselves for the benefit of ludic capitalism. In *Spectacle of Disintegration* I called the taking-leave the *language of discretion*. But I dissented there somewhat from the more metaphysical cast Agamben gives this.[36]

I think there's a bit of a danger in opting for the fourth quadrant of the political-aesthetic landscape. Incoherence in politics and aesthetics is as ambivalent as all the others in its implications. Sure it is partly this: "A harbinger of the truth regime, the whatever dissolves into the common, effacing representational aesthetics and representational politics alike" (142). But it is also the corporate nihilism of today's ruling, vectoralist class. I think it more consistent with Galloway's actual thinking here to treat all four quadrants of the aesthetic-political interface as ambiguous and ambivalent rather than exempt the fourth.

Ludic capitalism is on the one hand a time of that playfulness which Schiller and Huizinga thought key to the social whole and its history, respectively.[37] On the other, it is an era of cybernetic control. Poetics

35 See McKenzie Wark, "There is Another World," *Public Seminar*, January 14, 2014, at publicseminar.org.

36 Alice Becker-Ho, *The Essence of Jargon*, New York: Autonomedia, 2015; Giorgio Agamben, *Means Without Ends: Notes on Politics*, University of Minnesota, Minneapolis, 2000, 63–73; Wark, *The Spectacle of Disintegration*, chapter 17.

37 Friedrich Schiller, *Letters on the Aesthetic Education of Man*, Mineola, NY: Dover, 2004; Johan Huizinga, *Homo Ludens*, Kettering, OH: Angelico Press, 2016.

meets design in a "jurdico-geometric sublime" (29) whose star ideologues are poet-designers like Steve Jobs (on which see the movie, *Steve Jobs*). The trick is to denaturalize the surfaces of this brand of capitalist realism, which wants to appear as a coherent regime of ideology, but which is actually one of the most perfect nihilism—and not in the redeemable sense.[38]

I'm not entirely sure that the "good nihilism" of withdrawal can be entirely quarantined from the bad one of the celebration of naked, unjust power. It's a question that needs rather more attention. Alex Galloway, Eugene Thacker and I may be in accord as "nihilists" who refuse a certain legislative power to philosophy. As I see it, Galloway thinks there's a way to *hack* philosophy, to turn it against itself from within. I think my approach is rather to *détourne* it, to see it as a metaphor machine for producing both connections and disconnections that can move across the intellectual division of labor, that can find ways knowledge can be comradely, and relate to itself and the world other than via exchange value. From the latter point of view, these might just be component parts of the same project.

Software can now simulate the spectacle so effectively that it is able to insinuate another logic into it, the simulation of the spectacle itself, under which lies an abyss of non-knowledge. But I am not sure this was an inevitable outcome. As in Dean, I find Galloway rather erases the struggles around what "new media" would become, and now retrospectively sees the outcome as, if not an essence, then a given. This is partly what makes me nervous about a language of seceding or withdrawing (or Virno's exodus). One of the great political myths is of the outsider subject, untouched by power. All such positions, be it the worker, the woman, the subaltern, can now be taken as fully subsumed. But I think that means one works from an inside—for example via Haraway's figure of the cyborg—rather than looking for an exit back out again.

38 Mark Fisher, *Capitalist Realism*, Winchester, UK: Zero Books, 2009.

18.

Timothy Morton: From OOO to P(OO)

I have been reading the work of Timothy Morton with pleasure for many years now. Originally a scholar of English romantic poetry, I find his work reads best as poetry, or perhaps a poetics, as a singular Mortonian vision of the world—or in his book *Hyperobjects*, a vision of the *absence* of the world.[1] I have some problems with it as theory, however, and will try to outline here where my own thinking and Morton's both overlap and diverge. Perhaps bodies of work are a case of what Morton calls *hyperobjects*—spooky, nonlocal, pervasive entities that are at once in us and which we are in. In which case, the best way to proceed is simply to map one onto the other and find the edges where such things resonate.

One of the merits of Morton's work is its attention to twenty-first century problems. Morton: "To those great Victorian period discoveries, then—evolution, capital, the unconscious—we must now add spacetime, ecological interconnection, and nonlocality" (47). If one suspends disbelief and reads his texts as a science-fiction poetics, one starts to breath the (overly warm, possibly radioactive) air of the times. Branching off from Alphonso Lingis, Morton offers a phenomenology for the strange and untimely objects one increasingly seems to encounter—*hyperobjects*.[2]

1 Timothy Morton, *Hyperobjects*, Minneapolis: University of Minnesota Press, 2013.

2 See Bobby George and Tom Sparrow (eds.), *Itinerant Philosophy: On Alphonso Lingis*, Brooklyn: Punctum Books, 2014.

But first, *objects*. Morton:

> Objects are unique. Objects can't be reduced to smaller objects or dissolved upwards into larger ones. Objects are withdrawn from one another and from themselves. Objects are Tardis-like, larger on the inside than they are on the outside. Objects are uncanny. Objects compose an untotalizable nonwhole set that defies holism and reductionism. There is thus no top object that gives all objects value and meaning, and no bottom object to which they can be reduced. If there is no top object and no bottom object, it means that we have a very strange situation in which there are more parts than there are wholes. This makes holism of any kind totally impossible. (116)

In short, Morton declares victory in advance for the poets. The world is made of things that elude any other kind of knowing. This is even more the case with *hyperobjects*, which stick to being, are viscous, nonlocal, temporally weird, and are detectable only through the waves they make coming in or out of phase with other, more banal kinds of objects.

Mortonian poetics is a species of the genus *object-oriented ontology* (OOO), which claims to belong to the order *speculative realism*, like that of Meillassoux.[3] I read Morton as more a kind of poetic realism. One in which entities are shy and retiring, like an octopus squirting a jet of ink as it disappears. As one discovers in Galloway and Chun, *object-oriented programming* is indeed a world of objects that hide their own workings, although it turns out this is for industrial and commercial reasons, not as a matter of primal ontology.[4]

Through a deft bit of metaphorical *substitution*, Morton makes the opacity of objects, and in particular hyperobjects, do a lot of work. There's no transcendental leap outside of this world of hyperobjects, and as such a "world" cannot be said to appear at all, if by world we mean that which can be said to exist over and against me. There's no more bracketing off of a separate world, as "we are no longer

3 See Levi Bryant et al. (eds.), *The Speculative Turn*, Melbourne: re.press, 2011.

4 See McKenzie Wark, *Molecular Red*, London: Verso, 2015, 235.

able to think history as exhaustively human" (5). There's no outside. We're always inside hyperobjects and hyperobjects are always passing through us, whether the hyperobject is radioactive waste or global warming. This poetics brings us to an uncanny place—the end of the world.

Morton's aim is to wake us from the dream of a world ending, to the realization that it has ended already. There's no outside, no separation.

> Because they so massively outscale us, hyperobjects have magnified this weirdness of things for our inspection...What if hyperobjects finally force us to realize the truth of the word *humiliation* itself, which means being brought low, being brought down to earth itself? (12, 17)

Morton makes use of many examples from modern science, but I am resistant to the attempt to subsume such examples within OOO. Morton: "science doesn't necessarily know what it is about" (10). But surely the reverse is even more the case, as Morton almost acknowledges: "You have to wonder whether your poem about global warming is really a hyperobject's way of distributing itself into human ears and libraries" (175). One needs climate science to understand hyperobjects, as it is a key example, but not vice versa. As so often with philosophy, OOO comes after the labor of producing a knowledge of affairs, then adds a supernumerary interpretation to it.

As a genus of the order *speculative realism*, OOO wants to have an alternative to what Meillassoux calls (after Merleau-Ponty) *correlationism*, where for there to be knowledge of a thing there need be a corresponding subject. The OOO species approaches this by generalizing the Heideggerian theme of the *withdrawal* of the tool itself in the act of performing its tool-function, by positing that all objects withdraw from each other in this manner.[5] The subject-object relation then becomes just a subset of all object-object relations, in which objects always withdraw from each other, and relate to each other *aesthetically*, through the (inter)face they present.

5 See Graham Harman, *Towards Speculative Realism*, Winchester, UK: Zero Books, 2010.

Morton uses an example from Husserl. Holding a coin, one sees its face. But you can't see the other side of the coin *as the other side.* You can only flip it over and make it *this side.* But I think the thing to pay attention to is not the mystery of the other side or the limits of seeing just this side, but the *labor* of the flipping. Hence I would want to move on from the *contemplative* thought of OOO to what it cannot but acknowledge in passing but continually represses: the labor or *praxis* via which a thing is known.

But to say "labor" is not to say "subject." It is not to return to correlationism. For labor is always a mix of the human and *inhuman.* To say "tool" is to partly say, and then erase, labor. Particularly when one gets to modern means of knowing the world, the *apparatus* of labor and *techne* becomes a vast and inhuman thing. This is the case in a pertinent example such as climate science.[6] There it's an array of satellites, computers, terrestrial weather stations, forms of international cooperation of scientific labor, elaborately agreed upon standards and so on. Climate science, like all modern science, is an *inhuman* apparatus via which the *nonhuman* world is mediated in such a way that humans can comprehend it.

Contra Morton, I don't think Niels Bohr's "Copenhagen Interpretation" of quantum mechanics is correlationist at all.[7] Morton writes of "Bohr as thinking quantum events as if they were correlations to (human) instruments" (37). But why is the instrument "human"? Is not the instrument an inhuman thing that mediates the nonhuman to the human? Again, there's a collapsing of the space in which praxis occurs here.

For Morton, we are always inside objects. We are neither at the center nor the edge, and if they are hyperobjects they may be massive, pervasive and weird. But I don't think it's the object that withdraws; I think it's OOO that occludes the ways in which objects are known in the first place, which is in three steps.

First, there's the particular praxis that produces a knowledge. Whether the praxis is labor or science, it is always a cyborg mix of human effort and inhuman apparatus.

6 Wark, *Molecular Red.* See the chapter "Climate Science as Tektology."

7 Ibid. See the chapter "From Bogdanov to Barad."

Second, there's the generalization of that praxis in the form of metaphors and images. This is also a kind of labor, an intellectual labor, a mix of human talk and inhuman apparatus of communication.

The third step is the erasure of the other two. First there's the praxis of doing science about quantum mechanics or climate change. Second there's the production of the metaphor of the hyperobject, and third the erasure of the dependence of this metaphor on that prior praxis. In this case, the metaphor will then be claimed to be what precedes those other steps, for which it *substitutes*, when it is actually a later derivation.

Objects and even hyperobjects then appear as objects of contemplation, circulating all around us, free from the labor that produced a knowledge of them as such. Here I think Morton's version of a speculative realism has the same limitation as the work of Meillassoux. Where Meillassoux produces the spectacle of the absolute, Morton produces instead a contemplative relation to the ambience of the long duration. This is progress, however. As Morton wisely notes, it is harder to imagine the long duration than to imagine eternity.

Meillassoux thinks the problem with phenomenology is the finitude of the human subject that correlates to the object of knowledge. Morton thinks it's the privileged transcendental sphere. Morton:

> Kant imagines that although we are limited in this way, our transcendental faculties are at least metaphorically floating in space beyond the edge of the universe, an argument to which Meillassoux himself cleaves in his assertion that reality is finally knowable exclusively by (human) subjectivity. And that is the problem, the problem called anthropocentrism. (17)

What Morton offers instead is contemplative access to the immanence of the strange and the weird. But we're stuck with the problem OOO shares with speculative realism, and speculative realism shares with at least some orders of phenomenology: the erasure of praxis.

We're left in some version of the eternal gap between the phenomena of the senses and their contemplation versus the essence of things that cannot be known. Interestingly, Morton chooses to concentrate on the contemplation of the gap between essence and appearance itself: "a thing just is a rift between what it is and how it appears" (18). "Just is," that is, once we have erased the inhuman praxis that produced it as an object of contemplation in the first place.

This is where Morton's work is most interesting: as an aesthetics. By paying attention to the periphery of sensation, the ambient tone, the interference patterns, certain hyperobjects can be detected in everyday life (but only if we know in advance through other means that they are there).

> The ground of being is shaken. There we were, trolling along in the age of industry, capitalism and technology, and all of a sudden we received information from aliens, information that even the most hardheaded could not ignore, because the form in which the information was delivered was precisely the instrumental and mathematical formulas of modernity itself. The Titanic of modernity hits the iceberg of hyperobjects. (19)

Except that it doesn't. This is like a Platonic myth. Information did not come "from aliens" but from the natural sciences. What modernity hit was (for example) information produced by the praxis of the natural sciences about anthropogenic climate change.

There is already a name for that iceberg: the Anthropocene. What's with the compulsion of humanities scholars—even very fine ones such as Haraway and Stengers—to want to refuse this name we did not coin? Language is our job, of course. It's galling to have to admit that the relevant data here comes from without, from other ways of knowing, which bring with them other ways of naming, and other conventions about who has the right to name.[8] Somehow I just don't think that insisting on the right to name things we did not discover is going to cut much ice. One can indeed think (with Morton) the Anthropocene as a new historical age in which nonhumans are no longer excluded. Or one can do the reverse, which is perhaps more

---

8 In this case, naming requires the deliberations of the Working Group on the "Anthropocene" of the Subcommission on Quaternary Stratigraphy.

challenging, and is the point that earth sciences have arrived at: a new stage of geology in which humans are included. That to me is the truly strange thing to think. Our species-being is part of the rocky mantle, a kind of *coprolite*, perhaps …

However, there are elements in Morton useful for a twentieth-century critique of separation. He does not inquire much as to where they come from, but he is hard on the case of modes of thought that assume a prior distinction between the social and the natural, between self and world, between foreground and background. There are even forms of "environmentalism" that are caught up in this need for something separate, to be left alone. But this is no longer really possible. "It's oil we must thank for burning a hole in the notion of *world*" (34). Its products are now everywhere, not least as that metonym for the Anthropocene, the hyperobject of global plastic residue. The geologists now even find strata of plastic rock being laid down as we speak.

Morton offers a brief glimpse of an aesthetic adequate to the viscous, pervasive nature of the oil-based world. It's the rhapsodic, ambient, field-based art of a certain moment in modernism: Jackson Pollock, John Cage, William Burroughs. A contemporary extension might be Reza Negarestani's astonishing *Cyclonopedia*, a book in which oil is the central character, a malign stain, a memory of sunlight, erupting from the bowels of the earth to change the course of history.[9] Morton: "modernity is the story of how oil got into everything" (54).

But what I think is to be resisted in Morton is the gesture that makes this poetics a higher truth than that of other practices of knowledge. Borrowing an image from *The Matrix*, Morton writes: "The mirror of science melts and sticks to our hand" (36). He wants the viscous hyperobject to somehow be both before and beyond the realm of science, which as Karen Barad would have it, does require a kind of stabilizing of a closed space within an apparatus where observations can be made, repeated, recorded and then communicated.[10]

9 Reza Negarestani, *Cyclonopedia*, Melbourne: re.press, 2008; Reza Negarestani et al. (eds.), *Leper Creativity*, Brooklyn: Punctum Books, 2012.

10 Karen Barad, *Meeting the Universe Halfway*, Durham, NC: Duke University Press, 2007; Paul Edwards, *A Vast Machine*, Cambridge, MA: MIT Press, 2013.

It may be useful to have poetics (in the plural) that take the specific results of particular sciences and experimentally generalize them. This is what Bogdanov called *tektology*.[11] But I think we start to get into trouble when we assume that poetics is a higher power. Morton is far less attentive to poetry's limits than to the limits of scientific modes of knowing. So yes, let's attend to Jackson Pollock, but maybe attend also to how the promotion of his work in postwar America is tied to the suppression of an art that directly addressed the class struggle or racial oppression, or how it partook in the cult of the male genius which is the very opposite of any approach to creation as the product of a field or an emergence from an ambience.[12]

A good example of both the uses and the limits of a poetic and metaphoric extension of specific results from particular sciences is Morton's use of the *nonlocal* as a metaphor. Here he has in mind things like nuclear radiation and endocrine disruptors, things that are waste products of modernity but which can't be kept separate, which get into everything. Atmospheric carbon might be another example. They are examples of what I would call, following John Bellamy Foster, *metabolic rift*.[13]

It was Marx who opened this metaphoric substitution, thinking outwards from the *metabolism* of separate organism towards the thought that the whole planet is one metabolism. Marx was already starting to think the breakdown of such processes. In his time, it was flows of phosphorous and nitrogen. Now one could extend that tektology-style method of substitution to atmospheric carbon, complex hydrocarbon compounds, or radioactive isotopes produced by nuclear reactions. Thought of as metabolic rift, one can stay close to the science of geochemistry and need not add too many additional concepts.

11 Alexander Bogdanov, *Essays in Tektology*, 2nd edition, Seaside, CA: Intersystems Publications, 1984.

12 On the politics of art and letters in the Cold War, see Frances Stonor Saunders, *The Cultural Cold War: The CIA and the World of Arts and Letters*, New York: New Press, 2013.

13 John Bellamy Foster, *Marx's Ecology: Materialism and Nature*, New York: Monthly Review Press, 2000.

One kind of science that really does still seem spooky and weird is quantum mechanics. But again, this is only so if one tries to sustain some sort of nineteenth-century realism, from the point of view of which quantum mechanics seems to point to a troubling and contradictory reality. Niels Bohr really did have a solution to this, but it is one that meets strong resistance from those who really need to maintain a *faith* in a reality that is out there, and separate. One way to read Bohr is as offering a realism not of the *object* of knowledge but of its *practice*, but where its practice takes place within the *inhuman* space of the apparatus.

This is Bohr's *complementarity*: an apparatus gets a result; another apparatus gets an incompatible result. The results are a product of the apparatus. What is separate is the artificial space and time of the apparatus. One is to resist the temptation to say too much about what the results from within the apparatus might say about what we imagine to be the real and separate world beyond what the praxis of an experiment might say about itself.

But rather than affirm that the apparatus produces a phenomenon, something that has the status of a fact, Morton proceeds the opposite way. Rather than stick with the limited *recording* of an object that an apparatus can *produce*, he wants to say that the *real* objects *withdraw*. Fine, but this is to speak of something that in its very nature is beyond observation, beyond any knowledge, that can only be an effect of a poetic art or speculative discourse.

It is a poetics which runs many risks of simply substituting metaphors that unconsciously replicate current social relations onto the cosmic scale. It can lead to statements that are just not true: "OOO is deeply congruent with the most profound, accurate, and testable theory of physical reality available. Actually it would be better to say it the other way around: quantum theory works because it's object-oriented" (41). In the space of two sentences, an alleged congruence becomes by fiat a foundation.

Sometimes the praxis of science will simply blow a hole through our worldviews. Thus I agree with Morton that once one has even a poor layperson's grasp of something like quantum nonlocality, it is hard to call oneself a materialist, or even a "new" materialist anymore.

In the *Marx-field* there have been three responses to this. One was to sever any connection between what materialism might mean as a scientific worldview and what it might mean when applied to social and historical formations. A second was to formulate a "dialectical materialism" that could keep abreast of the sciences. A third was to shift from statements about the materialism of the world to a critique of the materialism of the production of knowledge about the world.

The first path was that of Western Marxism and of much critical theory today. I think Morton and I might agree that (call it what you like) the hyperobject, the Anthropocene or metabolic rift renders it obsolete. There is no separate world of the social. The second path was that of Engels, reinvented in a way by new materialism in a Deleuzian vein, and by OOO in a Heideggerian one. Rather than separate itself from the sciences, it claims to be about something prior to them.

The third is the tektology of Bogdanov, reinvented in a different register by Haraway and Karen Barad.[14] The merit of this third path is that it keeps critical thought in touch with the sciences, like the second path, but limits its ambitions. It respects the methods of the sciences and does not claim access to a superior reality. It looks critically at how ideas from the social world end up in the sciences, but also works creatively on how the sciences can produce figures that might be metaphorically extended to other domains. But it does not claim its second-order generation of such metaphors is a first-order knowledge of something more fundamental than what scientific knowledge might know.

The particular pleasure to be had in reading Morton is poetic: "Like God taking a photograph, the nonhuman sees us" (50). And: "We are poems about the hyperobject Earth" (51). Indeed, all life-forms become poems about nonlife, songs to the geo-trauma of being. Well and good. Until this: "Is the beyond of what might explain the poem more real than the here of the poem? There is no way to tell" (53). There are ways to tell, and they are partial and fallible. They are the various kinds of praxis of knowledge and labor, here as always rendered invisible to the contemplative soul. What *is withdrawn*

14 See Wark, *Molecular Red*, Part II, Section 3.

in OOO is always *labor*. In the absence of which magical thinking returns.

In a lovely metaphor, Morton has it that after relativity theory, "time and space emerge from things, like the rippling flesh of a sea urchin or octopus" (63). But here again, the significance of experimental proof is only fleetingly acknowledged. "Hyperobjects end the idea that time and space are empty containers that entities sit on" (65). No, physics does, once as theory, and then as theory confirmed by quite particular experimental apparatus.

Hyperobjects are not only spatially and temporally weird, for Morton they even exist in a higher dimension. They manifest through *phasing*, or interference patterns, when they encounter more mundane objects. This whole argument rests on an *analogy*:

> If an apple were to invade a two-dimensional world, first the stick people would see some dots as the bottom of the apple touched their universe, then a rapid succession of shapes that would appear like an expanding and contracting circular blob, diminishing to a tiny circle, possibly a point, and disappearing. (70)

Like the Tralfamadorians in Vonnegut's *Slaughterhouse 5*, "A high enough dimensional being could see global warming itself as a static object. What horrifyingly complex tentacles would such an entity have, this high-dimensional object we call global warming?" (71).

For Morton, the mathematical description is not what underlies the object, it is a paraphrase. Not being a Platonist on such questions, I can quite agree. However, I can't agree with Morton's attempt to make a poetics of the object an intimation of a higher reality. The thing to give up is the habit of substituting from our world of hierarchical social relations these attempts to make one's own intellectual labor practice into the "top dog." Like Bogdanov, I think the goal is not to assert a hierarchy of one form of knowledge over others, be it the sciences or philosophy or poetry. The goal might rather be a comradely cooperation of modes of knowing as a subset of ways of laboring.

Thus I admire the literary quality of this metaphoric leap: "hyperobjects are disturbing clowns in an Expressionist painting, clowns who cover every available surface of the painting, leering into our world relentlessly" (76). But I can assign no *a priori* truth value to this way of claiming a knowledge of the world. Unlike Morton (and, in a different vein, Galloway), I want a *consistently* indexical or metonymic approach to what a form of knowledge praxis does. A known thing is an index of unknown things. But one must always keep in view the means by which the indexical sign is made out of the world. And one should try to assume the bare minimum about that world beyond what the index traces.

Or, one could speculatively imagine a lot of objects, even "withdrawn" ones, but assign them no reality besides being possibilities in the mesh of language. And so one can say: "The abyss is not an empty container, but rather a surging crowd of beings" (80). Or, contra Morton, one can write as Meillassoux does of a universe after the style of Mallarmé that could collapse at any time and exists as and for no reason at all—as if the universe were modeled on the social relations of high finance.[15] To think that being reveals itself in such language, even in a veiled or withdrawn state, is really just the *via negativa* of logos.

To see it as something more Morton has recourse once again to a substitution. What if hyperobjects were to mind as base was to superstructure? "My thinking is thus a mental translation of the hyperobject—of climate, biosphere, evolution—not just figuratively, but literally" (85). Once again, notice that what is withdrawn from view here is praxis. The mind pulls the pattern of the world by reflecting on itself as itself.

Hyperobjects offer an ecology without matter, without the present, dwelling, one assumes, in the futurity of essence.

> The present is precisely nowhere to be found in the yawning Rift opening between the future and past, essence and appearance...The

15 See Quentin Meillassoux, *The Number and the Siren*, Falmouth, Urbanomic, 2012, his book on Mallarmé, a sort of Gallic version of Wilde's "The Portrait of Mr. WH"; McKenzie Wark, "The Nothingness That Speaks French," *Public Seminar*, November 13, 2014, at publicseminar.org.

> present does not truly exist. We experience a crisscrossing set of force fields, the aesthetic-causal fields emanated by a host of objects...Time is a flurry of spells and counter-spells cast by objects themselves... The unknown soul of things, the essence, remains on the hither side. (92–4)

Here we have *a*, rather than definitely *the*, way of thinking outside some kind of self/other or object/subject binary, even if that problematic dualism has been reinscribed on another axis.

There's no environment as something separate, out there. "The idea that we are embedded in a phenomenological lifeworld, tucked up like little hobbits into the safety of our burrow, has been exposed as a fiction" (104). Rather, there's an all-too-intimate relation with hyperobjects, which far exceed us yet pass through us, like radiation or dioxins. I agree with Morton that responding to all this with the rhetoric of "sustainability" or "resilience" is insufficient.[16] But unlike him I think this may mean more, rather than less, attention to molecular flows, such as oil or oil-based polymers. Earth systems sciences are never going to give us complete answers—like any verifiable knowledge they depend on the separations performed by particular apparatus—but more rather than less attention to such disciplines seems tactically the thing on which to insist right now.

Morton thinks we have to abandon the category of nature, which he takes to mean something like environment, a background, a thing apart. Hence his famous slogan *ecology without nature*.[17] I appreciate the rhetorical gambit here, but I don't know if in the long run this is a good tactic. One would have thought that ecology was an even more troubling term: *oikos* plus *logos*, as if there could be a logic or truth to metabolism within which the satisfaction of human social needs is achieved. I actually take the theory of the hyperobject to mean: *there is no ecology*. There is no homeostatic cycle of life that could be restored through the withdrawal of human interference.

---

16 On resilience, see McKenzie Wark, "Heidegger and Geology," *Public Seminar*, June 26, 2014, at publicseminar.org.

17 Timothy Morton, *Ecology Without Nature*, Cambridge, MA: Harvard University Press, 2009.

Nature is a rather more tricky term. To shorthand Raymond Williams, its root meaning is connected to birth (natality).[18] It has meant at least three different things. Firstly, the quality of a thing. Secondly, the force that directs the world. Thirdly, the material world itself. The human can be included or not in any of its definitions. It may not actually be possible to think ecology without nature, as ecology is just a point in the space of possible meanings of nature itself. As Morton himself says: "Home, *oikos*, is unstable" (117). But the hyperobject is still a theory of nature, one among the set of possible deployments of the term that refuses to see the human point of view as one that could claim a fundamental separation or externality of point of view on it.

It seems that Morton's resistance to the word nature has to do with Wordsworth's colonization of it. He prefers Keats's attention to the object.[19] But perhaps this was just a way to write nature poetry differently rather than a break with it. And maybe it's a path that comes with its own problems. "In OOO-ese, *reification* is precisely the reduction of a real object to its sensual appearance-for another object. Reification is the reduction of one entity to another's fantasy about it. Nature is a reification in that sense" (119).

But OOO responds to this with *reification in negative*. The futural, essential, withdrawn object becomes the fetish, at the expense not only of any particular sensory one, but of the collaborative praxis needed to work these partial, mediated apprehensions that are the real into some workable relation to each other. The insistence on a strange, spooky or weird kind of aesthetics is itself a product of this fetish in negative, which suppresses attention to praxis and contemplates a floating *phantasmagoria* of things.[20]

"Two hundred years of seeing humans at the center of existence, and now the objects take revenge, terrifyingly huge, ancient, long-lived,

18 Raymond Williams, *Keywords*, Oxford: Oxford University Press, 2014, 164ff.

19 See Timothy Morton, *The Ecological Thought,* Cambridge, MA: Harvard University Press, 2012.

20 Walter Benjamin, *The Arcades Project*, Cambridge MA: Harvard University Press, 2002.

threateningly minute, invading every cell in our body" (115). Well, yes, if one had not paid attention to the praxis via which the inhuman world of labor plus apparatus transforms nature into second nature (perhaps even a third nature), including all the things thus made that escape calculus of exchange value. These things appear then as akin to that most rarified of fetish objects, art.

As in Shelley, there's a wager on the ethical and political import of poetic vision: "This destiny comes from beyond the (human) world, and pronounces or decrees the end of the world. This decree marks a decisive point in Earth history in which humans discern the nonhuman and thus reckon the fate of Earth with greater justice" (148). One is reminded here of Shelley attaching his incendiary poems to a hot air balloon as a way to try and close the gap between the poem and its public, and between a public and action.[21] Everything is reduced to the rather idealistic project of countering a truncated view of the world with a *vision*: "This attitude is directly responsible for the ecological emergency, not the corporation or the individual per se, but the attitude that inheres both in the corporation or the individual, and in the critique of the corporation and the individual" (155).

What gives OOO its old-fashioned flavor is its attempt to give new life to this old metaphysical strategy. As Morton notes, we are confronted with limited options within the old possibility space, of which he lists three. Firstly, essence is everywhere. Secondly, there is no essence. Thirdly, essence is right here, yet it is withdrawn. Here I place myself with Bogdanov in the second camp, which declares an end to philosophy's attempt to claim a special object that is prior to and has more being that the objects produced within other forms of knowledge. Maybe we don't have to posit weird beings to understand evolution, ecology, quantum mechanics or climate change. Maybe we just have to *accept* these things as ordinary.

Morton has rather given us a variation on the *hidden God* (a version of option one, essence is everywhere). Lucien Goldmann's *Hidden God* is a study of Blaise Pascal and his contemporaries, and perhaps

21 Richard Holmes, *Shelley: The Pursuit*, New York: New York Review Books Classics, 2003, 149ff.

an instructive one for our times.[22] Pascal had a tragic vision of life. He accepts a world in which to act but its values cannot satisfy him. He is both in and out of the social. Its justice is not true justice, but he does not leave it as the mystics do. He maintains a faith in a superior realm, but this is not the ever present God of the middle ages. God does not manifest directly in his creation.

For Goldmann, Pascal has the worldview of an administrative class whose power is waning. They are within a powerful institution but not governing it. Rather like today's humanities scholars. Hence the *will to power* over the world through the staking of a claim to a higher reality, but a hidden one: in Pascal's case, God; in Morton's case, objects. The latter builds on the formalization of the former which for Goldmann was Kant's achievement. He made philosophy the legislator of what counted as a legitimate object of thought, of what belongs to appearances and what to essences. Morton banks instead on being able to speak in and about the rift between, the weird zone just beyond appearances from which to claim that they issue.

Perhaps this does have a value, in creating an illusion within which traditional forms of humanistic knowledge can continue to go on. And perhaps illusions have their uses when the dangers of losing them are too great. "Art in these conditions is grief-work. We are losing a fantasy—the fantasy of being immersed in a neutral or benevolent Mother Nature and a person who is losing a fantasy is a very dangerous person" (196). Morton's contributions to reviving old modes of affect and percept under new and pressing circumstances is certainly an important project.

For myself, I'm closer to the way Haraway goes about this, which likewise tries to *stay with the trouble* of our times, but stays also in the world of appearances. There're no additional claims for poetics as a way of knowing besides its ability to communicate between domains, and in particular to get actual knowledge about the nonhuman working within the spaces of humanistic and social thought.

In that vein I can agree with this version of Morton's project: "Nonhuman beings strike a devastating blow against teleology, a blow

22 Lucien Goldmann, *The Hidden God*, London: Verso, 2016.

detected by Darwin and celebrated by Marx, who wrote Darwin a fan letter for his opposition to teleology. The end of teleology is the end of the world" (95). But these nonhuman beings can be thought strictly in the world of appearances, the world of the praxis of knowledge with its cyborg apparatus of human labor and inhuman *techne*.

I would call this way of working not object oriented ontology, but *praxis (object oriented)*, or P(OO) for short. I would paraphrase Haraway's staying with the trouble as *staying with the poo*, meaning both staying with the praxis, but also meaning—staying with the poo. Stay with the waste, the neglect, the bad byproduct. Here I retain the metaphoric use of object-oriented, which as Galloway, Chun and others have pointed out, is a particular moment in the history of computation—but I retain it only as a metaphor, not an ontological claim.

19.

Quentin Meillassoux: The Spectacle of the Absolute

It's a zircon, the oldest rock in the world. It is about 4.4 billion years old. This particular planet is 4.5 or maybe 4.6 billion years old, so the oldest rock, a little bit of zircon, goes back a way. It is from the Hadean Eon, named after Hades, because it was an era that from any human point of view, or from the point of view of any kind of life, was rather hot and unpleasant. Or so it is generally thought.

When geochemists Mark Harrison and Bruce Watson studied this little zircon, they found some strange things. It's a crystal, and it grew as crystals do, and as it did it embedded in itself other atoms of whatever happened to be around—in this case, titanium. More titanium ends up in zircons when it is hotter than when it is cooler. So by counting titanium concentrations, it is possible to know how hot it was when the rock was formed.

What Watson and Harrison found is that this zircon crystalized at around 680 degrees Celsius, which means that it formed in the presence of water. As Watson explains: "Any rock heated in the presence of water—any rock, at any time, in any circumstance—will begin to melt at between 650 and 700 degrees. This is the only terrestrial process that occurs so predictably."[1]

I am not a geochemist, so I will have to take Watson's word for that. Two things stand out to me from this story. The first is that it is possible to have knowledge of something happening billions of years

1 Quoted in Robert Krulwich, "The Oldest Rock in the World Tells Us a Story," NPR.com, January 11, 2012.

before there were people. That little zircon is a lovely example of what Quentin Meillassoux calls the *arche-fossil*, a piece of evidence of a world that has nothing to do with our species-being.[2]

But there's one other thing of interest, to me if not to Meillassoux. It is the question of what makes it possible to have a knowledge of the arche-fossil. I can think about the arche-fossil. I can write about the arche-fossil. But neither thought nor language is all that central to its existence. Let's also bracket off from its existence the fact that there is a science called geochemistry, existing in departments of universities, communicating through peer-reviewed scientific journals and conferences. In a sense that's just the thinking and the language part of a knowledge of the arche-fossil understood sociologically.

The thing that is important to Meillassoux is mathematics: the zircon arche-fossil as a mathematizable description of the universe. From the Big Bang to the formation of its galaxies, its planets, and even its tiny rocks, the universe can be described mathematically, which to him means they exist outside of thought or language. It can exist outside of the knowing subject who thinks or writes—so long as one takes mathematics itself to be real.

The perspective on the arche-fossil that concerns me, though, is that it comes to exist via an apparatus that combines labor and technology, an apparatus by which a mathematical description of a cosmic process, even a geochemical one, is *tested*. The zircon mentioned above has been subjected to two such tests. At least one scientific procedure dates the fossil, and another measures the amount of titanium that crystalizes in it.

One can imagine a mathematical description of the world as something *nonhuman*, as existing without a human subject. The technical work of producing knowledge out of the arche-fossil also in a sense dispenses with the subject, resting as it does on an *apparatus*, an assemblage of labor and machine. This dependency on an apparatus I shall call the *inhuman*. It is, as we shall see, not quite the same thing as the nonhuman qualities of mathematical description.

---

2 Quentin Meillassoux, *After Finitude: An Essay on the Necessity of Contingency*, London: Continuum, 2008.

Once one starts looking into the technical part, one finds oneself in a world of company websites for hardcore geek machinery. Let me just mention the Cameca Company, which among other products makes Electron Probe Analyzers for Materials and Geoscience:

> The SXFive comes equipped with a versatile electron gun compatible with W and LaB_6. The beam current is continuously regulated, achieving a stability of 0.3% per 12 hours, thus enabling reliable long-term quantitative analyses. The beam intensity is accurately measured thanks to an annular Faraday cup and electrostatic deflection. The high voltage system operates at up to 30 kV for elements with high atomic number.[3]

I really have no idea what any of that means. Of all the websites on these things I found, I chose this one, because Cameca is a company that got its start producing movie projectors that could project sound films at the dawn of the "talkies." It then diversified into scientific instruments, but came back into the human-to-human media business briefly in the '60s with the famous Scopitone movie jukebox.[4]

The movies, as we know from Dziga Vertov, replace human vision with the kino-eye.[5] The movies show to human vision something that is already inhuman. The scientific instrument extends the range of perception even further, creating forms of inhuman perception across all sorts of scales and temporalities. Among other things, such instruments can perceive and measure arche-fossils, things which are completely alien to human sensory bandwidth and memory. Machine perception alienates the human from the human, by being the *inhuman* register of the *nonhuman*.

---

3 See www.cameca.com/instruments-for-research/sxfive.aspx. See also the "Early Earth" special issue of *Elements: An International Magazine of Mineralology, Geochemistry, and Petrology*, vol. 2, no. 4, August 2006. Scientific writing also regularly brackets off the specifics of the apparatus, but one can discover its presence in a journal such as this via the advertising, for machines by Rigaku, Australian Scientific Instruments, the wonderfully named Rockware and Comeca, among others.

4 Jean-Charles Scagnetti, *L'aventure scopitone (1957–1983)*, Paris: Editions Autrement, Coll. Mémoires/Culture, 2010.

5 Dziga Vertov, *Kino-Eye*, Berkeley: University of California Press, 1985.

If we ignore this machine vision, the media of the inhuman, we are left with a stark choice. On the one hand we have human thought and language, to which we might add human perception. It is a rather finite and bounded domain. On the other, we have the nonhuman domain of mathematics. Let's assume just for the moment that mathematics really can touch the absolute, that it is not limited to the human. Then one could, as Meillassoux wants, take the arche-fossil as a kind of emblem of the existence of an absolute beyond even the nonhuman that only mathematics knows.

Yet in between the mathematics of the absolute and the finitude of the human, there is something else. Something Meillassoux does not really even mention: the *apparatus*. It is neither human nor nonhuman, and it exists in a liminal, undecidable inhuman space. The apparatus requires human labor, but it is not reducible to the intersubjective realm of scientific discourse. It includes also the machine, that which perceives and measures far beyond the realm of the human, which registers the existence of a "great outdoors," but which does not touch the absolute.

With this question of apparatus back in the picture, as it were, it is possible to ask whether, when we claim that mathematics touches the absolute, it touches the absolute of a world that is real. Meillassoux approaches this by reviving the distinction between *primary* and *secondary properties*. The secondary properties of anything are its sensible ones. I see and feel the object, but is this really what matters about the object? And is this perhaps just the object as it appears to my senses? On the other hand, its primary qualities, its mathematical essence, exist independently of appearances. Or so Meillassoux, building on Locke and Descartes, would want to propose.

One could argue at this juncture, as Jay Bernstein does, that there is something fundamental to modernity about this split, about this sequestering of secondary qualities.[6] There is perhaps something inhuman about modernity, about its production of a whole apparatus for apprehending and transforming things, in which secondary

6 Jay Bernstein, *Against Voluptuous Bodies: Adorno's Late Modernism and the Meaning of Painting*, Stanford, CA: Stanford University Press, 2007.

qualities play little part. For Bernstein, after Adorno, the realm of the secondary quality is the realm of art. Art redeems what is sensed from calculation.

Or: one could argue that there's something of a sleight of hand involved in the idea of primary qualities. In Meillassoux's version, they are held to exist intrinsically in the thing, in mathematical form. Primary qualities can thus be held to be real in a philosophical sense. But they are not real in a scientific sense unless they can also be *measured*. The measurement of primary qualities requires an apparatus, of machines and labor, via which the primary qualities can be accounted for in terms intelligible as secondary qualities, as a numerical readout or a graph that can be seen, for example. Indeed, one might say that for primary qualities to be real in a scientific sense requires the primary quality to be made legible as a secondary quality via a *tertiary quality*. The tertiary quality of a thing is how the apparatus perceives it. It is an inhuman perception which makes the nonhuman primary quality legible via human secondary qualities.

What makes it possible for Meillassoux to loose a speculative philosophy from the constraints of a phenomenological one is the absence of a third kind of thought, which for the moment I will leave unnamed. Its preoccupation is not the absolute nor is it consciousness, it is the apparatus, that neither-nonhuman-nor-human thing, the inhuman media between them.

One thing I am trying to avoid here is a retreat from the great outdoors, the remarkable fact of the arche-fossil and all it represents, back into a phenomenology, for which "we cannot represent the 'in itself' without it becoming the 'for us' " (4). On the other hand, while I admire the elegance with which Meillassoux deploys the absolute to open up a speculative philosophy of the real, I want to argue that such a project can only be a *contemplative* realism, and thus an aesthetic one. As such it falls short of a certain project that for philosophy might be its last good calling.

Key to Meillassoux's argument is the attack on what he calls *correlationism*, defined thus: "Correlationism consists in disqualifying the claim that it is possible to consider the realms of subjectivity and objectivity independently of one another" (5). While there may be stand-ins for subject and object—thought and being, for example—correlationist thought proceeds in a circle. Meillassoux:

> Consciousness and its language certainly transcend themselves towards the world, but there is a world only insofar as a consciousness transcends itself towards it. Consequently, this space of exteriority is merely the space of what faces us, of what exists only as a correlate of our own existence. (7)

The result is a "cloistered" thought, in which the arche-fossil is no longer a nonhuman object of real wonder. Also gone, although not the same thing, is the absolute that so fascinated thinkers before Kant. Meillassoux's project is to revive precritical philosophy, but in a speculative rather than a dogmatic vein. The ancestral rock is his avatar of an absolute world. But there's a problem here. What constructs the knowledge of the rock as truly ancestral, as predating any human world, of pointing back, even to the origins of the universe itself? Namely: "an isotope whose rate of radioactive decay *we know*" (10, emphasis added). Well, how do we know it? Through the apparatus.

Meillassoux: "*Obviously*, it is not part of our remit to appraise the reliability of the techniques employed in order to formulate such statements" (10, emphasis added). Obviously? There is a slippage here. I doubtless know even less than Meillassoux about the science of geochemistry. It would not be my place to assess the reliability of a Cameca SXFive or any other apparatus. I am pretty sure that is not even the apparatus involved in this particular case. But I do take it as part of theory's remit to think the *apparatus in general.*

What we can say about the apparatus in general, is that there are no statements to be made about the ancestral that do not pass through its inhuman capacities to perceive and measure *tertiary qualities*. There is no correlation, but not because the object can be thought independently of the subject. Rather, because the object is produced via something else to which the subject, consciousness, language—call it what you like—is "secondary." Or in short, in this other view, *both* primary and secondary qualities are products of tertiary ones.

So yes, we can agree that "the ancestral witness is illegitimate from the viewpoint of strict correlationism" (11). And so much the worse for correlationism. But in freeing the arche-fossil from the correlationist circle while ignoring the apparatus, Meillassoux opens onto a great outdoors of a singly philosophical kind. It is not, appearances to the contrary, the great outdoors of science. Science can think a time anterior to giveness and indifferent to it, but speculative realism can only contemplate that time poetically (Morton) or mathematically (Meillassoux), but in any case as a *result* of an apparatus that remains unthought. It may turn out to be not the only way that Meillassoux exempts philosophy from certain kinds of engagement.

Correlationism has at least one virtue for Meillassoux. It wards thought away from dogmatism. Precritical philosophies offered all kinds of metaphysical absolutes. Critical thought holds itself accountable to a mapping of its own limits. But thought armed against dogmatism opened itself to another vice, what Meillassoux calls *fanaticism*. Correlationism put paid to philosophical means of speaking of the absolute, but not mystical ones, which install themselves again as spokesmodels for what is on the other side of the thing as it appears to consciousness—the thing-itself.[7] In so limiting what it says of the great outdoors, critical thought only enables certain kinds of mystical thinking.

Meillassoux:

> Against dogmatism, it is important that we uphold the refusal of every metaphysical absolute, but against the reasoned violence of various fanticisms, it is important that we rediscover in thought *a modicum of absoluteness*—enough of it, in any case, to counter the pretentions of those who would present themselves as its *privileged trustees,* solely by virtue of some revelation. (49 emphasis added)

For those who want a monist, secular or materialist thought, there's merit in this argument. But in shutting the door to revelation,

7 See for example Eugene Thacker, *In the Dust of This Planet: Horror of Philosophy*, vol. 1, Winchester, UK: Zero Books, 2011, for a contemporary mode in which this line of thought might be reanimated.

Meillassoux might actually open a portal to another kind of divinity, and another kind of "trustee"—one that plays dice.

Sheering away from correlationism, and its insistence on the self-monitoring subject's centrality in constructing the thought of the object, Meillassoux heads in the other direction, to the object, thought outside of correlation, but here he applies more than a modicum of the absolute. For him, if the arche-fossil stands for the ancestral, and is thinkable, then the absolute is thinkable. But again there's a slippage here, from the arche-fossil as it appears to science, to what Meillassoux wants to make of it. The arche-fossil is a thing from beyond human time, but the absolute need not enter into it. Knowledge of the arche-fossil is a product of an apparatus. It may come from 4.4 billion years ago, as in my example, or even from the beginnings of the universe, but it is a measurable thing. As Morton says, the very long duration may be even harder to think than the eternal.

Meillassoux: "How then is thought to carve a path towards the outside for itself?" (51). Like most philosophers, he does not take the road of the apparatus.[8] Instead he wants a rationalism of the absolute that is not dogmatic. This rationalism must extract itself on the one hand from the correlationist circle, and on the other, it must not run aground on what he calls *facticity*, or thought's inability to discover why what is, is. In other words, how can the absolute exist outside of thought or language? And yet, why *this* world and not some other?

There is a path already marked here that might escape at least from the first of these constraints, "the first metaphysical counter-offensive against Kantian transcendentalism" (51). Its most interesting version is the now little-known school of *empirio-criticism* of Ernst Mach and others.[9] From it descends the "tertiary" position from which I am approaching Meillassoux, which is even less well known today, but was certainly known in French philosophy schools a generation ago.

8 On this allergy philosophy has for the apparatus, or *techne*, see Bernard Stiegler, *Technics and Time, 1: The Fault of Epimetheus*, Stanford, CA: Stanford University Press, 1998.

9 For a critical assessment, see John T. Blackmore, *Ernst Mach: His Life, Work, and Influence*, Berkeley: University of California Press, 1972.

Its name is empiriomonism, and its central exponent is Alexander Bogdanov.[10]

As Meillassoux presents it, the original move of this school is to turn the correlation itself into an absolute. It begins with an acknowledgement of the Kantian constraint, that the thing-itself is not knowable other than by some dogma or other. But there is something knowable in-itself—the correlation itself. Meillasoux: "they converted radical ignorance into knowledge of a being finally unveiled in its true absoluteness" (52).

I would quarrel here with this use of the term absolute, as I think it is not necessary at all to think of Mach, and still less of Bogdanov, as making the correlation into an absolute. But it is the case that in Mach *sensation*, and in Bogdanov what I am calling the *apparatus*, replaces the dualist correlation with a monist concept which also restrains itself from making claims in advance about the real beyond the practice of the apparatus, and yet does not hold consciousness or language to be an external self-monitoring observer that might contemplate with disinterest what the apparatus produces in the labor of knowing the world.

In any case, for Meillassoux, such an approach passes the first test, avoiding the correlation, but fails a second one: facticity. For him, thought does not experience its limits in facticity, but rather its truth. Meillassoux founds his speculative, nondogmatic philosophy the same way Mach and Bogdanov did: by making a virtue of "necessity." In the former case, this necessity was thinking past the problem of correlation, in the latter, thinking past the problem of facticity.

In an original move, Meillassoux makes the *absence* of reason the ultimate property of facticity. There is no reason for anything to be or persist. All that is, is contingency. Meillassoux:

> Everything could actually *collapse*: from trees to stars, from stars to laws, from physical laws to logical laws, and this not by virtue of some superior law whereby everything is destined to perish, but by virtue

10 Alexander Bogdanov, *La Science, L'Art et La Classe Ouvrière*, trans. Blanche Grinbaum and Henri Deluy, Paris: Maspero, 1977. Published in the Théorie series, directed by Louis Althusser.

> of the absence of any superior law capable of preserving anything, no matter what, from perishing. (53, emphasis added)

Contingency here means how things persist or perish. Meillassoux revives the absolute in the form of contingency itself, but not in a dogmatic way. It is not that contingency is the new dogmatic answer to the problem of facticity. Rather, facticity is neither necessity nor contingency, but rather our non-knowledge of when one or the other applies. Even contingency is contingent.

Here comes the fun part: he goes on to argue, and rather convincingly, that correlationism presupposed the absoluteness of contingency. For thought to apprehend the thing without a dogmatic metaphysics behind it is to embrace the possibility, even if only for a moment, of its absolute contingency. Thus, the absoluteness of contingency must at least be thinkable for there to be a correlationism that dispels the illusion of an absolute of the dogmatic kind. Meillassoux: "this absence of reason is, and can only be the ultimate property of the entity."

Let's take stock:

First: there is certainly value in breaking out of correlationism. One of correlationism's limits is that it is not able to think contemporary science without expelling from it precisely that about which thought really should wonder, such as the ancestral evidence of a nonhuman world. But there is a problem with the thing on which Meillassoux wants to posit a new absolute. The *nonhuman*, mathematizable qualities of a thing could be thought as being outside of the subject and thus outside of the correlatonist circle, but only at the price of excluding also the question of detection and measurement, which I am here calling the tertiary qualities of *inhuman* sensation that properly belong to the apparatus.

Second: Meillassoux acknowledges two paths out of correlation, one being in my terms via the *apparatus*, by thinking that inhuman machinery of perception and measurement, and the labor by which it comes to us, of Harrison and Watson and so many others. This we might call the empirical exit from correlation. But Meillassoux takes the rationalist exit instead.[11] It rests on taking facticity to be as real a

11 As does Galloway. See his *Laruelle: Against the Digital*, Minneapolis:

problem as correlation, and answering that problem in an original way: there is no reason why what is, is. And better: there's no way of knowing why some of what appears is contingent and some not. This in turn is a tool for prizing open correlation, which in Meillassoux's argument has to entertain the possibility of a contingent world in order not to think it dogmatically, even if it settles instead for the cloistered world of the correlationist circle.

Let's conclude, as we started, with a particular example of an arche-fossil, if of a rather different kind. One perhaps not as glorious as the zircon, or even as identifiable as a thing. Let's consider not cosmology, but climate science, which gives us evidence of a very pertinent kind of *collapse*. Climate science tells us of past events, such as the climate of the Hadean Eon, but also of a future one, the imminent climate of the Anthropocene Era.[12]

Climate science abstracts from the fetishism of particular, contingent actions on a certain localized scale, that of the biosphere, to show us also a future event that has already occurred. The already transpired rise—among other gases—of atmospheric carbon has already raised global temperatures in the future. Climate science raises the alarm about an event that unfolds in slow motion all around us, but beyond the scale and memory of human thought or perception. It too is a thing which in its full wonder is outside the correlationist circle.

Climate science knows nothing of the absolute. It depends on an apparatus. Indeed, one of the leading histories of it is called *A Vast Machine*.[13] It has three elements: predicting the weather, modeling the climate, and the physics of how both weather and climate work. It took many decades to bring all three together. Gathering timely weather data from disparate locations and altitudes takes a huge, global infrastructure. Computing that data with an accurate model of the physics takes a vast amount of computational power. Both

---

University of Minnesota Press, 2014. See also McKenzie Wark, "Laruelle's Kinky Syntax," *Public Seminar,* April 23, 2015, at publicseminar.org.

12 Intergovernmental Panel on Climate Change, *Climate Change 2014*, Cambridge: Cambridge University Press, 2015.

13 See Paul N. Edwards, *A Vast Machine: Computer Models, Climate Data, and The Politics of Global Warming*, Cambridge, MA: MIT Press, 2010.

data communication and computation friction impeded the study of climate until the late twentieth century. At the base of our contemporary knowledge of climate, and climate change, is the evolution, from system to network to webs, of a global climate knowledge infrastructure, requiring coordinated global labors.

Climate science is our Napoleon at Jena, not the world spirit on horseback, but the biospheric totality via Comsat. If there is a short list of things calling us to a timely rather than a hesitant thought, then surely it is on that list. But philosophy has turned away from such things.[14] It grew bored with the double binds of the subject, but rather than lift its gaze toward this world, it conjured up another—the world of the *absolute object.* This *contemplative realism* provides a window through which to observe the beauty of a world that actually is collapsing, and the solace of knowing that the world will go on, even if the human does not. Philosophy has found a spectacle outside of history once again, while the sirens go off all around us, calling us to put out fires both conceptual and real.

This is why I choose to begin again, but elsewhere, with Mach and Bogdanov, and a quite other path out of the correlationist circle, toward the inhuman beyond phenomenology but falling short of the nonhuman and intimations of the absolute.[15] This other theory—in its engagement with the apparatus—might not even be philosophy. Yet it may have a few modest merits. It begins and ends with that mingling of labor and technology that characterize the times. It hews close to the problems that such an apparatus detects as the problems of the moment—such as climate change. It makes no claim to be the trustee of a portal between this world and another. It makes no claim that either it, or its subject, is a rare event. It seeks only to equip everyday life with the tools for its own sustenance and elaboration. It has no interest in rendering the contemplative spectacle absolute and eternal. It has an interest only in dispensing with the spectacle entirely. In this it does not hesitate.

---

14 But see Tom Cohen, *Telemorphosis: Theory in the Era of Climate Change*, London: Open Humanities Press, 2012.

15 This is the program of McKenzie Wark, *Molecular Red,* London: Verso, 2015.

20.

Isabelle Stengers: Gaia Intruding

Truth be told, nobody really knows how to respond to the slow-motion emergency in which we find ourselves. Even at the level of language. There's no rhetorical device that seems destined for clarity. In *Molecular Red*, I took the path of taking the language of the Anthropocene seriously, and looking for new genealogies from the archive to meet it. Haraway and Jason Moore prefer to call it the *Capitalocene*, to name the historical form of that which is killing the earth.[1]

Morton proposes an ecology without nature. In *Molecular Red* I thought it made more sense to think a *nature without ecology*, as nature is the more capacious and historically variable term, whereas the *logos* of the *oikos*—ecology—is precisely what can no longer be said to exist. John Bellamy Foster prefers to talk, after Marx, about *metabolic rift*. Rob Nixon speaks of slow violence. Isabelle Stengers revives and recasts the figure of *Gaia*.[2] Is that a better rhetorical gambit? Nobody knows. But it is a compelling one.

Rosa Luxemburg famously said that the choice of futures lay between socialism or barbarism.[3] For Stengers the choice has narrowed to a more infernal alternative: *barbarism or barbarism*. In the

1 Jason W. Moore, *Capitalism in the Web of Life*, London: Verso, 2015.

2 John Bellamy Foster, *Marx's Ecology: Materialism and Nature*, New York: Monthly Review Press, 2000; Rob Nixon; Isabelle Stengers, *Catastrophic Times*, London: Open Humanities Press, 2015.

3 Helen Scott (ed.), *The Essential Rosa Luxemburg*, Chicago: Haymarket, 2007, 24.

absence of a combined counterproposal from green and social movements, the choice becomes one between runaway climate change or a *geo-engineered* future, which mobilizes public finance for private gain.[4] The planet then becomes hostage to corporate interests.

It is time then for a new kind of movement that addresses itself to both what is usually thought of as the social and the natural. For Stengers the prototype of this is already in Félix Guattari's book *The Three Ecologies*, although one could think also of other examples.[5] For Stengers, as we shall see, it's a four-part plan: *naming Gaia*, *paying attention*, *calling-out stupidity* and *creating artifice*. "It is a matter of learning to inhabit what henceforth we know, of learning what that which is in the process of happening to us obliges us to do" (19).

We are suspended between two histories, the first being modern growth with its arrow of time and constant development. The second is more obscure and as yet without name or image. It is no longer a matter of protecting nature as an environment but of a nature that challenges our modes of thinking and acting. It begins from the stupefying contrast between what we know and what we can do.

Stengers wants a way to inherit the history of struggle against capitalism but without its grand narrative of truth and progress. This would be the problem with the figure of the *Capitalocene*. It tends to default to standard ways of thinking about capital and puts off to the distant future any project but its overcoming. But there is no longer time for that. Stengers wants to reach out to those who are experimenting with a new mode of production already, whether it is slow food, or permaculture or what have you.

Not much can be expected from what Stengers calls the *guardians*, and they know it. Whether elected or appointed, the guardians simply manage a state of "cold panic" (32). Their exhortations aren't even coherent: keep consuming but be "green" about it! They have lately added schools and universities to the list of institutions to be broken up for kindling and fed into the boiler room of commodification.[6]

4 Clive Hamilton, *Earthmasters*, New Haven, CT: Yale University Press, 2013.

5 Félix Guattari, *The Three Ecologies*, London: Bloomsbury, 2003.

6 Stefano Harney and Fred Moten, *The Undercommons: Fugitive Planning and Black Study*, Wivenhoe: Minor Compositions, 2013.

Even there, open-ended inquiry and collaboration is getting harder. Interestingly, Stengers thinks that rather than denunciation, the guardians deserve even less: laughter, rudeness and satire.

The model for thought and action on which Stengers dwells is the movement against Genetically Modified Organisms (GMOs) and its modestly successful attempts to get them banned from European food. The anti-GMO movement refused the guardians' mode of perception and refused to accept their good intentions. It came up with its own questions and created a genuine dynamic of learning. It questioned technical authority, and would not accept "trade secrets" as a reason for withholding information.

The GMO issue divided "expert" opinion, but for Stengers, too much of scientific and technical research has ceased to be in any sense "public" as it has been coopted by private interests through the patenting of the results. Hence questions about whether GMOs just lead to more resistant strains of pests can't really be asked or answered. Particularly when such resistance is itself something that agribusiness can profit from by selling more herbicides and pesticides. The general policy of agribusiness regarding public inquiry is in any case neatly summed up as: "Lie first, then say it is too late" (40).

That to which we have to respond Stengers names *the intrusion of Gaia*. We have to think in the manner this naming calls into being. In Hesiod's *Theogony*, Gaia is the first mother, who brought forth Uranus, the sky, and with him bore the Titans, including Chronos, their leader. Chronos overthrew Uranus and ruled over the Golden Age, before being defeated in turn by his own son, Zeus. For Stengers, Gaia is a blind and indifferent God, a figure for a time before Greek gods had scruples.

Gaia is a name that conjures up ancient myths, and became something of a hippie mantra, but oddly enough was popularized by a scientific theory offered by James Lovelock and Lynn Margulis, in which organisms coevolve with their environments and form "ecological, self-regulating systems.[7] For Stengers, the complicated

7 James Lovelock, *Gaia: A New Look at Life on Earth*, Oxford: Oxford University Press, 2000.

history of the deployments of the concept is actually part of its appeal.

Stengers wants a concept of a nature that is neither vulnerable nor threatening nor exploitable, but which asks nothing of us at all. Gaia is a "forgotten form of transcendence." Maybe a negative one, as Gaia is neither an arbiter, guarantor or resource. Gaia intrudes into human lives and perceptions, but there's no reciprocity. There's no channel for what elsewhere I called *xeno-communication*.[8] Nobody can claim to the high priest or priestess of Gaia. But there is no future in which we are free to ignore her. "We will have to go on answering for what we are undertaking in the face of an implacable being who is deaf to our justifications" (47).

It's a rhetorically risky move, perhaps especially in the United States, where talk of Gaia might naturally default to a kind of hippie romantic mysticism.[9] But then there are only rhetorically risky moves available, so perhaps it is worth a shot. Stengers insists that her invocation of Gaia is not antiscientific, and may even encourage scientists to think. But in general, she thinks that when it comes to the present danger, the scientists have done their work of warning us about where we really are.

One's sense of rhetorical tactics may be more a product of perceptions of local contingencies than of anything else. In the context in which I find myself, I feel obligated to tack a little harder towards shoring up respect for scientific forms of knowing the world. In the United States, the tactics being used against climate and earth scientists can only be described as a McCarthyite witch hunt.

But as Stengers makes plain, there're a lot of different things one can mean when one says "science." Some of which are not really forms or practices of knowing at all. There's no shortage of economic "science" being deployed to justify business as usual. Those who pledged their

8 Alexander R. Galloway, Eugene Thacker and McKenzie Wark, *Excommunication: Three Inquiries in Media and Mediation*, Chicago: University of Chicago Press, 2013, 160ff.

9 See for example Starhawk, *The Fifth Sacred Thing*, New York: Bantam, 1994. The example of which prompted Haraway to claim she would rather be a cyborg than a goddess.

soul to the eternal forward march of commodification are incapable of panic or reflection. For them, there is no situation, no matter how God-forsaken, that is not an "opportunity."

Stengers:

> Those who say to us "Marx is history," with an obscene, satisfied little smile, generally avoid saying to us why capitalism as Marx described it is no longer a problem. They only imply that it is invincible. Today those who talk about the vanity of struggling against capitalism are de facto saying "barbarism is our destiny." (51)

Capitalism fabricates its own necessity, which for Marx is what the rule of exchange value basically amounts to. Capitalism is a mode of transcendence that is not inevitable, just radically irresponsible. "Capitalism doesn't like noise" (54). It is hell-bent on eliminating signals that are not market signals, which are what appear to it as noise.

And yet for all that, Stengers is reluctant to collapse everything into the figure of capital. Talking about the Capitalocene runs the risk of ignoring certain new information, what Stengers calls the intrusion of Gaia, for which I have stuck the more conventional designation of the Anthropocene. Stengers:

> I also dread that it might incite those who resist only to pay lip service to the idea that global warming is effectively a new problem, following it immediately with the demonstration that this problem, like all others, should be blamed on capitalism, and then by that conclusion that we must therefore maintain our heading, without allowing ourselves to be troubled by a truth that must not upset the prospects for the struggle. (56)

It is a matter of learning to compose with Gaia instead: "Naming Gaia, she who intrudes, signifies that there is no afterwards" (57). That means letting go of an epic materialism in which nature is there as a resource for human conquest. Where obstacles exist only as the narrative pretext for Promethean leaps—as in children's stories.[10]

10 J. B. S. Haldane, *Daedalus*, London: EP Dutton, 1924, famously preferred a mortal to a supernatural figure from Greek myth for scientitic and technical leaps.

One can no longer claim a right not to pay attention to all that Gaia stands in for. Both those who think capital can be negated and those who think it can only be accelerated are called to account for their inattention here.

This civilization, such as it is, turns out to be as blind as its predecessors. Even when there is attention to the "environment," it is so often still framed as a question of a resource to be preserved rather than used. Precautions against dangerous products do not really challenge the "sacred right of the entrepreneur" (63). Which is to not pay attention to anything much other than the aura of the brand, and tactics of competitors and maximizing shareholder value. Risk is the price of progress. The entrepreneur makes the Promethean leap, even if nobody much believes anymore that anyone else is likely to benefit.

The dirty secret however is that these magnificent men in their profit machines don't really want to take risks. They want security. This is what for Brown and others is the characteristic of neoliberalism: the role of the state becomes the securing of profit with minimal extra-economic risk. They want to be indemnified against the results of their own actions. They want everything to be an opportunity for them.

What Stengers calls the *entrepreneur* I would call the *vectoralist class.*[11] It is no longer much interested in making things, let alone growing things. It just wants to skim the interest off from *asymmetrical flows of information*. It wants the state to foot the bill for basic research while it reaps the rewards when it is privatized as patents. It wants to shape the agenda for state-funded research to the template of its own interests. And it wants the state to go to extraordinary lengths to privatize the information commons and police its enclosure. To me that's a whole new regime of commodification to what Wendling identifies as Marx's *thermodynamic* model of capital.

Stengers has an interesting read on what happened to science in all this, although in this text it gets very abbreviated treatment.[12] One

11 McKenzie Wark, *A Hacker Manifesto*, Cambridge, MA: Harvard University Press, 2004.

12 For a more extensive treatment see Isabelle Stengers, *Cosmopolitics* I and II, Minneapolis: University of Minnesota Press, 2010 and 2011.

way to express it might be to say that she defends the sciences against Science. Stengers: "It was a matter not of attacking scientific practices but of defending them against an image of authority that is foreign to what makes for their fecundity and relative reliability" (69).

In her version, Galileo conducted an all-too successful propaganda mission on behalf of a rather limited and idealized version of the scientific method, which then got elevated into a kind of authority to be wielded against mere "opinion." This had the unfortunate effect of giving capital-S Science the role also of determining the real questions as those that can be settled objectively. One is reminded here of André Breton, who dared declare that Science is useful for the solution of many problems, unfortunately all of them of secondary interest.[13]

The problem for the sciences is that many had aligned themselves with the state, and with agendas in part set by the state. But with the hollowing out of the state they are unable to defend themselves against new regimes of management. Resentful researchers feel betrayed by the state, losing their little niche. But the state is not a bulwark against the intrusions of Gaia, on the one hand, or the demands of commodification, on the other. The state enables commodification without any reference to progress anymore. It still produces rules and norms, and in the process eliminates the local, traditional, the commons, and destroys resources that might nourish an art of attention.

But Stengers is wary of institutionalized Science, not the practices of the sciences. "We need researchers able to participate in the creation of the responses on which the possibility of a future that is not barbaric depends" (73). She is not a critic of an abstract technical rationality, as if it were to blame for all our predicaments. For "to attribute all that to technical rationality is to go a bit too quickly. As practitioners, technicians could be capable of many other things than subjecting everything that moves to categories that are indifferent to their consequences" (74).

This is however a crucial problem. The very terms of public debate are set in advance by what is in the interests of the entrepreneurs,

---

13 Paraphrasing from André Breton, *What Is Surrealism?: Selected Writings*, Atlanta: Pathfinder Press, 1978, 166.

aka the vectoralist class. "What has been conquered for all has been redefined by categories that are addressed to whoever, categories that produced amnesia and which are then vulnerable to the infernal alternatives concocted by capitalism" (75). Nobody's particular needs or interests or desires are taken into account. The state maintains public order; the entrepreneurs maintain a right to responsibility. Between them they generate a hostility to *paying attention.*

And so what needs to be collectively reclaimed is an art of paying attention, something with which the state can't help. We need consensual narratives about what is supposed to matter. Stengers highlights the narrative of the ongoing enclosure of the commons. The so-called knowledge economy—what I would call a vectoral rather than capitalist mode of production—erases the line between public and private research. The state lets the vectoralist class appropriate public knowledge production, while making the state responsible for enforcing its version of "intellectual property." Or as in the case of the Trans-Pacific Partnership and similar treaties, creates para-state formations to do it. There's a need to invent new modes of resistance to enclosure.

But for Stengers, there are two kinds of story one can tell here. One version, which one might find in Boutang or Lazzarato, restates the Marxist "conceptual theater." This is a story about something like a proletariat of the immaterial whose use value is immediately social. Cognitive capitalism exploits this sociality itself, which is a sort of postindustrial commons that is anonymous and abstract. A new figure, such as the multitude, replaces the worker as the agent of liberation.

I have always dissented from part of this narrative. I think the category of the "immaterial" is meaningless, and modifiers such as "cognitive" and "semio-" don't really capture what is distinctive about the forces of production and reproduction in our times. I also think it best not to assume in advance some sort of collective or class unity when really one is talking about quite different experiences and implications within the production process. Thus, in *A Hacker Manifesto* I was careful to see the hacker and worker as different figures that need to find ways of combining their interests through cultural, political and organizational means.

Nevertheless, I think Italian and French writers such as Virno, Boutang, Lazzarato and Berardi are at least asking the right questions and trying to capture in a conceptual net some of the features of this stage of commodification. It would appear that Stengers also accepts part of the shared terrain here. She draws attention to those working in computation who invented a form of resistance to the appropriation of what was common to them, of which Richard Stallman and the Free Software movement might be the most conscious element.[14] "It was as 'commoners' that they defined what made them programmers, not as nomads of the immaterial" (85).

However, to Stengers, the commons is not a new conceptual guarantor of a universal beyond oppositions. She is resistant to the reinstalling of a teleological version of the narrative in which the socialization of the commons must burst through the fetter of private property, even in its advanced "intellectual property" form. In *A Hacker Manifesto* I relied on a kind of ontological argument about the nature of information itself as something inimical to property and necessarily existing only as something shared. I'm not quite ready to give that up, but Stengers certainly puts me on notice as to the problems with this line of thinking, as she does with the kinds of arguments of the workerists and autonomists. I think she obliges us to confront a world without guarantees, in which barbarism or barbarism may well be an accurate description of the political-economic choices. The challenge is to respond to the intrusion of Gaia in a way that isn't barbaric and that makes no appeal to a pregiven outcome.

Certainly one form of barbarism attends the decline of attention occasioned by the transformation of both the arts and the sciences into endless versions of the same *gamespace* for professional "moves."[15] The sciences in particular have had the ability to "populate reality with new beings and agencies" (91). But not when they are constrained by capital-S Science to a kind of gatekeeping role for the state and the vectoralist class. Science becomes a kind of totem for Promethean

14 Richard Stallman, *Free Software, Free Society*, Boston: GNU Press, 2002.

15 See McKenzie Wark, *Gamer Theory*, Cambridge, MA: Harvard University Press, 2007, the "Agony" chapter.

man, able to brush aside all obstacles in the race to turn all of nature into a resource.

This is why Stengers is reluctant to concede too much to Science as a mode of practice and belief. It isn't really what the sciences at their most creative were about, and it forecloses other ways of knowing and organizing. So on the one hand, the sciences have to be uncoupled from belief in Science, while other forms of organizing "in the streets" have to be uncoupled from the epic grand narrative of liberation or romantic belief in spontaneity.

Stengers: "we live in a veritable cemetery for destroyed practices and collective knowledges" (98). But while trying to create new or revived forms of commons, one has to bear in mind that it is no guarantee. The commons has its dangers too—one of which is fascism. As Mouffe reminds us, the democratic commitment to a shared substance usually comes with a strong sense of who is excluded from it, with all the dangers Gilroy identifies of treating the excluded as *infrahuman*.

We may have had enough of the figure of the *pharmakon*, but Stengers deploys it here as a name for the undecidable, for that which can have good or bad effects that can't always be known in advance.[16] Those from the world of computing who challenged its rather narrow commodification with free software are one of her examples of thinking one's practice as a pharmakon.

But why did the sciences not respond in the same way as some of the programmers? Why did Science link itself so completely with the state and the vectoralist class? Actually, this is just as true, if not more so, of programming today, as Chun reminds us. But the question remains. One element is a hatred of pharmakon, of the undecidable, a desire for scientism even where Science has no viable methods. Another is an ethnocentric belief in Science as a rationality of the West—Joseph Needham's debunking of the myth of a China without science notwithstanding.[17]

16 Jacques Derrida, *Of Grammatology*, Baltimore: Johns Hopkins University Press, 2016. My reading of it is in *Gamer Theory*, sections 219–22.

17 Joseph Needham, *The Grand Titration: Science and Society in East and West*, Toronto: University of Toronto Press, 1969.

It is time then for a way of paying attention that is not wedded to guarantees in advance, be they of Science or some sort of ontology of the political as one finds it in different ways in Mouffe, Butler and Virno. "Every creation must incorporate the knowledge that it is not venturing into a friendly world but into an unhealthy milieu." It has to be an experimental era. "The pharmacological art is required because the time of struggle cannot postpone the time of creation. It cannot delay until 'after,' when there is no longer any danger" (104).

This could be an enlightened age, but only if enlightenment is thought once again as a taste for free thought and imagination as insubordination. It cannot continue in any useful way under the sign of the Enlightenment as a rentier, as the representative of established privilege, combatting with critique any forms of mystification or regression, but at the expense of attacking forms of social life that have not been entirely obliterated by reasons of state and exchange value. Stengers offers, paradoxically enough, a critique of critique, in the name of a more constructive and constructivist thinking, after the style of Deleuze.

It is time to declare a truce in the "science wars." The critique of the "social construction" of knowledge was unable to see how, as it is in Haraway, sciences can at one and the same time be saturated in social and historical forms and yet still crystalize out stable results that point to a nonhuman world. On the other hand, Science really does need to be held to account for its pandering to industry and complicity with the state.

The enemy of both humanistic thought and the open inquiry of the sciences is a kind of *stupidity*. This now even affects the rentiers who defend the Enlightenment, who really defend privilege, and have lost all sense of adventure and risk. (Stengers gives no examples, but I can't help thinking of the sad trajectory of Richard Dawkins.) Rather than critique which claims to see through to the root or the essence, or to ground everything else in an ontology of first things, Stengers like Deleuze prefers the world of second and third things, of thinking through the middle, or the milieu.[18]

18 Gilles Deleuze and Claire Parnet, *Dialogues II*, New York: Columbia University Press, 2002.

It is a time, then, for *minor knowledge*, which questions the order words of Promethean modernization.[19] The guardians keep the floodgates—as they see them—closed to questioning. We have to learn to pose our own questions. And refuse the answers when the questions to which they answer are answers for nobody, for whoever, rather than answers *for us*. And all that without investing too much faith in one or other belief that we know what we're doing: "it is not a matter of converting us but of repopulating the devastated desert of our imaginations" (132).

Among the traps to avoid are being captured by expertise, and avoiding confrontations that polarize the terrain and empty them of everything but the interests of opposing camps. One must try to "make the experts stutter" in a milieu poisoned by stupidity (138). One must fabricate trust which not only respects differences but also *divergences*. We're not on the same path or ever going to be. There's no way to totalize differences. There's no way to "penetrate" appearances and get to the whole truth in advance. "The desperate search for that which, being 'natural,' would supposedly have no need of any artifice, refers in fact, once more and as ever, to the hatred of the pharmakon, of that whose use implies an art" (144).

I would count Stengers (as I count myself) as a realist of the procedure rather than of the object of knowledge. We can know something of how we got the result. We can't know much about ontology, or nature, or the real. As I argued against Meillassoux, it takes an *inhuman* apparatus to make the *nonhuman* appear to the human. Stengers: "a scientific interpretation can never impose itself without artifice, without experimental fabrications, the invention of which empassions them much more than the 'truth'" (146), Stengers goes elsewhere than the recent ontological turn in thought, but not back to the old obsession with epistemology, which was just as prone to wanting rules for proper ways of knowing as ontology wants methods for the proper way to the unveiled object.

Hatred of *artifice* is hatred of pharmakon. It's a desire for guarantees in advance for the true and the good. It can be a hatred, in particular,

19 Gilles Deleuze and Félix Guattari, *Kafka: Towards a Minor Literature*, Minneapolis: University of Minnesota Press, 1986.

of democratic artifice.[20] Stengers: "those who feel themselves responsible demand that the only legitimate means for political action be those that are guaranteed to be without risk, like children's toys" (147). Politics as that which forms a disjunction with the "natural" order.

None of this will appease Gaia, but might help with a less barbaric future. *Naming Gaia*, confronting *stupidity*, *paying attention*, honoring *divergences*, creating *artifices* might be a recipe or an algorithm (for that is what I take *pharmakon* to mean) for mitigating the barbarism to come.

---

20 Here Stengers gestures towards Jacques Rancière, *Hatred of Democracy*, London: Verso, 2014.

21.

Donna Haraway: The Inhuman Comedy

When my daughter was little, we played a game on the way to her preschool called Count the Dog Poo. It was a game about counting, as you would play with any child, but also a game for a little New Yorker, to teach her to watch where she steps. Living in New York, pretty much every day one can expect the pleasure of watching shit extrude out of a dog's asshole. Hence it is with a certain amusement that I learn from reading *Manifestly Haraway* that in California, Donna Haraway picks up her dogs' poo with the blue plastic wrapper of the *New York Times.*[1]

Besides a different relation to dogs, I find there are many ways my sensibility differs in interesting ways from Haraway. She describes herself as a "Sputnik Catholic" (283). While raised religious, she says, "My Catholic girl's brain got educated, as opposed to my being a pro-Life activist mother of ten, because I became a national resource after Sputnik. My brain got valuable" (283). I think I might describe myself as a Mercury Marxist. (While it is the Apollo rather than the Mercury space program that I remember, that's the wrong god.) Something about the agonistic rivalry of the Cold War space race points to the possibilities of the human becoming something else.

Being a secular Protestant to Haraway's secular Catholic, I'm a bit less interested in mediating figures. The naked confrontation with the problem of totality is the thing I take to be what endures from the

1 Donna Haraway and Cary Wolfe, *Manifestly Haraway*, Minneapolis: University of Minnesota Press, 2016.

Protestant sensibility.[2] Devotion to one's labors was not supposed to be an end in itself, but rather a means to make bodies comfortable enough to open toward the sheer sublime alien otherness of the world.

So I read Haraway's writing from a situation a little askew to some of its topics. And that's what makes it interesting. *Manifestly Haraway* offers three moments from her evolving work. It takes the form of three meditations on the manifesto. The book reprints the famous "Manifesto for Cyborgs" (originally 1985), the "Companion Species Manifesto" (2003) and a fresh conversation with Cary Wolfe that can be read as notes for a "Cthulucene Manifesto."[3] I want to read these starting from the most recent, working backwards.

The impulse to rename the Anthropocene something else—*anything* else!—is a powerful one and perhaps even its own pathology. For a humanist, there's every reason not to want to be centered again on Anthropos, after spending so long trying to decenter him. But it was biologists and earth scientists who named it, and it might sustain ongoing conversations to respect that. Haraway: "I wish that it hadn't been their term. But it is their term...We will need to continue to operate within this discursive materiality as well as others that name our urgencies better in key respects" (242–43). It's helpful to be able to speak with the natural sciences in language that plays there.

In any case, as Haraway says, "I don't have to choose one term." If she did, it might with Jason Moore call this the *Capitalocene*: "the players in the Capitalocene are, at a minimum, situated plants, animals, humans, microbes, the multiple layering of technologies in and among all this" (240). It's a way of naming that identifies a power at work in climate change, ocean acidification, mass extinction and other signs of living and dying very poorly. My only hesitation about the name is that were capitalism to be abolished tomorrow, nothing is really solved by that mere negation.[4]

2 McKenzie Wark, "Kierkegaard's Frenemies," *Public Seminar*, December 23, 2013, at publicseminar.org.

3 See also the excellent Haraway interview-book by Thyrza Nichols Goodeve, *How Like a Leaf*, Routledge, New York, 1999.

4 Jason W. Moore, *Capitalism in the Web of Life,* London: Verso, 2015.

So let's think through another name. Let's live also in the *Chthulucene*. Haraway is no great fan of Lovecraft, for whom Cthulu is the name of the ultimate monstrosity, at the far reaches of his racist fantasies of the other.[5] Rather, she chose the name because it was given to a species of spider local to her in California. It is curious how the languages of fantasy fiction and scientific classification can criss and cross.

Here is how Haraway further roils the language:

> My Chthulucene is the time of mortal compositions at stake to and with each other. This epoch is the *kainos* (-cene) of the ongoing powers that are terra, of the myriad tentacular ones in all their diffracted, webbed temporalities, spacialities and materialities. Kainos is the temporality of the thick, lumpy "now" which is ancient and not. (294)

Let me just pick out the word *diffracted* here. This is a scenario populated by many earthy godlets, but whose relations to each other are neither mystically withdrawn nor a theater of representation, but more like waves breaking and ramifying against each other.

It is a way of getting into the world with one's feelers that is a bit aslant to some seemingly similar things. It isn't a *new materialism*, it is a quite ancient one.[6] It isn't *post-humanism*, as there never was much to say about the human here. It isn't *ecological*, as there's something a bit off about ecology's obsession with healthy reproduction. It is not quite the *Gaia* of which Stengers writes, but a wilder one, from before Hesiod made her a—more or less—respectable God. The Chthulucene is more snake-head Gorgon, one that can even shatter mirrors. "I want to cast in my lot with the ongoing, unfinished, dreadful powers of the Earth, where the risk, terror, and promise of uncategorizable mortal ongoing can still be found" (288).

Haraway is interested in practices that gather up and make worlds. "I think my proliferating words and figures are flesh and do a lot of

5 Carl Sederholm and Jeffrey Andrew Weinstock (eds.), *The Age of Lovecraft*, Minneapolis: University of Minnesota Press, 2016. See the China Mieville essay in particular.

6 See for example Rosi Braidotti, *The Posthuman*, Cambridge: Polity, 2013.

things" (277). But it is a nonidentity of word and flesh, a resistance to the name that sticks and becomes a fetish, a stand-in, a double. It's a version of the *via negativa* of religious thinkers, but not one aimed at the gesture that marks by its absence where the infinite might be, but rather where the finite might be.[7] This *via negativa* is as injunction to humility that not only refuses representation but also the indexical and the holistic. "You will not come together from two, or many, into one, because that is precisely the idolatry that the negative way tries to block" (279).

This is perhaps a residue of the material semiotics of Catholicism that Haraway might share with Stengers and Bruno Latour.[8] Haraway: "For me, the incarnation and sacramentalism were overwhelmingly about a shared meal, in and of the flesh. Carnality is seriously Catholic. Both cyborgs and dogs, both manifestos, bear witness to that!" (270). In the absence of the Void, the Real, or Name of the Father that might speak the final meaning of things, there's no end to the slippery copresence of words and things.

It is a refusal of the structural—or perhaps Protestant—turn in semiotics, initiated by the Swiss linguist Ferdinand de Saussure.[9] This separates an abstract plane of signification from the plane of things and events to which language refers. In place of which, here is "the extraordinary tentacular closeness of processes of semiosis and fleshiness" (268). It is like a game of rock-paper-scissors: there's no trump move over all the others; the sign and the hand are inseparable—but not one.

---

7 On the *via negativa*, see Eugene Thacker's contribution to *Excommunication*, Chicago: University of Chicago Press, 2013.

8 Bruno Latour, *On the Modern Cult of the Factish Gods*, Cambridge, MA: Harvard University Press, 2010.

9 Ferdinand De Saussure, *Course in General Linguistics*, Chicago: Open Court Classics, 1998. Curiously, one of the origin stories one could tell for structuralism is the meeting of Claude Lévi-Strauss and Roman Jakobson at the New School during the war. Most of the Francophone refugees were working on how to restore the continuity of Catholic French culture after the Nazis. This did not appeal to Jakobson and Lévi-Strauss, of course. Instead, they developed a theory for the structural analysis of cultural forms. See Peter Rutkoff, *New School: A History of the New School for Social Research*, New York: Free Press, 1998.

But there's another way to go here, and it leaves its trace in Haraway, in her alternate naming of the Capitalocene and the Chthulucene. The latter might foreground the slippery, fleshy, protean world, but the former still point towards the background, toward more abstract and disembodied figures of totality, particularly of *bad totality*—one that wills itself to completion and exclusion beyond the moment of disaster. Rather than pluralize the foreground particulars, it might be interesting to pluralize the background generalities. There's the generality of capitalism—if that is still what this mess is—and it has forced enclosure of thing after thing in and as the commodity form.[10] But then there's the generality of climate science, the passage of actual molecular flows of carbon through atmosphere and ocean. One can see the dance of particulars as twisting in the violent wind between whatever it is those two abstractions try to name.

The Greeks and the Romans had a series of moon goddesses: Selene, Phoebe, Artemis, Hecate, Luna and Trivia. Just imagine if the moon shot had been named after Trivia rather than Apollo! She was a goddess of crossroads, whose presence was known only by the barking of dogs. What might an ethics and a politics be like that was a "secular" version not just of the chthonic mud gods but also the more ambient ones? The emphasis in Haraway's recent works has been on an ethics for the Chthulucene. But perhaps one needs both an ethics of the Chthulucene and a politics of the Capitalocene, not to mention some rhetorical generosity for working with those who call it the Anthropocene.

To start with the ethics, and its questions: How are we all to live in "non-innocence?" (236). And: "How to truly love our age, and also how to somehow live and die well here, with each other?" (207). Perhaps it's a matter of meeting across differences that don't resolve dialectically, yet don't return to separate enclaves either. "We must engage—must dance—ontological choreography if we are to live and die well with each other in the troubles" (224). Haraway gives it a queer twist: "Make kin not babies!" (224). Which I would rephrase as: make *kith*, not kin! Haraway: "We need other nouns and pronouns

10 McKenzie Wark, "The Sublime Language of My Century," *Public Seminar*, May 14, 2016, at publicseminar.org.

for the kin genres of companion species, just as we did (and still do) for the spectrum of genders" (187). Or kith genres, perhaps.

Can an ethics of partial relations scale up to a politics? Or does a politics have to entail, maybe not as an ontology as Mouffe would have it, but just as a tactic, an *agonistic* relation to an-other? Perhaps we're all up against the Carbon Liberation Front and its takeover of the air and oceans.[11] That is not how Haraway approaches politics, however. "I think an affirmative biopolitics is about finitude, and about living and dying better, living and dying well, and nurturing and killing best we can, in a kind of openness to relentless failing" (227). But this is not a biopolitics after Butler and Brown, who focus on the politics, so much as out of Lynn Margulis and Evelyn Hutchinson, who focused on the biology.[12] Hence it doesn't fixate on the power to kill or the otherness of death. "Death is not the problem but cutting the tissue of ongoing-ness is the problem" (232).

In its affirmative mode, this might be a politics à la Préciado of pleasure lived publicly, coming from queer activism. In a less fun mode, this might be about confronting biopolitics as "the violence of making live when the possibility of living well is actively blocked" (229). Here Haraway does connect to Butler's category of that which can be grieved, but rather more broadly, extended beyond human bodies throughout the connections among the living and dying.

Climate change effects various worlds very unevenly. Some things adapt slowly, some quickly, even too quickly. Questions of what to let live or let die, make live or make die, are pressing. What exactly does it mean to call something an *invasive* species? Haraway: "this question of ecosystem assemblages is the name of the game of life on Earth. Period" (249). Politics might not be, or might not just be, a matter of critique of some abstract thing, but also "affirmative relations to worlding" (265).

Politics in Haraway is always connected to "learning to compose possible ongoing-ness inside relentlessly diffracting worlds. And we

11 Bill McKibben, "A World at War," *New Republic*, August 15, 2016, at newrepublic.com.

12 Evelyn Hutchinson, *The Art of Ecology*, New Haven, CT: Yale University Press, 2011; Lynn Margulis, *Symbiotic Planet*, New York: Basic Books, 1999.

need resolutely to keep cosmopolitical practices going here, focusing on those practices that can build a common-enough world" (288). The key words here include caring and learning, diffracting again, but also *partial connection*.[13] "All of us who care about recuperation, partial connections, and resurgence must learn to live and die in the entanglements of the tentacular without always seeking to cut and bind everything in our way" (295).

Looking back on the "Companion Species Manifesto," from the point of view of the Chthulucene, it seems to me as a text structured around an allegory. It's about love between dogs and humans, who are kith but not kin. It is not love as perfect unity, symmetry, identity, or purity—those residues of the old patriarchal sky god. "Besides, you never have a correct love, because love is always inappropriate, never proper, never clean" (275).

While others try to rethink what liberty or equality might mean today, to the extent that Haraway remains within the undead matrix of modern euro-thought, it is about "fraternity." Or what might possibly go in its place when not only God the father is dead, but so too are the human brothers who thought they could think the world and order it in his place. Hence the word *companion*: "We are companions, *cum panis*, at the table together. We are those who are at risk to each other, who are each other's flesh, who eat and are eaten, and who get indigestion" (215). Companion species "make each other up, in the flesh" (94). They are also *kith*, with its clingy, clammy senses of the friend, neighbor, local and the customary. Companion species eat together, parasite off each other, eat each other, but also collude and collaborate with each other.[14]

Species might be more nominal than real. It's a word with several senses. In biology it means gene flow, selection, variation, population. But there's an older sense of the word, going back to Thomas Aquinas, where a species is a *generic*, a series of abstract forms, through which to define differences. The two senses collide in something

13 Marilyn Strathern, *Partial Connections*, Lanham, MD: AltaMira Press, 2005.

14 See here that other modern Catholic philosopher, Michel Serres, *The Parasite*, Minneapolis: University of Minnesota Press, 2007.

like the practice of dog breeding, where the *genetic* is made to yield the *generic*, the breed. "Discourses of pure blood and nobility haunt modern breeds like the undead" (160).

Species might also, after Marx and Freud, refer to something more abstract, and touching on the totality again: *specie* as gold and as shit, and a general economy in which the human as species-being might be multiply implicated. But Haraway always pulls the reader back from a too quick flight to the abstract. Her concepts and figures are about finitude, impurity, historicity, complexity, cohabitation, coevolution and cross-species solidarity.

In a delightful détournement of Althusser, Haraway asks if maybe animals hail us as we hail them into our constructs of nature and culture.[15] Maybe Althusser's *interpellation* works not just on humans, calling them into ideological and imaginary relations to their real relations, but animals as well. If a human knows itself as itself when called, and becomes a subject of that call—maybe a dog does too. And then what about when a doggy bark calls a human? And perhaps, over a very long time, it becomes a kind of *metaplasm*, a remodeling of dog and human flesh, not in each other's image, but differentially, bouncing off each other's abilities and needs. What if that human and dog relation, including all its abuse, was an allegory for multispecies life more generally?

There are both dog stories and dog histories here. The stories are about dogs Haraway knows personally; the history is about how those kinds of dogs came to be in America. The former has some queer dog sex-pleasures and lots about how dogs and humans shape each other. They are about dogs and humans training each other for the sport of agility, where the human guides the dog through a series of obstacles. These are stories about respect and trust, not "unconditional love" between humans and dogs. It is about nonsymmetrical relations that don't turn the animal into a surrogate human. It is about "situated partial connection" (140). Dog and handler reaching for excellence as concrete beings, not abstractions.

---

15 Louis Althusser, *On Ideology*, London: Verso, 2008; on détournement, see Guy Debord, *The Society of the Spectacle*, New York: Zone Books, 1994, chapter 8.

The dog history has multiple actors, including dogs, coyotes, wolves, government departments, ranchers, scientists and dog breeders. Both at the particular and the historical level, species shape each other through flexible and opportunistic moves. "Relationship is multiform, at stake, unfinished, consequential" (122). It is not just a matter of Man subordinating Nature to His will, as both techno-optimists and—weirdly—deep ecologists—both seem to believe.

Haraway is resistant to seeing historical actors of any species as raw materials for capital or empire, but maybe sometimes the dense net of relations or figures in the foreground crowds out the background. One could retain the commitment to narrating history as co-history, in which the narrator is always implicated, while painting in more horizon. "Again and again in my manifesto, I and my people need to learn to inhabit histories, not disown them, least of all through the cheap tricks of puritanical critique" (181). I can't really speak for my Puritan kith, but if I could, I might point out the irony of an inclusiveness that requires excluding us to make its point about including everything else.

Not that the abstract ground is absent from Haraway. It is just that when she writes of love, it is about particulars; when she writes of rage, then it is about the abstract. What might be interesting would be to complete the semiotic square: to find points of rage among the particular; and even a difficult love of the abstract.[16] The abstract, and rage, come together in the figure of the *cyborg*.

> Care, flourishing, differences in power, scale of time—these matter for cyborgs. For example, what kind of temporal scale-making could shape labor systems, investment strategies, and consumption patterns in which the generation time of information machines became compatible with the generation times of human, animal, and plant communities and ecosystems? (113)

The companion species text puts the stress on situated partial connections. The "Manifesto for Cyborgs" leans a little more on imagined

16 A. J. Greimas, *On Meaning: Selected Writings in Semiotic Theory*, Minneapolis: University of Minnesota Press, 1987.

totalities. The latter are still *situated*. They just tune in to the background of a situation rather than the foreground. The temptation to resist is seeing the imagined totality as a ground in the sense of an ontology, as if it were something prior to the situation (as in Morton). It is rather something secondary and speculative.

The *cyborg* appears as an everyday figure, an aspect of women's experience, one might also say of the experience of labor. The more common way to imagine the cyborg is as the other, as that which infiltrates, against which the human fights a border war to preserve its essence. We are supposed to imagine we are Deckard the blade runner, cutting the inhuman from the human, but perhaps we are all Rachel the replicant, laminated aggregates to flesh and tech: "we are all chimeras" (7). So perhaps we could assume the pleasure and responsibility of life and love among confusing boundaries.

Among other things, this is a choice between genres. It means letting go of narratives in which the decoy or the infiltrator is exposed, leading to a restoration of lost wholeness. No more Eden: "the cyborg is resolutely committed to partiality, irony, intimacy, and perversity. It is oppositional, utopian, and completely without innocence" (9). It is implicated in troubling boundaries between the human and the animal, the organic and the machinic, and between matter and information: *the inhuman comedy*.

Haraway stays close to the slippage zones between two perspectives, one about bodies, one about relations. She does not completely flip the script and subordinate bodies to relations. What if we did for a bit? Not in a moralizing or critical genre, but a speculative and ironic one? That's one of the things going on in "A Manifesto for Cyborgs" that is less common in Haraway's later work, but which might have its uses.

Haraway: "'Advanced capitalism' is inadequate to convey the structure of this historical moment" (27). It was a bold and prescient claim. "I argue for a politics rooted in claims about fundamental changes in the nature of class, race, and gender in an emerging system of world order analogous in its novelty and scope to that created by industrial capitalism" (28). It has implications for both narrating the form of the bad totality and for seeding terms within which to make alliances in and against it that might tend towards a more habitable one.

> From one perspective, a cyborg world is about the final imposition of a grid of control on the planet…From another perspective, a cyborg world might be about lived social and bodily realities in which people are not afraid of their joint kinship with animals and machines, not afraid of permanently partial identities and contradictory standpoints. The political struggle is the will to see from both perspectives at once. (15)

Or rather four perspectives: the uninhabitable particular and general; the habitable particular and general.

There's thus more to it than the good particulars against the bad totality. Particularly in an era in which the particulars themselves became the form of the bad totality itself: "we risk lapsing into boundless difference and giving up on the confusing task of making partial, real connection. Some differences are playful; some are poles of world historical systems of domination. 'Epistemology' is about knowing the difference" (27). One might add: some situated speculations on the totality might be part of domination; some might not.

Haraway does a good job of playing across the boundaries that structure certain enervating habits of thought, but there is one terminological duality I think might be worth bringing back into the mix. "The boundary-maintaining images of base and superstructure, public and private, or material and ideal never seemed more feeble" (36). There's a way in which the first of these pairs is not like the others. Thinking about how one is situated in a base or an infrastructure is itself a way of refusing binaries, so long as one keeps the concept of infrastructure open as a question. Maybe we don't even know what's infrastructural in a world that runs on the information vector as much as on coal mines and blast furnaces. Maybe we don't even know whose labor is implicated in its workings.

The "Cyborg" text is actually rather good on the emerging infrastructure that I call the vectoral, which monitors boundaries, and measures flows, and manages what Galloway calls *protocol*, which polices what can connect with what.[17] The vectoral is not interested in the integrity of natural objects, as it reaches into objects of all kith or kin, extracts a measure of its value and authorizes connections and disconnections.

The vectoral produces, as a secondary phenomenon, the appearance not only of *objects*, but as Lazzarato shows, also of *subjects*. Haraway was already saying this: "Human beings, like any other component or subsystem, must be localized in a system architecture whose basic modes of operation are probabilistic, statistical" (32). Not just bodies but situations are subordinated to the vector. Home, work, market, public, body, all are traversed by it. It is basically what the military used to call C^3I: command, control, communication and information—but for civilians.

Is this still capitalism, or something worse? Haraway was already grappling with a new language for it in her "Cyborg" text. Whatever it is, it produces a new worldwide proletariat, new distributions of ethnicity and sexuality, and new forms of the family. Haraway was writing about an earlier moment in Silicon Valley, when it was still a major center for chip fabrication, using mostly women of color as an industrial workforce. Much of that production has moved on, leaving toxic Superfund sites behind, but the global, distributed labor of making these digital means of production still exists, on an expanded and globalized scale.[18]

The word *precarity* had not yet been coined, but Haraway was already describing it. Work has in a paradoxical way been feminized.[19] On the one hand, women get to work; on the other, the work is precarious, powerless and toxic. The vector has the ability to route around any stoppage or strike that workers might deploy as leverage.[20] "The success of the attack on relatively privileged, mostly white,

17 Alexander R. Galloway, *Protocol: How Control Exists After Decentralization*, Cambridge, MA: MIT Press, 2003.

18 Andrew Ross, *Bird on Fire*, New York: Oxford University Press, 2011.

19 Here Haraway perhaps escapes Préciado's complaint about the concept of feminizing labor, as that labor also changes what the "feminine" is supposed to be.

20 Timothy Mitchell, *Carbon Democracy: Political Power in the Age of Oil*, London: Verso, 2013.

men's unionized jobs is tied to the power of the new communication technologies to integrate and control labor despite extensive dispersion and decentralization" (39).

Haraway identified some important symptoms of this world, including its "bimodal social structure," or what we now call inequality (44). Not least for women workers. The electric mega-church might now be the OxyContin of the people. Then there's the "permanent high-tech military establishment" (42). Or what we now call the surveillance state. It spawns an ideology that is in part "sociobiological origin stories" (43). Now mixed with Ayn Rand. The limited vision of this world, as Haraway already notes, could already be found best expressed in the form of the video game. In *Gamer Theory* I added that so too are some of its possibilities.[21]

Haraway: "Most Marxisms see domination best" (50). They are less good about everyday life. But rather than subsume all the bad signs under a kind of totalizing pessimism, it helps at the same time to work on a "subtle understanding of emerging pleasures, experiences and powers" (51). Dialectics may be a dream language rather than a magic key to the real. But perhaps if one knows it's a dream, the speculative and totalizing vision can have its uses. Haraway mostly finds this in utopian science fiction, but maybe theory can offer some of the same situated perspective on the useful and harmful, the foreground and background, without collapsing everything into one of those four quadrants of ways of thinking and feeling.

Haraway opts for a cyborg politics of noise and pollution, but I think that's only one of the tactical styles it enables. In a world enclosed by the vector as a gamespace, a cyborg can be a player, a spoilsport, a cheat, but also a trifler.[22] One can accept the rules and the goal. One can refuse the rules and the goal. One can accept the goal but not the rules. And one can accept the rules but not the goal.

Each of those tactics can do with some shareware terms, concepts, stories, affect: "race, gender, and capital require a cyborg theory of

21 McKenzie Wark, *Gamer Theory*, Cambridge, MA: Harvard University Press, 2007.

22 Bernard Suits, *The Grasshopper*, Boston: David Godine, 1990.

wholes and parts. There is no drive in cyborgs to produce total theory, but there is an intimate experience of boundaries, their construction and deconstruction" (66). Maybe that's just one mode. One can think ambivalent boundaries or one can think ambivalent vectors. Maybe cyborgs also write total theory but take it lightly. A good fact is *mostly* true, about something in particular; a good theory is *slightly* true about a bunch of things.

Hence when Haraway says "the production of universal, totalizing theory is a major mistake," one can separate totalizing from universal (67). As Henri Lefebvre proposed, to totalize can be a situated act that knows it isn't universal, which comes into friendly or agonistic relations with other totalizations.[23] Relations between particulars are partly made out of particular articulations, but also out of the more or less playful encounter of broader worldviews. Everyone works outwards, substituting from where they are and what they do to toward the absolute.

What Alexander Bogdanov called *tektology* is the sharing, comparing and testing of component parts between divergent worldviews generated in particular situations.[24] All we have to agree on is a shared task of making a possibly livable world. We don't even have to agree to forego a grand confrontation with the world, which for those of us who are temperamentally "protestant," isn't going to happen anyway.

It seems vital in the Chthulucene that the shared task of making a possibly livable world include those who work in the natural sciences, and who tend to have the worldviews that grow outward from those kinds of labors. Haraway: "taking responsibility for the social relations of science and technology means refusing an anti-science metaphysics, a demonology of technology" (67).

That calls for thinking through what Haraway describes with "the odd circumlocution the social relations of science and technology" (37). There was a time when this would not have been odd. The *social relations of science* was a whole movement in the 1930s, started

23 Henri Lefebvre, *Critique of Everyday Life*, London: Verso, 2014; McKenzie Wark, *The Beach Beneath the Street*, London: Verso, 2015, chapter 8.

24 Alexander Bogdanov, *Essays in Tektology*, 2nd edition, Seaside, CA: Intersystems Publications, 1984.

by once-famous Marxist and leftist scientists such as J. D. Bernal, Joseph Needham and JBS Haldane, but which included also Dorothy Needham, Charlotte Haldane, Dorothy Hodgkin and Kathleen Lonsdale.[25] It did not survive the Cold War purges of intellectual life. Science studies has reinvented many of its themes and in many ways improved upon them. Yet perhaps, as Haraway once noted in passing, the "liberal mystification that all started with Thomas Kuhn" has erased a little too much of its radical past (69). We are very fortunate that Donna Haraway and her kith reinvented it.

---

25 Gary Werskey, *The Visible College*, New York: Holt, Rinehart & Winston, 1979, does a great job with this story, but it might look different if one put the women back into it. See also Georgina Ferry, *Dorothy Hodgkin: A Life*, London: Bloomsbury, 2014; Judith Adamson, *Charlotte Haldane: Woman Writer in a Man's World*, Houndmills: Macmillan, 1998.

Acknowlegements

All but one of these pieces appeared in *Public Seminar*, the free online journal of the New School for Social Research. I would like to thank its founder, Jeff Goldfarb, for inviting me to join that adventure in the free general intellect. It was an invitation to write freely and without looking over one's shoulder, which proved most stimulating. My thanks also to the other editors and workers who keep *Public Seminar* live and lively.

The Meillassoux piece came out of a conversation with Suhail Malik and originally appeared in Christoph Cox, Jenny Jaskey and Suhail Malik (eds.), *Realism Materialism Art*, Berlin: Sternberg Press, 2015. My thanks to the editors.

My thanks to everyone at Verso Books, particularly Leo Hollis, who first suggested the idea for this book. Also to Mark Martin on the production side, and copy editor Mike Andrews. The pieces are all much improved from their rough form as impromptu 'letters' on the *Public Seminar* website. All of that labor needs to be paid for, so if you like this book, but are reading it for free, please think about buying a copy in one format or other. A shout out to Versovians past and present, who have been and remain a joy to work with.

Finally, my thanks to colleagues and particularly students at Eugene Lang College who have made such a great intellectual home for me this last decade or more. Many of these pieces started life as my class notes for upper level students at Eugene Lang College and graduate students in Liberal Studies at The New School for Social Research, and all have benefited from our discussions of them. This book is for you, and for students everywhere – the general intellect to come.